MW00813651

COME HOME

finding comfort in who you are

MEGAN DOYLE

Know Thyself

COME HOME

Appreciation and Dedication

Some years ago, I stumbled into an opportunity to teach U.S. Military Veterans about yoga. Most of them had never even been to a yoga class. Because the program was supported by their GI Bill, the students appeared. In the beginning, most of them weren't interested; they just appreciated the money. At the beginning, most of them weren't really interested; they just needed the money.

Then they got started.

The program was intense: four hours a day, four days a week, for six months. The yoga wasn't branded. The students learned the yoga that served them, as my teachers taught me. This is yoga tailored to the practitioner, full of thoughtful modifications to postures, and appropriate variations in breathing, focus, meditation, and prayer. This is yoga entirely concerned with its original purpose: to make the sacred journey toward our own peaceful freedom.

And the students learned. They started to enjoy the material. They discovered they *were* the material. They inquired into their bodies, minds, energy, personalities, and hearts. They found their yoga. In the very first cohort, I understood what they were teaching me. The students had been trained to journey toward conflict. They'd never been taught to come home to peace.

These amazing students (and, of course, my mom) inspired this book. I won't name them; they know who they are. They are the 150 and more students who learned yoga in their beautiful, wise ways, and brought it to their families, neighborhoods, churches, and schools. Thank you, my dears, for learning to come home.

This book is dedicated to all returned and returning warriors who have trained to become extraordinary in the world without being taught to appreciate the precious treasure that awaits them at home.

Table of Contents

Preface

Realize the Self, the shining goal of life!

If you do not, there is only darkness.

See the Self in all, and go beyond death.

—Kena Upanishad

For a time, imitating everyone else,

I preferred myself. Unaware,

I only heard my own name.

Because I was in myself,

I did not deserve to know myself.

Not until I left myself, did I see myself.

—Rumi

Forgive yourself for not knowing what you didn't know before you

learned it.

—Maya Angelou

The Path Toward Home

First, let's remember how we laugh. We smile and sing and wonder. Together and apart. We all do this.

Now, let's think of how we suffer. Think of how we hurt, ache, cry, and languish. It's also what we do.

We can suffer together, and we can move beyond suffering together. We can smile gently at how we've suffered and begin to laugh more.

Life gives us every opportunity to do all of this…and more. We tend to overlook the gifts of life until we learn to understand our despair and our joy. Realizing and shifting our attitude toward life itself is the path that brings us home.

To walk that path, we have to let go of every idea that keeps us from a deep, full, wild appreciation for life itself. We have to be willing to recognize how much we don't know about the way we live our lives.

Are you ready to acknowledge that you may not know as much as you think? Is it possible that you haven't investigated who you really are? Perhaps you haven't said thank you to life itself?

We all pretend to know something because it gets us through the day. When it comes down to it, we don't know much. We pretend our pretense is enough. And while limited knowledge is certainly not a problem in itself, it becomes a serious limitation when we confine ourselves to these limits. We refuse to accept that the world out there has something to offer us. As if, somehow, we know more than life itself how life itself lives.

What if we looked into life more directly and discovered ourselves there?

This is how I walk my path. This book is an effort to share the best of what I've learned in a conversation with you. I don't know much, but I love a good conversation—with whatever form of life is available to listen and share.

It's time we help each other out. It's time we connect and consider our ways. Life holds us all; we share that. We have access to infinite wonder beyond the walls of our limited knowledge. The world is always ready to offer an experience of refinement, illumination, and freedom. Our task is to figure out what keeps us from seeing the world clearly.

So let's go. Let's travel together and find our way.

Here's a word to bolster our courage.

None of what follows is new; mostly, it's ancient. And timeless. Ready for us at every moment we decide to listen and learn.

What follows is information that's been passed among attentive, seeking humans over a few millennia. I like to imagine millions of shared moments passed over coffee, tea, in joy and in grief, in wonder and in despair. If we're overwhelmed by any of it, may it be the endurance of the guidance and the way it resonates when we find it. It strikes us, and we hum. We already know all this, and when the guidance finds us, we feel it.

That's our legacy; our responsibility is learning how to use it. This will include making every effort to acknowledge and address the obstacles that keep us from accepting our gifts.

3

... if true freedom were readily available and could be found without great effort, how is it possible that it should be neglected by almost everyone. But all things excellent are as difficult as they are rare.

—*Baruch Spinoza*

We are a stubborn lot. In our resistance we've confused cynicism with skepticism. As skeptics we're discerning and careful about what may be appropriate to us. As cynics we refuse to consider the potential of kindness and good advice.

Our acceptance wanes; we refuse our gifts.

It's okay. The enduring persistence of our human quest finds its way. We all want to be okay; we all are, actually, okay.

Let's start with this premise: we are perfect. More on this later. For now feel the possibility.

Next premise: we don't have to suffer so much.

Life will give us plenty of opportunity to despair. We don't have to become desperate. Our experience with hardship and crisis reveals the work we're meant to do. While we may not have control over the challenge, we each have a say in our response. Our task is to learn how to transform our attitude toward the challenge. This means that we work with the mind to shift its patterns of reactions. We learn to carry our histories a little more easily. To choose our own adventures. Even to enlighten ourselves.

Slowly or quickly, depending...

Depending on what?

On you.

You are the conditional event. Or aspects of you. Parts of you. Some parts will be willing, and some will be reluctant. The method always depends on you and your cultivated relationship with all those parts—you and your willingness to work with yourself in relation to everything. It is precisely as rigorous or as easy as it must be to move yourself into a position where you can honestly say *thank you* as you engage with everything.

Can you think of anything more frustrating than being told to be grateful for the people, places, and events that you dislike the most? For most of us, it's challenging enough to give thanks for the best parts of our life.

But *thank you* is always the prayer that guides us toward home.

Did you say thank you when you opened your eyes again this morning?

Do you realize you're breathing, and do you offer deep appreciation for your breath?

We forget sometimes. We don't spend the energy to remember. We might even scoff at gratitude, preferring a worldview that awaits deliverance by someone else. I call this outsourcing. Businesses do it to save their resources. We do it to conserve our energy…a highly precious resource that we haven't realized is completely renewable and infinite. In our mistaken view, we expect someone else to deliver to us what must be done. We wait.

We are the ones we're awaiting.

The human story, regardless of how or where it originated, is rich with wisdom on discovering peace, solace, joy. Universally it involves a journey without a geographic destination. Where we're meant to go is within. We go inside to go home. We make the choice to go home. We choose now over later to go home. The path we follow will depend on who we are. To understand who we are, we start asking.

For this reason, I wrote this book.

I prefer to think of it as a really, really long love letter. It's meant to offer a hand as you make your inquiries. And to share my own. I don't have any answers for you; that's your job. I do have decent questions. Your role is to proceed with curiosity, compassion toward yourself, and honesty as you answer them. It's your path. How you navigate it is for you to decide.

Choose wisely.

You're the one who has to pay attention. You're the one who has to discover your methods. You're the one coming home.

This is your journey.

May we learn, along the way, to recognize the guideposts that remind us to care for ourselves, to love ourselves, to realize ourselves. May we commit ourselves, moment to moment, to the wonder of being alive, to being ourselves, to being connected. May we realize that the journey into a grateful awareness of this precious life is the destination itself. This is home. When we arrive there, we discover relief from suffering and a deep pull to cherish the world.

As you read, perhaps remember this: we are.

That's it.

All of us together are in the process of being. We simply are. This long love letter is my way of using language to remind us that we're the same. You're as special as I am. I'm a reflection of you. We're all incredibly fortunate to exist. We all sometimes forget for a bunch of different reasons. We are so alike in our idiosyncrasies.

So please don't let the words become a distraction. I could have written *I love you* over and over again. It would carry the same message, and eventually you would get the point. You'd shake your head first, roll your eyes, and protest. But ultimately you'd get it.

You're perfect. You're always okay.

How does it feel to read that?

And this?

I love you.

Whatever we're feeling is just a little dirt on our windows. We can't see clearly through the dirt of our beliefs, opinions, judgments, and training. With our vision so impaired, we can't fathom that love is plainly here for all of us to share because we've been told it may be a heavy experience. We've been taught to believe that love is a merit badge: earned or deserved. We worry it may disappear when we fail or misstep.

Truly it doesn't go anywhere.

Love connects me to you. And you to me. And everything.

Love is persistent and pervasive.

Love all, please. And know that you are loved.

Prologue

I remember these things: my chemistry homework on my lap and my dad's hand brushing it away. He said, "Everyone is worried about you. Your mother is on her way." We both sighed.

I was barely sixteen, an enthusiastic student...awkward, curious, slightly fanatical about despair. I devoured all the works of angsty European writers—Nietzsche and Sartre—and acted out their inconsolable dramas in monologues at school competitions. Sometimes to friends. Poor friends.

I was that kid. I wore a veil sometimes, to mourn the futility of life. And I had acne. I was a tall, gangly goblin.

I enjoyed debates about sorrow and nihilism. My family found me exasperating. I pushed anyone to tell me their ideas of God or gods. In long-winded journal entries, I demanded justification for our existence. I cared more about these concerns than homework or university plans. As for me, I considered a creator irrelevant, whether a power existed or not. I refused to attend to, or respect, any higher power who required so much suffering in exchange for life.

I was into the woe.

The cool kids weren't into me.

I'd been that way for a couple years. I was feeling the futility of it all. I had been making threats and experimenting with the means.

I'd cultivated a tedious habit of planning my death. It was a creative exercise. I wrote poems about it, considered the methods and the aftermath. I wrote letters to explain. I always apologized. I gave them suggestions on how to heal.

Ultimately the letters nudged me toward life. Why bother causing the despair I wanted to cure? Why not stay put and be a helper?

So…life it was.

Still I tempted fate. I drove fast. I went days without eating. I cut myself. No one was paying much attention, so I cut deeper and deeper. Finally a friend got worried and called my brother. He called my mom. That was when my dad interrupted my homework.

We sat on the bed until the paramedics came. "Are paramedics necessary?" I asked.

He sighed. He said, "You know your mother."

We actually laughed, and he held me, his arm heavy on my back. I remember his smoky cologne. I explained to him that I thought chemistry was taking the world apart too minutely. He said, "I prefer physics." Pretty soon the house went wild with uniformed men holding their belts and unnecessary medical bags.

I spent two weeks in a hospital, watching my parents disagree about pathologies. My mom wanted me medicated. My dad wanted me released. I wanted a hug and maybe a congratulatory pat on the back. Many of the kids in the ward were exploring drugs, crime, and sex. I was just curious about death. I wanted someone to acknowledge the importance of the topic.

I tried to share what I knew: that we all come assured of death, that the mortality rate among humans everywhere has always been 100 percent, that life keeps going even when we don't.

My family didn't love this conversation.

Fortunately the psychiatrist at the hospital respected it and gave me this advice: don't impose ideas about difficult subjects on anyone who isn't ready. It was a valuable bit of wisdom that I urge all of us to adopt. The doctor and I spent our time together discussing Walt Whitman and easier ways to coexist with my family.

Almost two years later, on a foggy October night, my dad shot himself.

My sister was sent to tell me. She drove three hours and arrived at my college dorm room. I don't remember anything about the conversation or the following days. I have one memory of that night: looking out my dorm window to see my boyfriend and my sister's boyfriend chugging beers in the parking lot.

My dad had been found dead at a place where we'd picnicked. It was unclear if it was the bullet or the shallow pond where he'd fallen that had killed him. He left me the gift I didn't want to leave him. I could never heal him, and he could never heal me. A consistent thought of mine as we went through the motions of mourning: I will never get over this.

I was wrong. I healed.

It was a slow process to become whole again. I love him still, every day. I thank him, every day.

The death of my dad is one of the most provocative lessons I've learned. I'm grateful for his guidance every day, as a father and a man who suffered. He was my catalyst.

It took many years—of distancing myself from him, pulling him close, raging at him, emulating him, grieving for him, understanding him, and finally accepting him with deep gratitude for all he is—before his lesson landed. The person to forgive was me.

So, on another foggy October night, two decades after my dad's passing, I forgave myself by accepting every gift my dad shared with me. There was the yellow bicycle and the drinking. He introduced Buddhism to me and realized his own suicide. My dad gave me true wealth.

After his death I fought depression, anxiety, panic, anger, guilt, jealousy, shame, disappointment, and insecurity. These are all fertile grounds to tread on. If you've been there, and I bet you have, you will know what I mean. They're so fertile that we resist passing through them. They stink. But tread we must. This is the journey home.

It isn't easy. But it's rich.

After my dad's passing, it seemed that every negative emotion compelled me in one direction or another. Often at the same time. And I wasn't dysfunctional. On the contrary, I was ambitious, capable, competent, confident. I wasn't content, but to most observers, I was a successful woman in a good career with a loving husband. I had friends. I did yoga. I was indignant often. I expressed my emotions like I was vomiting. I couldn't even fathom that I could truly appreciate life.

I found a miserable comfort in negativity and always wondered quietly: Will I relieve myself someday and do what my dad did?

I had limited faith—what the hell did it mean? I laughed at people who celebrated God. I wrote cruelly about them, ridiculing their belief as a dismissal of intellect. I didn't even realize I was in the process of searching. And yearning for mystery.

And then a teacher and friend helped me see. On an October night, two decades after my dad's passing, when I reached a point of overwhelm that I wasn't sure I could bear, my friend reminded me to look inside. He reminded me of something I'd known but never been told: the divine is within me.

And I understood. Immediately I understood.

The mystery consoled me.

I never doubted again.

That was the moment when I ended and began. That was the moment I came home.

We all have these moments available to us.

What I discovered inside has held me in awe ever since. The awe inspires me to write to you. Please look inside. Please remember the place from which you're searching. That's home.

Please join me in coming home.

This beautiful life we share is crammed with shits and giggles. It is not an either/or proposition. The better we become at accepting these shits, the sweeter the peal of our giggles. The trouble these days is a trendy conviction that we are meant, somehow, to be persistently happy. We think what makes us unhappy is an injustice.

Truly, what makes us unhappy is a treasure.

Paradoxically, expecting happiness is something like expecting wealth. If we wait for its arrival, our disappointment is assured. Conversely, our efforts often bear fruit. Most often, the fruit is different from what we anticipated. Still, fruit is fruit. Abundance tends to wait for our acknowledgement. Then we see how ever-present it is. It doesn't limit itself to wealth or happiness. It exists in everything.

Until we make our acknowledgments, we become increasingly frustrated. We may even suspect that we're somehow failing. The life we expected—the happy life—eludes us, and we want to blame someone. Maybe we blame our parents, our teachers, our spouses, our friends. Often we blame ourselves.

We don't realize the gift of life.

When we believe life is acting against us, we feel brutalized and powerless. We believe we're victims without power. When we believe we're meant to control the phenomena of life, our inability to do so can feel like overwhelming defeat. Our perceived failures sadden us, but they aren't the cause of our suffering.

We suffer because we don't realize where our power rests. We may not be able to control life, but we have a say over our response to it.

And yet the only time and space holding our lives is the one immediately available. We only ever live right now.

We are perfectly placed to live. Right now.

But we won't until we decide.

We'll never understand the way things work if we don't *stand under* every experience and simply observe it. It is our privilege in life to discover not just the gifts of life but also our manner of perceiving them.

We attend to our experience by perceiving it.

The questions we must ask ourselves are these: Do we remember that we control our awareness? Do we remember that whatever we expose in the light of our attention takes on the tint of our attitude? Do we remember we choose the attitude?

For now it's enough to start suspecting that we've been casting our light a bit willy-nilly. The light show is confusing and stress-inducing. We've lost our ability to discern the difference between importance and distraction, between worthwhile and detrimental, between real and unreal. Until we learn how to work with the light of our attention, we might be missing the best parts of the show.

How did this happen?

We are encouraged to look in every direction but one: within.

Turning inward—toward the insight of our own self-awareness—is not only difficult but also frightening. The world around us chatters, fidgets, and sleeps with difficulty. If we do something, anything, we worry we'll miss what is undone. If we quiet down, we worry we'll hear what we've been told doesn't belong in the prattle around us. Or we regret that our voice is not in it.

We are educated to believe ourselves free, with vast potential; we're instructed to rein ourselves in to conform with expectations, norms, laws. For a while, or for much of our lives, we proceed from day to day in these straitjackets, upset only when someone else disrupts our careful balance. We never think the uniform itself may be the issue. We consider the uniform a mark of our accomplishment and stability.

Despite our relative safety and security, we're captives. To remove the bind, we have to muster a few moments of unpredictable strength. Psychological and physical and emotional strength. Of course, we each have the requisite strength, but we've been counseled, educated, informed, fed, and sometimes medicated to diminish it. All aspects of it.

We've been taught to mistrust ourselves.

These days our greatest courage is often stoked by a bottle of wine, a bit of drugs, or some wacky activities that get us ample attention and, ultimately, injury.

We are, simply, ridiculously out of touch with ourselves. In response we have trained our nervous systems to erect veritable fortresses around us to prevent harm. We are stressed, with poor digestion, with little patience, so tense that we could break at the slightest push because we look at the world around us and perceive it as something to be pushed away.

From this place we tremble at the peephole. We are incredibly judgmental about what we let out and absurdly foolish about what we let in. We end up hiding behind a growing heap of rubbish—material, emotional, behavioral. We hunker down behind our barricades. We have no idea that it's safer without them.

We are, always, home. It's time we decide to shift our attention so we can see it.

It's time we come home.

The world is waiting to play with us.

Coming home, making ourselves comfortable, we can delight in the game.

For those of you eager to get going, you'll find techniques in every chapter, in the study guide at the end, as well as recorded and available online at knowthyselfyoga.com/homepractices. Try them. Maybe they'll inspire you to learn more, or maybe they'll be enough.

For those who enjoy a little context, read along. Please read the whole book, and maybe look at it again when you're done. Some things will come clear later. That's the nature of learning.

And if you take a certain delight in this book, please share it with a friend whom you suspect will also take a certain delight. Please don't bother sharing it with anyone who won't. Let them find it on their own, at a time that's right for them.

For now let's send a message of appreciation to ourselves. In the words that feel right to you, please offer a *thank you* to all that you've weathered, all you've destroyed, and all you've cultivated. May we marvel that we find ourselves together, united by these words. Your arrival at this moment is meaningful and important. I'm happy you're here, and I'm grateful to share this precious life with you.

May we learn from each other.

May we always be friends.

May we show each other the way home.

1. Who Are You?

Do you ask crows why they steal from your untended garden?

Do you blame aspiring rain or the goddess of dirt

for teasing life from the ground?

Do you ever wonder at all what you might learn from creepers

and wild things?

A forest welcomes you, wild thing,

when you take its gifts.

Then, like a good guest,

leave before the first bird shares secrets

about the night.

Not a single family of trees would refuse to foster you.

And when you're gone, your brothers and sisters

will remember

your small admiration.

As will you.

—Megan Doyle

This journey starts with our decision. We make a choice. We make it now. Then we make it again and again, always.

Destination: You

We'll start with a shared decision: let's head home.

The way home is right smack into the center of you. Whatever you see around you—the trees, the flowers, the lovers, the friends and family—are your guideposts, trailheads, and signs. These markers aren't your destination.

Home is the destination. Your destination is you.

Now we're getting somewhere.

You may have noticed the one constant in life is change. Change affects our bodies: we get old, we get injured, and we get sick. Change affects our living conditions: we marry and we divorce, we buy a house and lose it, and we get a career and abandon it. We want to be something, call ourselves something, and then everything changes again. Many of us spend much of our lives wishing for stable conditions and find ourselves falling all over the place when they evolve.

What if we count these evolutions as helpful guideposts?

With every condition in flux, we have an opportunity to consider our direction. We have a chance to determine how we'll respond to change. We don't have much choice in the fact of change, but we do have a means to influence its direction.

Fortunately, on this adventure the goal and the means of travel are the same: to become self-aware, we turn our awareness to ourselves. To go home, we look within. When we get lost along the way, we return our attention to the space inside.

We are the subject of our journeys. Despite years of education into every other subject, all of them awesome and worthy of our pursuits, our true contentment won't arise until we inquire into our own natures. Our truly awesome natures. Your inquiry into you will be your loftiest and most meaningful endeavor.

The redirection of our studies can seem worrisome at the start.

We may not want to look at ourselves. We're highly trained to look elsewhere. We might even think it's selfish to evaluate our own well-being. Self-obsessed or even narcissistic. To which I gently reply, whatever rationalizations we use to deter our progress are important to notice. Get to know them. These are our sweet efforts to protect ourselves from our ultimate responsibility: the work to be done is right here. It's you and you and you.

We look at ourselves.

We may find this inappropriate. With so many concerns plaguing our times, how can we prioritize ourselves?

Listen, I know.

I've heard friends, and I've heard myself, over the years. We have to care for others. We have clients, jobs, families. We want to save everyone. And we will. We just have to learn how to do it correctly. When we realize the work to be done starts with us, our world shifts on its axis.

We can all agree: we're kind to share our attention toward others. However, let's honestly consider whether the kindness comes from an altruistic place. Meaning, are we kind because we're good with ourselves? Or are we kind because we're making amends that we owe to ourselves?

Often we're so dependent on saving others because we don't want to save ourselves. We can see precisely how to fix and remedy others but have no interest in applying the remedy to our own existence. It asks too much of us. We'd have to acknowledge the sources of our pain, our weakness, our anger, fear, despair, and doubt. We may see these qualities clearly in others but prefer not to see them in ourselves.

These are the shadows we avoid.

Let's bless our protective instincts and ask them to step aside.

Consider...is it possible to help anyone else before we help ourselves? Do you really think you have any chance of saving someone else if you can't save yourself? And have you noticed that no matter how many friends you try to save, most of them keep on doing what they do?

That's what people do. They do what they do. Until the moment that they don't. And it's always their decision, regardless of whatever persuasion or force you applied.

I was a frequent practitioner of that forceful persuasion. I remember feeling frustration, sorrow, and a very insidious resentment toward anyone who wouldn't take my advice. In short, I was unhappy in most relationships that didn't let me control them.

Even those that did were less than satisfying. I lost friends, growled about ungrateful clients, and spent long, lonely spells in an angry silence waiting for anyone to agree with me about the error in their ways.

Why would anyone listen to me? I wouldn't even listen to myself long enough to hear how annoying I was.

There is no need to lament the suffering of the living or the dead.

—*Bhagavad Gita*

It took a pretty serious redirection to discover that I was the one who required my attention.

The impetus for the redirect came in the wake of persistent panic attacks and serious confusion about the purpose of my life. I realized in that period that all the solutions I was offering to everyone else were hints from some place deeper in me.

The solutions were meant for me. My help was meant for me.

Is it possible that you may be seeking to fix everyone around you with solutions meant for you?

In time I found a great deal of peace in the discovery that this precious life is best spent attending to myself first. When I take care of myself, I can care effectively and wholly for others.

Our lives are so special and certainly worthy of our attention; there's no need to become an intruder into the lives of others.

Your life will captivate you, and what you learn from yourself will help you become more conscious of your actions and the energy underlying them. You'll find stability and ease in your authenticity. Everyone and everything around you will appreciate you for that authenticity. You will become honest.

What does it take to dedicate this precious life to your own discovery? To be your honest, authentic self?

It requires a readiness to gather every bit of you and bring it all home.

God is at home, it's we who have gone out for a walk.

—Meister Ekhart

For one moment imagine yourself in all your fullness.

You are human. You've existed a number of years with various family members, friends, teachers, workmates, neighbors, and strangers. These relationships have been wonderful at times and challenging at others.

You have certain physical qualities, some of which you may love and others not so much. You have emotional habits. Again, some may serve you well, and some may be past their expiration date.

When you gaze over the landscape of the life you've lived so far, can you see how you are a beautiful composition of being? This being is composed of your body; your interactions with it and the world it inhabits; your experiences in the world; and certain yearnings, beliefs, and ideas shaped by all of it. Can you see in this beautiful composition that there are some parts of you that you routinely prefer to ignore?

You may have certain aspects you don't even acknowledge or remember. Likewise, you may enlist other aspects that give you a sense of self that no longer serves you.

We are, all of us, so amazingly complex. At the same time, we are, all of us, capable of becoming so powerfully whole.

These lives are treasures. They allow us to realize our best qualities, our worst qualities, and every quality in between.

We are these wonderful assortments of possibility and response, accumulated from past events and our current reality. Every single one

23

of them springs from various yearnings that formed into patterns, whether these are physical, physiological, energetic, experiential, or spiritual. We are all a set of longings and expectations that have come to life through our behavior.

When we become friends with every little quality in us, we become full, whole, and authentic. We become robust and peaceful. We discover the feeling of home.

Thus to begin, we must commit to ourselves.

To be of consistent, enduring, and purposeful service to others, we must first serve ourselves. Through our efforts, we become capable of tending to our needs. As we cultivate ourselves, we grow. We become like a garden. We will have plenty to share, thanks to the efforts we make to plant appropriate seeds, nourish our roots, and patiently allow our growth.

If we don't tend to ourselves well, our garden will have little to offer.

Someone else will have to feed us. Despite their generosity, we'll feel the discomfort of that reliance. We may not understand our discomfort at first, but if we're willing to examine it, we'll see. We thrive when we learn how to nourish ourselves.

Yoga with Presence

Here's your first practice. Please follow along.

Take a deep breath. Realize the fact of your existence.

You are, right now, a human being. You exist.

You dwell within a composite of some tens of trillions of cells that create the form of you over and over again. Smile at the wonder of this form.

You are breathing. You expand and contract with every breath. Notice this. Smile at your breath, coming and going.

Your attention is noticing. Notice this as well. You may have a dull awareness or a sharp recognition of the fact that you're watching you. That's you too.

You may like it or not. Also you.

And you may, possibly, experience a comfort in the exercise. A sweet gratitude to see and be seen. You.

You are someone who has loved, been loved and loving, regardless of reciprocity or propriety. You.

Notice you, among everything in your surroundings right now. And notice how you are, remarkably, connected with all of it. As soon as you put your attention on every form and face around you, you establish a relationship in this very moment. It may be as fleeting as the moment itself, but still. You.

Please smile at the presence of you.

That's it. The most basic exercises are not the easiest. But they are worthwhile.

Will you commit to practicing every morning for a week? A good time is when you first wake up. You can make note of the practice and keep it next to your bed. You might choose the following shorthand message to yourself: remember all of you.

When you wake up, read the words and remember: you.

This is you deciding to connect.

See how this works? It starts with a decision. The action follows.

We have all these sensations and emotions because we're meant to experience life. We're meant to know ourselves.

Our families, friends, jobs, and the whole world enhance our experience of life and self, but they can't be the ground from which we observe. We are that ground. We must decide to stand on it, to claim it, and become still upon it. From this place, moment to moment, we experience life.

We house the instruments that allow us to sense, perceive, and become conscious of who we are. We're home. The entire universe is at home in us. Everything we've been looking to find has always been with us.

Until we arrive in this moment, on our ground, it's much easier to complain.

Or quit. Again and again.

We resent the work we do, the people we do it for, the obligations that call upon us. In this resentment we always find the means to abandon our efforts eventually. That's how we survive. Maybe after we've recovered some energy, we try again. Most likely, we repeat the cycle again. And again. Until we find another way.

Resentment is like drinking poison and waiting for the other person to

die.

—St. Augustine

Familiar? Why is our feedback loop so faulty?

Because most of the time, we put our efforts toward mastering the work we do, the people we do it for, and the obligations that call upon us—instead of mastering ourselves. Essentially, we become masters of obstacles. When a new obstacle presents itself, we become afraid, anxious, and overwhelmed because here is one more obstacle we don't know how to overcome. As masters of ourselves, we may not know the fine details of every obstacle, but we know how to organize ourselves in response to it. A master knows how to clear the path.

In many yoga classrooms, the focus of a whole practice is placed on poses ranging from simple seated positions to confusing contortions. Yoga students can become obsessed with mastering postures, often to the detriment of muscles, joints, and tendons. The poses become the obstacles.

When not seen for what they are—maybe surmountable or maybe worthy of total bypass—yoga students may prioritize the mastery of the obstacle over the entity attempting it. They become hurt, fatigued, frustrated, and grumpy.

They blame the pose, and it becomes their master. They don't see their responsibility in the endeavor.

I've been there. I once dislocated my shoulder moving into a challenging pose to impress a teacher. I wanted to prove my mastery.

Consequently I had to master shoulder rehabilitation. Thanks to the injury, I learned about mistaken priorities. And pride.

Sometimes the wise way to overcome an obstacle is to simply walk around it.

My yoga practice shifted on that painful morning.

The gift of yoga's silliest poses is in the metaphor.

A beautiful application of yoga's postures will guide us toward greater self-awareness, confidence, and comfort. To understand how to apply a posture, we must be willing to pause and ask for its purpose. How does the position serve our body and breath? How will it guide us into a profound relationship with our body, mind, and identity? Perhaps it will teach us about our relationship to our great stumbling blocks. Perhaps it will illuminate our current condition so we may appreciate how it serves or challenges us. Perhaps it will demonstrate to us a persistent pattern of conquest.

Appropriate application of yoga postures leads us toward clarity and self-awareness. Moving through the positions with an aim to perfect the pose guarantees that we'll face a fight whenever a new challenge arises. It is not the pose to be perfected. It's our relationship with it. It is our posture toward the posture that counts.

If you're ready for the self-awareness, welcome to your unique array of stumbling blocks.

Your duty is to recognize what your obstacles truly represent.

I like to think of obstacles as detours guiding us toward those aspects of ourselves that have, for various reasons, scattered away from us. They lie like shadows beyond us. We may not like the way the detours present themselves. We often feel judgmental, confused, averse, or even afraid as we see these obstacles arise in our path. But each of these feelings is telling us a story that leads us to some part of us that isn't healed. Somewhere down that detour is the potential to make peace with ourselves.

We discover the means to become whole.

We decide.

This journey starts with the decision. We make it now.

But seek ye first the kingdom of God, and his righteousness; and all these things shall be added unto you.

—Matthew 6:33

When we choose to proceed, we walk toward ourselves to find ourselves. We perceive and accept that we have obstacles in our paths. We laugh when we realize we're the ones who put them there. We consider how we might remove them.

At every moment, we are grateful that we have a path so full of opportunity to learn more about ourselves.

When we walk, we naturally go to the fields and woods: What would become of us if we only walked in a garden or a mall?

—Henry David Thoreau

What else would we want to do with this life?

Who Are You?

We have a strong tradition these days of outsourcing just about everything to do with our care. Or we do nothing. When something goes awry, we have no idea how to solve it.

Obesity, insomnia, anxiety, depression, pain—these things come upon us, and we're at a loss. We say we don't have enough money. Or if we have money, we say we don't have enough friends. Or if we have enough friends and money, we regret climate change and worry that our kitchen isn't up-to-date. We install solar, fix up the house, and then we wonder why we just aren't happy at all.

We go to doctors. Therapists. Healers.

We call on anyone who promises a balm, a pill, a device. Even better, a panacea.

Many of us presume someone out there will make it right. We're seeking that one missing link to a better world. A workout routine. A supplement. A whole pantry of supplements, barefoot shoes, and a meditation app on our phones.

And maybe yes. But mostly no.

What may be right for me may not be right for you. What works for you may not serve your neighbor. Which is why the most important player in this drama is only you. Always you.

You're the keeper of the balm. Just as I keep mine, you have yours.

It's you. It's in you. As we learn to know ourselves, to help ourselves, to change ourselves, we see. What we discover is illuminating because who we discover is ourselves. The kicker? We don't see until we choose to make the effort. That's the way it works. If you don't look, you won't find.

It's a truth reiterated in our shared wisdom traditions. We evolve as we discover it.

You may not have heard it because our culture doesn't sponsor or promote a robust wisdom tradition.

Or you've heard it but weren't ready to listen. It happens.

Here's some truth, so listen: You're part of a lineage that has passed along guidance to help human beings for as long as humans have communicated. Some of this has been recorded in sagas and scripture. Imagine, prior to that, the wisdom shared around fires, on long walks, at the close of day when the sun disappeared yet again. Maybe the truth came in stories at bedtime or letters from father to son. The truth is our birthright and destiny.

We all carry it.

The Self in man and in the sun are one.
Those who understand this see through the world
And go beyond the various sheaths of being
To realize the unity of life.
—Taittiriya Upanishad

We have only to decide to remember it.

So, here we are. Shall we remember together?

The Truth and the Pattern

We follow these patterns in our lives. We're patterned beings.

Some of the patterns are ingrained in us seemingly from birth, and some systems of thought point to previous incarnations as a source. Some patterns arise as we're nourished by our mothers and fathers in infancy. Some patterns strengthen because they allow us to strengthen into adulthood.

Our systems of education and livelihood deepen our patterns in a variety of ways. So do our interactions with others, our loves, our traumas, our successes and failures.

The patterns determine our behavior. Their sources will come clear as we give space to healing from them. The time-space reference for them is not as important as our willingness to inquire into the patterns. This is the start of healing.

The source will reveal itself. Listen carefully.

We exist in a pattern of persistent movement. We are in constant motion—physically, energetically, emotionally. We drive here and there; our eyes dart from screen to screen to screen; our mouths chew and chew; we jump from worry of the future to nostalgia for the past; our emotions rise and fall.

In all this volatility, we've forgotten our agency. We don't realize that all of this motion is initiated on a choice we make. Our allegiance to the patterns is so strong that we forget we've bowed our heads to follow them.

The truth is, we choose to move.

As we hear that, something rises up in us to justify our actions.

We resist agency because we see the woven universe around us as a tapestry hanging on a gallery wall. We don't realize we're implicit in its warp and weft. We feel it looming over us: the places we have to go, the people who depend on us, the way things were and could be. We imagine ourselves trying to rise up to the art on the wall, to protect it, to wonder if it's even real. But we're the art.

Looking inside may feel irrelevant, selfish, or even frightening. This is simply another belief that's become a pattern. We simply aren't trained to do it.

Instead we've been trained to keep busy. We pretend like we have so many important things to do when the things we do are only important because of the urgency we've given them. This makes us feel important, which is another pattern we maintain because it helps us feel purposeful. That purpose, unfortunately, often demands that we look toward others for approval, acceptance, comeuppance, and gratification.

What a strange predicament. The world we want to improve, conquer, or control is the world we wish would applaud us. We sit and watch the show and want the players to give us the standing ovation.

We're looking in the wrong direction for our accolades.

The result? We've made ourselves captive to ideas of little consequence. You may be raising children or curing cancer or amassing wealth or all three at the same time—thank you for your hard work—but these roles will shift and eventually end.

What will remain? Would your importance diminish? Would you have all the requisite approval to feel satisfied?

We're loyal adherents to a system that tells us consistently that we aren't enough. So let me reveal this subversive and absolutely open secret: you are perfect, and you are important. Regardless of our roles, we have a purpose. Each and every one of us.

Now that we've discovered this good news, shall we share it widely?[1]

Our discoveries, as we translate them to our experience, very often change the direction of our lives. Or at least highlight the purpose of them.

As we experience for ourselves the potential of our own discoveries, may we too become compelled to pass along the possibilities of peace within. It is only from peace within that peace beyond will reign. May we all learn from each other and share broadly what we find.

You're the One

You're the one living your life. You're the one experiencing the world. You're the one, whether you regard yourself as special or flawed, worthy or wallflower. I promise this: no one, ever, will live your life as

---

[1] We can all take heart that people throughout history have endeavored to guide us toward the stability to acknowledge and live these truths. Teachings persist despite our collective will to ignore guidance. Somehow, we eventually find our way. Our teachers appear. We humble ourselves to accept what they share, and it often changes the direction of our lives and highlights the purpose of them.

perfectly as you do. No one, ever, will know with precision what it is to be you.

Which means, the first question must be: Who are you?

I'll start.

I'm Megan.

We can agree this reveals nothing more than an inclination of my parents. For example, I was meant to be called Monique. My mom met a woman named Megan when she went into labor. She went with it. Done. I've known *Megan*s and *Monique*s. I am no more related to either by nature of my name.[2]

Who are you?

Most of us probably don't remember ourselves as infants, and most everyone but our mothers would find us unrecognizable from then to now. Can you remember yourself at seven? The material form you took at seven years old has been almost completely refreshed every ten years or so since then. Very few cells from your childhood exist in you today. Most of our physical forms have died and regenerated many, or at least a few times, over the course of our lives.[3] We live on.

This is the process of our embodiment. We come into the world with a soft and rubbery body that may, if we're lucky, grow rigid and dry. Our tissues firm up as our engagement with the world lengthens. We progress toward death. This is the trajectory of the body. In the process

---

[2] The relationship we share is much deeper. More on that later.

[3] Stomach cells, skin cells, blood cells: these die and are replaced in days or months. The cells in our bones and fat may last up to ten years before they die. Some cells in the eyes and central nervous system may endure through the whole human life span.

of living, our cells continuously die and renew. Our bodies are in a constant state of birth, death, and rebirth.

You remain. We come and go; something in us remains constant.

Who are you?

Do you recall your perceptions as a kid? Did something live under the bed? Did you talk to summer lizards as they sunned themselves? Or make friends with every neighbor? Did you jump out of trees and imagine flight or listen to the stories of the birds?

When I was seven, I visited two friends daily. They lived in a lush, overgrown jungle in a yard across the street. I would climb into shadowy caves beneath a thicket of suburban overgrowth. There, I would sit in the dirt and share stories with an old couple named George and Georgina. Retired and still in love, they listened and offered space for art in mud and flower petals. George could be stern; Georgina was the Earth Mother herself. I spent time with these two until I was maybe eleven.

That was when a boy down the street informed me that imaginary friends were for babies. I pretended to agree. But I also chose to forgo one friendship to avoid the teasing in another.

George and Georgina understood when I apologized and said I would no longer visit. They said I was always welcome. And I kept them in my heart to guide me. To this day, occasionally, I think of what they would advise when considering my options.

I modified my behavior, but I didn't really change. Specifically, I learned to work with a rule that says the unseen—however supportive it may be—may be doubted by others. Someone else's doubt need not become our guiding star, but we can still appreciate the moment of light it sheds on our path.

I learned about society's expectations, and I made an alteration. A little subversively, but maybe that's the way we should engage with most of society's requirements. I maintained my perception of two faithful friends, and I offered discretion so no one would be concerned.

The girl I was at eleven hesitated to abandon George and Georgina. The woman at twenty may have pretended they never existed. The woman at forty knows they're ever present, available with a simple thought.

This is the evolution of the mind. It perceives, it restricts, and if we let it, it expands.

Consider: What do we allow our perception to pick up, how do we restrict what it shows us, and how do we put it to work to expand our awareness? At a certain point, we discover that the mind is simply an instrument: we can learn to direct its focus, or we can suffer our clumsiness and become distracted by the lack of restraint.

So, who is this entity using the instrument of the mind?

You.

Who are you?

Are you this thing you do? An engineer, teacher, student, accountant, lawyer, doctor, wage earner? A gardener, baker, cook, cleaner? Do you do so you may be? Or do you do because you have to and wonder what else is out there for you?

Maybe you recognize yourself as a creator? Someone less associated with doing, someone awed by her creation. A mother. A father. An artist, poet, writer, musician. You cultivate and see yourself in the artwork.

Or do you use general terms? You are not what you do but how you inhabit this world. As a child born to a mother. As a sibling, a cousin, a colleague. A lover. A friend. A neighbor. You are someone in relation to another.

In all of these identities, an interaction with something or someone is required. We may not like to admit it, but these are projects. With work, it's obvious. With creation, maybe less so.

With relationships, it depends on the day. All three, however, are absolutely the same in that they require relationships outside of ourselves.

Our patterns teach us that anything outside us is separate and occasionally burdensome. It may not be the events, circumstances, and interactions that deplete us but rather the parameters we establish around them. Instead of feeling stable and at ease in our relationships, we build boundaries that prevent honesty, compassionate listening, and clear self-expression. When these relationships become troublesome, we wonder if we wouldn't be happier just living alone somewhere with cats and dogs.

Sorry to say, misery in company eventually becomes misery alone. The misery, you see, comes from inside us. The root of every beastly condition is in us, seeking nourishment in our every interaction. This is why so many of those obstacles seem intractable.

In our unique ways, we perceive our obstacles as beasts guarding the gate. We don't move forward because the beasts demand our attention. In our unique ways, we feed them well.

Let's look away from the snarl and cast our sights within. Let's stop nurturing the beasts. The beasts grow weak when we feed ourselves love.

The beasts thrive on fear, anger, hatred, judgment, scorn, resentment. We thrive on love. Food, water, air are requisite to survival; a profound experience in life demands abiding, unconditional love.

We are perfect; we do the best we can; we have purpose.

Love this incredible fortune.

It's as simple and incredibly demanding as that.

Every relationship on which you base your identity will be shifted immediately when you choose to engage it with pure, unfiltered love. No need for competition, mistrust, comparison, or hurt. Only love.

From this perspective, the separation between you and every activity dissolves. There is no longer a *you* and an *outside*. There is only a you, nourished and strengthened in every interaction by the love you share regardless of time, space, screaming ego, or adverse circumstance.

It isn't easy. It's your purpose.

I ask again: Who are you?

As you consider this question, begin to examine what would happen to you if the projects you've undertaken were to end. In other words, if you couldn't do your profession, would you be you? Who would you be? If you couldn't create any longer, if your child should pass…who would you be? And if your relationships ended and you were the last person on the earth, who would remain? Still a daughter or son, but what more? Who are you at the source?

A code?

That changes too. So what remains as the code rewrites itself?

What remains of you between infancy and now? What remains from your first home to your last? What remains as the breath comes and goes? As you learn and let go?

This is for you to discover.

Please acknowledge this paradox: We're told that a spiritual life requires our selflessness. But maybe the spirit is the self.

If we ignore ourselves and look everywhere else to make sense of this life, we won't see it. Discovering the spirit is a process of realizing the self. And in this process, we find out how we evolve and how we stay the same. We learn to be discriminative in our thoughts and behaviors as this evolution happens, and the foundation for this discrimination is compassion, kindness, love. Selflessness is truly invested in the self. Let's find the self.

Let's find unconditional love.

First, we study our dimensions. We get a sense of who we are from head to toe, birth to now, and remain invested in this very moment. We study the body and understand how it works, how it holds, how it compensates for injuries—physical and emotional. We study our energy and discover how it ebbs and flows throughout the day, throughout a season; we become acquainted with accessing energy to nourish our efforts, heal our wounds, and strengthen our commitments. We look at our patterns of behavior and discover how repetitive we are when we settle ourselves in a groove.

Also, how our patterns are amenable to modification. Other grooves await.

Eventually, or quite suddenly, we see that what we think ourselves to be is actually constantly in movement. We are bodies decaying, energy zapping, thoughts and moods arising and fading. There's no consistency there.

We are passing away from our very first moment. What we think we are is completely irrelevant because it is only in flux. Within that flux is something else. Your home. You. Love.

The same entity that has loved consistently since moment one. This is your true nature. This is where you can learn to rest. From this resting place, you can become grateful for constant change, as you're grateful for the growth of your garden and the quiet zip of the hummingbird passing through it.

To get there, we have to ask: Who am I?

When we've exhausted all possible answers, we arrive at knowledge. We are not this; we are not that.[4] We are.

It is imperceptible, for It is never perceived;

Undecaying, for It never decays; unattached for It is never attached;

Unfettered—It never feels pain and never suffers injury.

—Brihadaranyaka Upanishad

We are, simply, home. We rest there.

---

[4] In the Brihadaranyaka Upanishad, this is "neti, neti." Not this. Not that. The Upanishads are sacred texts that evolved and distilled ancient Vedic tradition of ritual into dialogues and verse. The Upanishads share wisdom into universal inquiries and contemplations to foster our self-awareness and realization.

I long, as does every human being, to be at home wherever I find myself.

—*Maya Angelou*

When we learn to rest at home, we become selfless.

We realize that everyone has a home and their homes are as beautiful as ours because there is no longer a separation between us. Their source is ours. We are represented in all others. What we do to ourselves, we do to others. What others experience, we also experience with compassion and kindness. We are love.

For most of us, we can't get there until we do the work, contend with the obstacles and the shadows they cast, find stability and ease on our path, and see our light.

We need to learn how to move through the darkness that obscures our comprehension of self.

The darkness is our ignorance of who and how we are.

The light is us.

We've seen it before. It reflects in the smile of a stranger when we pass with a smile of our own. It beams in our laughter. It brightens every time we choose to be kind, and then it spreads beyond us. We know who we are when we're home.

Wisdom to Bring Home...

- You're the one. Every inquiry in life starts with you, and every answer will come because you're ready to acknowledge it. We must be willing to look within, to center our attention on ourselves and observe who we are.
- The decision we make to attend to ourselves is one we make again and again.
- We are patterned beings. Some of these patterns will counsel against self-inquiry; some will benefit our inquiries. As we start paying attention to our patterns, we can determine which are useful and apply them.
- We each have a purpose in this life, and we are entitled to live our lives as expressions of and in service to this purpose.
- Although it seems like a journey, we are, actually, always home. The journey is our process of discovering this eternal truth.

To continue contemplating who you are, please see the study guide at the end. The questions presented in this chapter reappear for your consideration. Sit with them. Be with them.

2. What Is This Body?

Somebody should tell us, right at the start of our lives, that we are dying.

Then we might live life to the limit, every minute of every day. Do it! I

say. Whatever you want to do, do it now! There are only so many

tomorrows.

—Pope Paul VI

Rest assured, life has you.

Your Body is Constantly Dying

My dear friend, I want to share an open secret with you. Please feel strong.

You and I share a fate: we both exist in bodies in a process of decay. To be blunt, we're on our way to death. We share that fate. We are, with every breath, closer to our last exhale. Please savor this next one. Please say thank you to the inhale that follows. It wasn't guaranteed.

What is guaranteed is this: at some point you and I, and everyone we know, will die.

In fact, we have both been dying, along with every other person each of us has ever encountered, since the moment of our birth. Some of those you've known are gone. Some of those you know will last longer than you. But all the bodies around you and on this earth, from moment one until the last, are meant to pass.

44

The way we ready ourselves for this inevitability proves a valuable method for enhancing our experiences in the interim. In other words, the more we accept the fact of death, the more freedom we find to live.

We can cherish the body while we have it and respect that it will fade. We can care for the body appropriately when we honor its cycle.

Whatever it is we're meant to do for our bodies requires our attention. Very often, our attention to physical issues is taken up with the resolution of discomfort, pain, injury. In this chapter on the body, we aren't going to learn how to fix, improve, or preserve the body. Instead, we'll contemplate the ways we might befriend our bodies. Healing happens in the friendship.

How do you relate and honor your beautiful body? Do you realize it houses you so loyally and will hold you as long as it can?

Yoga with Breath

Let's do a small practice together.

Please become aware of your breath.

As you feel the breath moving into your body, silently say, "My body receives this breath."

When it feels right, please exhale. As you feel the breath moving out of your body, silently say, "My body releases this breath."

Do this about five more times. Feel both sides of your breath in your body.

Where do you feel your body receiving and releasing the breath?

As you inhale again, please thank your body for breathing.

"Thank you, body, for breathing in."

Feel your thanks expand as you acknowledge how precious, fulfilling, and lifesaving every breath actually is.

As you exhale again, please thank your body for breathing.

"Thank you, body, for breathing out."

Feel your thanks expand as you realize how much relief every exhale offers.

Please do this about five more times.

Every breath—your inhale and your exhale—gives you access to your most essential nutrient in this life. We can live without food for a while, without water for a shorter time. Without breath, we don't last long at all.

"Thank you, body, for letting every breath arrive and go. I'm grateful you breathe."

What If...

What if our parents taught us from the beginning that our bodies will change and eventually perish? What if we were all educated about the trajectory of our bodies and encouraged to influence our maximal well-being throughout the journey?

What if we were taught to honor all of life as a process of birth and death?

What if...

The body of every baby born in the world and alive today is on a path toward death. Somehow, we insist on ignoring this bit of wonder in favor of an impossible alternative. We love to pretend that one of the only promises life makes to us is sure to be broken.

We are all children, afraid of the dark.

We hold tight to life.

We want life to hold us as dearly.

Rest assured, life has you.

As surely as life offers growth, so too does it offer decline. We are in the midst of it at every moment. We're held dearly in life's constant movement, embraced by its change.

Look around and observe for yourself.

Life moves lifeward.

You've certainly seen a flower bloom and pass. You've eaten a tomato that started from a seed that became a plant that flowered, fruited fragrantly, and finished up at the end of summer. You may also have eaten a burger that was once a calf who grew and became a cow, whose body produced the muscle you ingested to nurture your body.

See the changing leaves on trees, your aging friends. Attempting to grow without marveling at the space made by loss is like trying to contain water without a vessel. Or to know sound without appreciating silence.

Feel your body for a moment and realize its constant shift. The body is a wonderful teacher of change.

Life in our physical world is a constant balance between poles. Its most basic polarity is creation and destruction.

The physical world comes and goes. We are part of that.

If you're willing, see how it feels to you for a moment. Your body is in the process of dying.

The body of your lover is dying. The body of your child is dying. Your dog's body too. Your neighbor's body. And everyone you know.

You aren't alone in the process. We're all in it together. Look to the strangers around you. You can spot a bird in a tree, a sleeping cat, and a man on a bicycle; all of them, with you, are moving together toward a moment when everybody now alive will expire.

Long may we last.

It's enough to make you want to hug everyone, no?

We share a finite space in time in these bodies.[5]

As we await the bell's final toll, we might want to treat all the bodies we perceive—ours and those of others—as kindly as possible. In this camaraderie we may find ourselves more present to the plight of others. You may feel profoundly those events and circumstances that limit the tenure of bodies you've met.[6]

People living deeply have no fear of death.

—*Anais Nin*

Can you imagine the solace you might find by becoming present to every moment our bodies share together? It's your choice.

---

[5] And our perception of separation from every other body becomes much more suspect as we consider that each of them is headed, with our body too, toward infinite dust.

[6] You may even want to say thank you to all those bodies who have endured along with yours to keep you company.

How shall we live and die together in these bodies?

May we never rush the final bell. May we last as long as we learn.

And may we cherish these bodies for carrying us through every wonderful encounter. And I mean every...single...one.

Your Body is Constantly Born Again

But how do we cherish these bodies? How do we hold them dear?

First, please know this. You, my dear, more than anyone else in the world, are the best-placed person to answer that question. Just as you, good friend, are the exact person to tend to your body with the greatest care.

Every moment, your body may be dying, but it's also in a process of renewal. Cells turn over. This is the way life works. We grow and decline; we come and go. Every part of us. Breath inspires us and departs. Nutrition is consumed and turned into movement. Waste is eliminated and becomes space created for more.

The energy of being alive is a constant ebb and flow.

Unfortunately, so much of the energy of our aliveness—our current of being—is limited in some way. Maybe we have pain. Or tension. Or weakness. Or obesity. Many of us dissociate from our bodies for various reasons—trauma, disease, disaster. As a result, our experience of sensation and expression in the body is a little foreign.

Some of us even acknowledge our bodies as strangers. We say things like, "I don't feel right in my skin." The distance we keep from our bodies is reflected in our well-being—both physical and psychological. We may find ourselves struggling with protective weight, with anxious trembling,

49

with chronic indigestion. These conditions are the body's way of communicating its comfort or discomfort with the way they're being tended.

Learning how to cherish the body asks that we first befriend it. It asks for a new perspective.

I sing the body electric,

The armies of those I love engirth me and I engirth them,

They will not let me off till I go with them, respond to them,

And discorrupt them and charge them full with the charge of the soul.

Was it doubted that those who corrupt their own bodies conceal

themselves?

And if those who defile the living are as bad as they who defile the dead?

And if the body does not do fully as much as the soul?

And if the body were not the soul, what is the soul?

—Walt Whitman

Let's consider for a moment our friendship with our body. How are we in its presence?

Notice how we play a silly game while we live. We come into the world, figure out how to run, and just as quickly are told not to fall. We learn to talk, and someone tells us what we shouldn't say. We begin thinking for ourselves, and we're told to shelve it or stop.

Each of the reprimands carries an introduction of fear. The risks we naturally take—celebrated momentarily—are quickly tempered by an abundance of caution. We prove our caution by holding our bodies overly tight. We cling, and the tension takes its toll. Our friendship suffers.

A friend of mine leads a fairly privileged life. She's wonderful Amelia.

Amelia has a husband and two children and ample financial stability. Despite her security, she bears some pretty hefty grudges. In the recent past, she stopped communication with her family following an uncomfortable dinner, she sued an employer for an offhand remark, and she boycotted a restaurant after a host seated her near the kitchen. For a long time, she kept her grudges like badges of honor. By the time her kids were in middle school, she'd taught them, consciously or otherwise, to bear her grudges in dutiful ways.

Although healthy and active, Amelia has convinced herself—and her children—that there are threats to her children that require her constant vigilance. As little ones, these two were reluctant to go outside to play. A bit older, they kept their distance from strangers and spoke dismissively of them—their clothes, their behavior, their hair, or anything that seemed different.

The kids became overweight. They had these funny inflexible attitudes that you don't often hear in kids: make believe was silly; climbing a tree had no point; worlds of the imagination were ignored. The only place they were allowed to play was in organized sports, and they both suffered a number of injuries.

I wondered aloud to Amelia one day: "Would your kids ever want to stretch their bodies in a little yoga routine?"

It's clear that Amelia is the queen of her children's resistance, and I didn't intend to challenge her reign. I simply wanted to make the offer of a safe place to soften. Plus, I love those kids and my friend.

To my surprise, the kids came along to yoga once a week for a few months. They moved like Tin Men when they first arrived. Neither could touch their toes. Both had sore backs. Still, they moved. They explored. They grumbled. And then they started laughing. They called themselves Gramma and Gramps and told the elderly students in the class they would be flexible by the time they were seventy.

As it is for most students, moving with the breath, relaxing and paying attention was strange for these kids. The first week they thought it was slow. The second week they fell asleep. Then the seeds took root. They loosened up and lightened up. The body's comfort opened the door to easing the mind.

Both of them incorporated a few principles into their routines, and now that they're heading to college, it's endearing to see them choosing to carry their lighter ways with them. Their mother—bless her—continues to keep her grudges. These days she laughs at the habit a little more. She's learning from her kids.

When the student is ready, the teacher will appear.

—Unknown

Some of us hold tight. It's a learned behavior. We can learn otherwise. We can start with the body, offering it movement, softness, kindness, and support. When the body finds softness, our experience with the world softens. Until then we'll keep holding tightly and feel the world squeezing us.

We hold tightly when we run and hate the feeling. We hold tightly when we speak and can't utter what we really want to say. We hold tightly when we contemplate, and it becomes a burden so great, we'd rather watch movies all day. And then we hold tightly when we love and decide love feels too challenging to support.

All that holding with all that tension leads to all kinds of resentment. Frustration. Anger. Guilt. Shame. Pain too. It's like an equation: no matter what the variable is, if you multiply it with holding tightly, we suffer.

The insult to the injury is that these are the experiences that demand we tighten our grip. They are patterns, and they strengthen every time we employ them. Every time they manifest, we hold on more tightly and enhance the experience. We turn toxic. We hold so tightly that nothing can move us out of it.

Over many years, I've seen highly trained athletes, soldiers, and executives find their way to peace by giving peace to their bodies. Those who engage with physical relaxation are the ones who start to see things differently. As they soften into whatever they feel, the feeling softens too.

A former marine and bodybuilder with raging neck tension and chronic anger practiced a few weeks of quiet, guided body scans. She returned to see me with a broad smile. She said, "I don't need to be mad anymore. And my neck pain is so much better."

An attorney with back pain rested his body mindfully every day for two weeks and later shared, "I don't even remember what the pain feels like."

Whether the bodybuilder's anger had overstayed its welcome in her neck or her neck was making her angry is irrelevant. They both distracted her from peace. By cultivating peace, she relieved the distractions, so peace could remain.

In her comfortable moments of rest, she discovered that she didn't have to host pain or persistent anger.

Likewise with the attorney. He learned to cultivate the calm he needed.

They each shifted their patterns by loosening very strong grips.

Frequently we're wound up. We are not at ease.

Often, the older we get, the tighter we become.

Oh, the body.

When I say we hold tightly, hear me clearly: I mean in the way we hold our bodies *and* the way they hold our emotions, memories, illusions, beliefs, opinions. Each affects the other.

Each is the other, just differently expressed in its manifestation.

Maybe you've experienced this before? A headache is inseparable from the experience of anxiety on a particular day. A sprained ankle may be acted out in despondency as the world becomes less navigable. That tight neck limits our ability to turn and to patiently consider a different perspective.

We are all suffering in these bodies. They are miraculous and prone to injury. They are a treasure, and we want to keep them safe.

The Buddha validated us all with his acknowledgement of our suffering. We feel aches and pains; we get sick. We also experience loss:

people we love die; jobs we enjoy end; our bodies weaken with disease and age.

In Christianity, too, suffering is understood as our shared plight.

The fact of it, however, is simply the provocation for inquiry. Our suffering is our launchpad.

We are not meant to bear our crosses in eternal misery. We are meant to realize a way to rise above it.

Through many tribulations we must enter the kingdom of God.

—Acts 14:22

We can learn how to relieve ourselves of the burden. We can learn to share our relief with others who ask for help.

Instead we stand awkwardly and rigid in a two-part game plan: 1) we commiserate and impose the weight of our suffering onto others, and 2) we secretly or not so secretly believe that no one else suffers as profoundly as we do.

We think we suffer, and it's a punishment. We're convinced our punishment is worse than everyone else's. We won't even consider that we might look at our suffering and see how we might lighten its weight.

Maybe this is simply momentum. Mass times velocity. We suffer until another force comes along to change its direction. We don't realize we are that force. Maybe this is also addiction or, at least, obsession. We prefer that we have our suffering. We may feel special in the misery we assume no one else can completely appreciate.

The answer to the problem of suffering is not a way from the problem but

in it.

—*Alan Watts*

Please listen closely. We are special for sure. Just not for the depth of our suffering.

We're special because of the natures hidden beneath the suffering. Not for our suffering but because of our very natures.

Each one of us.[7]

Consider again the body. Shall we come to a dear friendship with the body?

Your Body Is a Precious Gift

Our bodies are absolute treasures. Take a moment to consider how closely your body has remained to you. It is the most loyal friend you'll ever have. It will not abandon you regardless of the abuse, the scorn, the distaste cast on it.

These beautiful bodies that house us are not meant to last. Our bodies fade. They go. We want them to last.

But why? Well, that's obvious. They shelter us. We inhabit them, and they provide us with a means of experiencing the world.

---

[7] The universality of our beautiful, special selves does not in any way diminish ourselves. If we acknowledge it, it is the loveliest connection you'll find in life. But let's embark on that in due time. Or skip ahead to the chapter on "You."

From this network of bones and muscles, of tissue and blood, we are a finely tuned organism of sensation. A highly sophisticated world, in fact, populated by a whole network of operators that know what to do and when to do it to keep the mechanism functional. We are, all of us, difficult beings to replicate, and yet these beings that house us know exactly how to do it, over and over and over again. We couldn't make a liver, but our cells are well-informed of the proper procedure. Thank you very much, treasured cells.

The very fact of our existence is so statistically unlikely.[8] Just marvel for a moment at the incredible fact that you came to be in your body.

First all of our ancestors had to survive and make babies. Back in the day, mortality rates were such that being born didn't give you great chances of making it to five years old. But somehow your ancestors made it. Well done.

Then your mom and dad had to stumble upon each other. They had to enjoy each other's company for some period of time sufficient to procreate. That's magical enough, or at least wildly unpredictable— approximately equivalent to the chances of bumping into a certain person at a party attended by the entire population of California.

After that it gets wild.

When we start dealing with eggs and sperm, we're working with huge numbers. The chance of one sperm meeting one egg is 1 in 400 quadrillion. That means 400 with 15 zeroes after it. All combined—from ancestors to you—you are the privileged existence that managed to surmount essentially almost zero chance of being.

[8] Look for a great infographic published by Business Insider in 2012 using the research of the Happiness Engineer, Dr. Ali Binazir. The following estimations come from there.

The chance of any of our singular existence is unfathomable. The number is exhilarating. You are not simply one in a million. You are one in a 10 to the 2,650,000. The number of zeroes following the one would fill 10 books. Who knows how to say it any other way than you're special?

You, me, and all of us exist in highly unique and specialized bodies whether we've realized it or not. We've done much better than win the lottery just by being alive.

It's no surprise, then, that we want to prolong our lives. Sometimes we even pretend that we're going to have them forever. This, my friend, is the great conundrum. In this primary ignorance, we hurl ourselves into the waves of life before sobering ourselves to the fact of mortality. As we've seen, we haven't been trained to comprehend our mortality. Nor have we refined the discernment to care for ourselves appropriately for whatever duration the physical body has.

We forget to be proper custodians of our bodies. We fail to prioritize our health until we're ill at ease. *Dis*-eased, even. We consume too much without an idea of need; we do too much without a sense of purpose. Our bodies become overweight, overstressed, and stuck in pain cycles while digesting poorly. Still, we won't wise up until injury puts us on the bench or disease pushes us to bed. Even then, we may not learn the lesson.

We rarely, if ever, pause to consider whether a meal, a hobby, a home, a commute, a schedule, a partner, or a career is right for the vessel that will transport us through the experience. We commit, again and again, crimes and misdemeanors against our health, happiness and wisdom.

Most of us are more considerate of our cars.

Consider, for a moment, your body as your most wonderful friend. You will never have a more constant companion in your life than your miraculous body. Your body has taken you everywhere you've ever been. Despite some of our worst decisions, our bodies persist. Despite broken bones and overburdened livers, overtaxed nerves and inappropriate fuel consumption, our bodies persevere toward life. Long may these bodies carry us.

Instead of learning how to love and nurture our bodies, we cultivate habits of protecting them from potential peril. We are wise to prevent future suffering where we can. We are loving when we acknowledge the condition of the body from place to place, from moment to moment.

We worry over dirt and germs, but perhaps we can remember the joy of contact and the strength of our immunity. We become enraged and combative over cracks in the sidewalk and hot coffee, but perhaps we can watch our steps and be attentive to our choices. We demand legislation that forces seat belts, helmets, and speed limits. What if we also realize the kindness of treating our bodies with care without the force of law making the demand?

Who do you think is in the best place to care for these bodies? Who, actually, is meant to live in these bodies? Are we willing to cultivate a deeper connection with these wonderful friends who carry us?

The fear we have of the world's ability to destroy our bodies shows our basic instinct to trust in our care for them. We just don't quite know how to do it. We don't come with an owner's manual, and we haven't realized that we're the ones meant to write it.

We may be a bit overprotective and misguided. Parents learn that children need freedom. Our bodies do as well. Some of us who have experienced the confinement of doting parents or the rigors of sports or military life may go to the opposite extreme. We may push our bodies to excessive activity, risk, and finally injury. In either case we're trying to avoid an essential truth: we are gifted with life in the body, and it will only be as comfortable in here as we decide to make it.

Our responsibility is to know our bodies' conditions, limitations, and needs. In response, we must offer our care appropriately.

Life happens moment by moment. Whether we confine our bodies to a windowless room or wander the world barefoot, everybody now on Earth, including ours, ultimately will perish. Our fear of their demise diminishes our courage to live fully, kindly, and wisely in them.

So, how shall we make friends with our bodies? What will we include in our owner's manual to promote health, happiness, and well-being?

Life in a physical body wants experience. Our role is to care for the body wisely by learning to sense how every experience serves us.

We are meant to eat food, to drink the various elixirs of life, to consume and receive nourishment through each of our wonderful senses. But we are also meant to have discernment in the foods we eat and in the elixirs we sip. We are meant to savor every breath.

We are meant to cherish our bodies.

These bodies of ours give us precise and precious instruments for engaging with life. These instruments are the senses. We gorge on a beautiful rainbow through our eyes. Our ears devour music. Gentle, loving touch will nourish us as well as a home-cooked meal, even a delicious one whose smells carry out the window to excite the neighbors.

Keeping your body healthy is an expression of gratitude to the whole

cosmos—the trees, the clouds, everything.

—Thich Nhat Hanh

We are made to consume the content of these experiences and to discover how they serve us. We are meant to feed ourselves with the entirety of life, not just food.

When we discover the nourishment of life around us, we don't feel the same compulsion to overeat, overcommit, or overwork. We realize abundance is all around us and our bodies are in connection with it.

How do we make this discovery?

Initially we simply practice saying thank you to our bodies. We thank them for their service, for their strength, for their resilience, for their continued efforts. With every thank you we utter, we pause for a moment to listen in to our body's response. This is a felt sense. We may feel our shoulders release. We may find an enlivening in the chest. For some of us, we'll discover brighter views, stronger scents, and a greater connection with the ground beneath us.

As we develop thanks for the body, we amplify sensory perception. Through the strengthening senses, we'll hear our bodies more clearly. This is the body's means of communication. We pretend like it's a one-way street, but we talk to our bodies all the time. As with any relationship, kind communication nurtures deeper communication. We hear the messages our bodies convey and begin to understand the patience required to respond well. Because bodies, unlike minds, are always in the present and weighted in the material world.

My friend, this body is His lute.

He tightens the strings and plays its songs.

If the strings break and the pegs work loose,

this lute, made of dust, returns to dust.

Kabir says: Nobody else can wake from it that heavenly music.

—*Kabir*

When we start to communicate with our bodies, we naturally slow down.

It's a relief. We feel it.

We commit to becoming the wise guardian of our bodies. Our gratitude deepens. This is when we realize how we've confined our bodies in patterns of abuse, neglect, and fear. It becomes more than uncomfortable; it becomes unacceptable.

This doesn't mean we become sheep, following every trend promoted by health and wellness coaches.

It means we become wise. We listen.

We become aware of what serves us and what continues to promote the patterns that hold us captive.

In our improving relationship, we learn what the body needs, and we take the time to offer it. We understand that this is always a conditional exercise. In other words, no one can tell you what's right for you but you. Guides can give you options, but it's up to you, conscientiously listening to the senses instead of reeling from them, ducking and dodging them, indulging them. Sometimes, this means we have to be a little lighter with these bodies. We can appreciate them for what they are instead of pretending they might someday be otherwise. For example, you may want to be tall but you're short. You may want smaller feet. I think my ears could take me sailing. Still, I'm happy to have them. Thank you, ears, for helping me hear.

Isn't this what true friendship is? We listen carefully to each other as we are. We accept, encourage, laugh, and love. We let go of our ideas of what should be and appreciate the connection for what it is.

The body is composed of what we eat, what we consume through the senses, and what we think. If we offer it junk in the form of food and vision and sound and touch, the body will become a junkyard. If we offer it food made by loving hands, visions of those we love, touch inspired by love and loving sounds, the body becomes a vessel of love.

Let's be friendly.

When this kindness is cultivated, we appreciate our good fortune to have these vessels transporting us around. We begin to relish opportunities to learn more about existence. We may even realize how privileged we are to exist. And what an honor it is that we have our freedom to tend to this existence.

When you experience things like heat and cold, pleasure and pain, you only feel them because your senses are in contact with them. These things come and go. These things have the nature of impermanence, so watch them come and go with patience and an even mind.

—Bhagavad Gita

Your Body Is Unique

From this grateful space, we can ask with total sincerity: If I cherish my body, how do I best care for this vessel of experience?

These days many folks only want the vessel to be something other than what it is. The question of caring for it doesn't arise because our distaste for it leads to interests in improving, altering, changing it. We don't start where we are—beautifully housed.

When we don't appreciate our residence, we take risky steps. If we persistently betray our bodies, should we be surprised when our bodies betray us?

I know an amazing woman in her forties. She astounds me with her stories of solo adventures over mountain peaks and marathon hikes under the summer sun. I have awe for her courageous feats, as well as compassion for the lows that consistently follow.

She loves to do a million things. She's magnificent in whatever physical activity she undertakes as a hiker, cyclist, swimmer, partier, surfer, doer, doer, doer.

She was also magnificent in depriving herself of rest.

When we first met, she asked for guidance for chronic back pain. Surgery had done nothing for her. Physical therapy brought no relief. Her shoulders, held high near her ears, suggested the confinement of an electric fence. I asked if she felt pain in her shoulders too. She answered with an immediate (slightly offended) no.

Later, after a little bit of work together and a little bit of quiet together, her gazed dropped to her tightly clasped hands. She acknowledged the tension. She admitted she had pain almost everywhere. What's more, she admitted that she was more worried about confronting what her body was holding so tightly than continuing to live in its confinement. She said she kept herself very physically active because it was the only way for her not to listen to her thoughts.

I asked about the pain. She said, "The pain, I can tolerate."

"Really?" I asked.

After some hesitation, she sighed. "Not really."

Like my friend, some of us push our bodies too far. We think we're supposed to stay aggressively active for various reasons: to appear busy, important, dominant, wild. We demand a lot from ourselves, expect ourselves to soar beyond competence, and often expect others to rise with us. We find ourselves disappointed often, and we demonstrate it in frustration. Our bodies feel this heat as indigestion, migraine, and inflammation in the joints.

There are also those of us who thrive on erratic energy to move here and there. We are like the wind. We may not be entirely dependable, but we are a good time. Electrifying company. And when we feel pain—also electrifying—we wear ourselves out ignoring it. Our bodies experience these high winds much like the earth might feel a dry desert storm. Our skin grows dry, our muscles weaken, and our joints feel stiff and immovable.

Some of us may not like all that movement so much. We like to sit around. We get dull, heavy, stagnant like a murky pond. We were kids who sat still on the laps of our mothers. We're the people who give the softest hugs, the kindest pats, the biggest meals when things get rough. We may also like to eat a little too much and forget that activity feels good. As a result, our bodies may experience stable, deep, and aching pain. It scares us a bit more because it lingers.

The reality is, we're all embodied, and all our bodies have unique ways of experiencing the world. We all tolerate stress in unique ways, and we all have variable levels of comfort and being overwhelmed based on variable conditions. We need to learn to read our gauges. When we're close to low energy, will we rest? Likewise, if we know the body has been sitting a bit long, will we take it out for a spin? The body well-tended is a considerate friend; it doesn't demand our attention unless something is amiss. Ideally we learn to read its signals before they become alarms. We learn to listen carefully to understand the source of the stress affecting it. And then we learn to soothe the body of its distress.

Our bodies are intelligent and responsive.

And we all have natural tendencies in the way we use and abuse these wonderful bodies.

In the ancient science of Ayurveda, these natural tendencies are considered pragmatically to keep aware of the potential stumbling blocks they can create. These tendencies are metaphorically, poetically, and very realistically discussed as an amalgam of elemental energies. This amalgam determines our form in the physical world. We may be small-boned, dry, airy, and eccentric. Or heavier, with supple skin, thick hair, and as slow and deliberate as continental shift. Some of us may be a bit more fiery, with ruddy cheeks, bright eyes, and prematurely thinning or graying hair.

We're all a little of everything, but we each have our energetic signatures.

The stumbling blocks appear when we fail to appreciate that we can work with these energies—to reconcile with our constitution and use it wisely. In Ayurveda this means we learn to use opposites to provide us with balance. Some simple examples? A desert vacation to restore someone who is feeling very dry and depleted may not be appropriate but a trip to a warm, tropical beach would feel wonderful. A person feeling overwhelmed with hot anger may not want to indulge in spicy foods but instead could choose to cool down with cucumbers and mint water. Someone feeling the weight of the world in their body may want to eat comfort food on the couch to feel better but a better option might be raw veggies and a brisk walk.

We don't have to be victims of how we are; we don't have to regret it either. Instead we can learn to understand how we are, and how to help ourselves.

What if you pay attention to how you are, instead of shunning, shaming, hating it, hurling it away, or forcing change on it?

What if you reconcile with yourself? If you don't mind this suggestion, this is how you could consider cherishing your body.

You accept it, work with it, nourish it, and love it in the ways appropriate to your body. Not someone else's body. Not an evidence-based body. But the body that you live in, feel in, are in. You may have bones that are dense or brittle. You may have skin that gets hot or stays cool. You may digest fast or slow, hold weight or lose it. Your body is special in so many ways.

Have you ever met a body like yours? And have you ever felt what it was like to be in someone else's body?

Even though we only have ourselves to experience deeply, we've become accustomed to outsourcing our wisdom to anyone else. Experts and scientists and personal trainers and yoga teachers. Psychologists and doctors. A whole bunch of people who aren't actually us. Some of those folks may give decent suggestions. Some of them may have important guidance to share. But their expertise, no matter how extensive and well-intentioned, will never replace your own wisdom with regard to your experience of being in your body.

This, my friends, is our first adventure on the way back home: explore the body.

What does it have to say? How does it say it? Have you listened in carefully? Have you found areas that sing more loudly than others? Have you discovered both tension and ease in there?

More simply, what do your feet feel like on the ground? How do you shift your weight when you stand? Where are your hands, and what is the position of your head?

There is so much more sensation to feel than pain. Let's pay attention. Sensation is your body's language, and it is always communicating. Our attention gives us the means to listen, perceive, and consider what it has to share with us.

Our neglect often provokes the body to communicate more forcefully. You may know this form of communication as pain.

Do you have pain? Do you have comfort? Can you locate places of ease in your body? Can you allow yourself to acknowledge that pleasure and pain coexist? Likewise, they may not be discontinuous. In other words, if you're willing, you can trace a feeling of discomfort all the way to a place of ease. You can even invite the ease to move toward the tension.

Our bodies appreciate our attention. We are meant to listen to our bodies. All its noise. All its ruckus. And its peace.

The pain and the pleasure too. The quiet tingles. The flutter of our eyelids. Our hunger pangs. The air on our skin.

Each message has something to tell us. We may be surprised that the sensations are not strictly related to physical movement. The body's messages deliver guidance. The body is wise and highly responsive. Whatever predicament you may be in, the body will often suggest a way out. It may be that the predicament is an old emotional wound or an ongoing confusion. The body will offer pointers. Your job is to learn its language and listen in.

A man I know—midforties, smartest guy in the room, athlete and math dude—says his priorities shifted when he discovered the feeling of his feet on the ground. He'd been on pain medication for years for discomfort his doctor associated with degenerative disc disease. This man was tired of the complications. He felt chained to the diagnosis, the medication, and the relationship with a doctor who didn't do anything.[9] My friend called me, pretending—not convincingly—to be much less anxious than he was. Then he confided he was in panic. He'd become scared of the drugs. He wondered what they were doing to his liver, his intestines, his brain's ability to process.

---

[9] The doctor did what doctors are expected to do these days. He offered medication and shots. As we collectively remember our many interweaving dimensions, may all healers realize how to gently hold the hands, minds, and hearts of their patients.

I asked my friend to take a deep breath, to slowly exhale and feel his body. I listened to him breathe into the phone for a few minutes. When he spoke again, his voice was thin but calm. He'd realized a simple fact, he said. He realized the only thing happening at that moment was the experience of feeling his feet on the ground.

In that instant he changed his course.

He asked his doctor for support to come off the medication. He wanted to try yoga and asked for guidance.

Over a period of six months, with his doctor's approval, this man committed to a progressive decrease of his medication. He never said he was quitting; he said he was reducing the dose as much as he could. We worked together to develop comfortable movement practices. He committed to a short series of yoga poses to strengthen his back, a breathing exercise, and a prayer to repeat as a reminder of his strength.

It was a simple prayer that we created together based on his ideal vision of his relationship with his body: *I'm in perfect health and always healing. My body is a ready, willing, and strong friend. I'm grateful for this strength, and I use it wisely.*

As he started to move his body again, and to feel his body moving, he often returned to the feeling of his feet on the ground. It was a link for him—to the ever-present foundation of the earth, to his own roots and the growth they'd nurtured in his life. He'd known this before, as a highly ranked martial artist, but he'd forgotten. When he felt his feet on the ground, he remembered himself: his strength, his balance, his focus. His concerns—about pain arising, about people knowing his pain, about the physiological effects of the medication, and about who he might be without these worries—dissolved. His feet on the ground reminded him that he was established in his life.

It also gave him a stable foundation from which he considered the sources of his pain.

He observed that he was honoring a family legacy. In pain, he, his siblings, and his parents found fodder for conversation and complaint. He also saw that his pain increased with his frustration at his family's financial choices. He discovered that his skepticism toward his family's choices coincided with his sharp pain. He learned he couldn't change his family. He had to accept their choices and recognize that whatever followed would not be his problem to solve. He finally understood how angry he'd been believing that he would have to save them.

Three months later his family was the same as ever, but he suffered no back pain. His body gave him the effects of drug withdrawal instead. I offered him another breathing exercise to fortify his resolve and soothe his nerves. He was diligent in his practice. He meditated daily and checked in when he worried over his ability to become free.

Of what? I used to ask. Free of medication? Of pain? Or free of worry?

Your Body Is a Gateway to Freedom

Freedom is a funny, wonderful, misunderstood, and always evolving concept. Freedom starts with our friendship with the body. Freedom is available at every moment. It requires a constant choice to remain friends with the body before we strive beyond it. What we think of as freedom most often is a greater confinement than we might realize.

A home comes with a mortgage; a car comes with expense; our every desire leads to suffering, even if it's fulfilled.

Friendship with the body, however, takes us toward contentment. We realize how well the body houses us. Whatever we may have on our list of desires pales in comparison to the treasure we already have.

Take a moment now to realize how fortunate you are to have a body.

Today I am fortunate to be alive,

I have a precious human life,

I am not going to waste it.

—*Dalai Lama*

In the possibility of not wanting so much, we discover the freedom of contentment. Contentment can be a highly threatening concept for those of us who continuously strive for status and financial success. We resist contentment because it feels passive or apathetic. These ideas bolster our defenses against freedom by keeping us tightly wound, too busy to listen to our bodies, and too tense to feel anything beyond discomfort and pain.

My friend found his freedom by making a daily choice to celebrate the feeling of his feet on the ground. He committed to the effort of befriending his body. He followed a simple but effective practice. Every day he made time to relax and listen to his body. Every day he said thank you to his body at the end of his practice.

Years later he's found a new stage of freedom: he is now a man with a self-care practice that doesn't require numbing agents to subdue the very loud shouting his body relied on to catch his attention. The pain that once required epidurals and daily opioids is nonexistent. He runs daily and enjoys backpacking.

Most importantly he cherishes his body. He feels it, listens to its messages, and responds. When it asks for something, he provides it— simple movements, simple breathing, simple visualizations to focus his energy toward calm and healing intentions. And when pain arises, he listens carefully to discover its source.

Every day he makes a point of feeling his feet on the ground.

And this, I think, is the best kind of story. It's about a man remembering himself. He followed his own wisdom toward his potential. No one could do it for him. He suffered obstacles along the way, but none were insurmountable, and indeed, all of them became light posts letting him see more clearly into his darkness.

Your Body Is Your Best Friend

Our body is a trustworthy guide. To trust it, we must learn to trust ourselves with its wisdom. We must become friends.

Healing the body comes by way of a commitment to healing the relationship we keep with it. It requires patience, inquiry, and practice.

It is an adventure on our journey toward home. We take one step and then another on the path. Each step is measured by our condition and context. We don't force ourselves to run if we aren't ready. We allow ourselves to rest when we need it. Our bodies' needs are for us to discover. We want to offer them a balance that places them in harmony with their natural rhythms and keeps them in rhythm with the conditions around them. To do this, we pay attention to our bodies' reactions to the experiences we give them, and we offer thoughtful responses.

People, ideas, beliefs, and patterns will occasionally get in the way, but we remain less interested in their intrusion than the learning we take from them. We learn how to kindly and courteously excuse ourselves as we step around them, thank them, invite them along. We learn how to see every experience as a beacon in darkness; if we pay attention, we will watch the light grow brighter and see more clearly how to step forward with confidence.

Most importantly we keep the peace as we go. As we come home, we don't need to do so with aggression or apprehension. Instead we take a deep breath and remember that we've made it this far. If we maintain a peaceful attitude as we journey, the journey will be peaceful.

Peace includes a light heart. We may want to remember to laugh a bit more at bodies' physical forms. They will burp and shit. They will occasionally smell. We all share these potentials, so take delight. We are sometimes gross in these bodies.

Likewise, we might laugh at the language so frequently used around us to describe attempts at wellness. What a joke. We *fight* obesity; we wage *war* on substance abuse; we *kill* cancer. We take ourselves to early morning *boot camps* as though we're preparing to become warriors. But who are we going to fight? It's just you in there.

Why would we go to war against ourselves for our own health?

Whoever won a war for health? A better question: Who wins any war?

When it comes to the body, every effort to kill something is killing a part of the body itself. This is a grand paradox when we remember our instinct to live and live and live. Cancer itself is life gone haywire: our own cells replicating inappropriately.

As we seek to save our lives from the glitch, we often bet our own endurance against…well…our own endurance. The cells are ours, gone renegade. So we wage war. And we suffer the consequences deeply. Maybe we get lucky and survive the battles. Or we don't, and the whole body succumbs, as much to the treatment as to the life that ran amok.

Which isn't to say that we shouldn't do our best to address cancer and any other physical disease or imbalance. We must.

Whatever imbalance arises, may it be a message to all of us that our friendship with the body is seeking renewal. What would it mean if we looked into the imbalances that cause life to run amok?

This is the process of cherishing the body. We come to know it intimately and care for it passionately. Our friendship with the body moves past effort and into a thoughtful dynamic conversation about the source of our conditions and sensations. We aren't limited to seeing the body as an entity separate from our experiences, emotions, thoughts, and feelings. Instead, we cooperate to investigate the source of our imbalances and discomforts. We learn how our experiences, emotions, thoughts, and feelings have impacted the body. We do what we can for ourselves—appropriately and with loving regard for our unique conditions in life.

Finally, as in any good friendship, we learn to accept the various ways our body communicates with us and to become moderate in our responses. As our bodies progress through life, may we experience all the sensations they offer us with profound curiosity. Every tense muscle, indigestion, kiss, goose bump, pain, and tingle is guiding us to a deeper awareness. May we release our defenses and receive them all.

Be in Your Body

Some of us may feel that we're completely body aware. Some of us may have no clue. Whether you know all or nothing, try these practices as though meeting your body for the first time.

For example, we've all been breathing since our birth. But let's pretend for a second that it's a brand new experience. What does it feel like for you to take a deep inhale? And to release a long exhale? Do you use your nose or mouth to breathe?[10] Where do you feel the breath in your body? Can you feel the expansion of your ribcage as you inhale? What happens when you exhale? As you breathe, can you also notice that there's a pause between the inhale and the exhale? Can you distinguish the sensation of this moment from the pause between the exhale and the body as it prepares to inhale again? Approach these inquiries to the best of your ability, with a mind as open as your heart.

Why not? It's you examining you. I promise there will be no subject more interesting for you in this world than you. See what happens.

---

[10] The benefits of nose breathing are extensive. We experience greater immune response thanks to our nose hairs, the mucosal lining, and the chemical reaction of bringing oxygen in through the nasal passages. Oxygen is better absorbed by the body when it enters through the nose. Nose breathing has been shown to stabilize mood, improve blood pressure, and diminish sleep troubles.

Yoga with the Body

Let's practice yoga with the body.

In a comfortable position, either on your back or in a chair, please consider these questions, one at a time, for a few moments before you continue with the sequence of simple movements below.

- What is this form you inhabit? What is your body made of?
- Can you feel its weight, any areas of tension or ease?
- Can you sense its layers, the movement of your breath through it, and the subtle vibration of energy in it?
- How do you treat this body? What do you commonly say to it? What don't you say?
- How does it feel to say thank you to this body? Let "Thank you, my good friend" be your mantra as you continue to the exercise below.

Now try these simple movements.

<u>Position One</u>

Rest on your back, with your legs gently straight on the ground or with knees supported by a pillow.

Find your breath. Recognize your inhale and exhale. You'll move with the breath.

On an inhale, please bring your arms up and over your head toward the floor behind you. As you exhale, please bring your arms back to your sides. Do this about eight times, moving carefully with your breath.

<u>Position Two</u>

Stay on your back, but bend your knees, so your feet are flat on the ground and about hip-width apart.

Find your breath again. You'll continue to move with the breath.

On an inhale, gently lift the bum up by pressing the feet into the ground, strengthening your legs and lengthening the spine. On an exhale, slowly lower the bum back to the ground.

Do this about eight times, moving carefully with the breath.

<u>Position Three</u>

Still on your back, bring your knees toward your chest. Place your hands on your knees.

You'll continue to move with the breath.

On an inhale, feel the expansion of your ribcage. Let the knees move gently away from your chest, just to the point where your fingers can still rest on your kneecaps. On an exhale, let the knees move gently toward the chest, keeping the knees hip-width and the feet relaxed. Once again, do this eight times, moving attentively with the breath.

Now, feel the sensations in your body after these small simple movements. It doesn't take much to enliven our bodies. Please say thank you to your bodies and then take some time to rest for a bit.

Thank You, Wonderful Body

These beautiful bodies of ours are instrumental to our journey home. They carry us and allow us to experience the wonder of this life. They also help us deal with life's greatest challenges. As you do these exercises, you may notice old memories arising where pain once lived. Or you'll feel an increasing comfort where tension used to reign. Our bodies house us and our history. Some old traumas may be carefully enclosed and others less so.

As we begin to cherish our bodies, we learn to understand how they carry the stories of us—those experiences that taught us love and those experiences that taught us fear. Our job is to celebrate this role and live in gratitude. If the body hadn't held on occasionally, we might not have made it as far as we have. When the body learns to let go a bit, we learn how to do more than survive.

Feel your body every day. Listen to it. Thank it and cherish it in every moment.

It's the only one you have. Long may it last.

Wisdom to Bring Home...

- You are not your body. The body is but one dimension of the existence we lead. It is an important and precious dimension that deserves our gratitude, but it's a temporary home.
- Our bodies are all, at every moment, in the process of dying and renewing. Our life in these bodies is finite, and we all share the same diagnosis. As we live, we can realize how precious it is that we and everyone we know are all

walking together toward the end of our bodies' time on earth.

- Realizing the reality of our bodies' journeys can help us choose more carefully how we want to treat them while we have them.

- Our bodies give us access to the sensations of life. When we pay careful attention to the ways our bodies function, we can experience life more deeply and thoroughly. We discover the body has much more to share with us than discomfort and pain; it is also the gateway to pleasure and our sense of connection, calm, and peace.

- We can practice becoming better attendants to our bodies and the personal histories they store. As we attend to the body, we can discover its loyalty and service to us. We remember to offer our appreciation.

To continue contemplating this body, please see the study guide at the end. The questions presented in this chapter reappear for your consideration. Sit with them. Be with them.

3. What Is This Mind?

As a tethered bird grows tired of flying

About in vain to find a place of rest

And settles down at last on its own perch,

So the mind, tired of wandering about

Hither and thither, settles down at last

In the Self, dear one, to whom it is bound.

All creatures, dear one, have their source in him.

He is their home; he is their strength.

—Chandogya Upanishad

Your thoughts have the power to ruin the most beautiful day. Your thoughts are not you.

Please Remember: You're a Miracle

Please remember that you and I and everyone we know suffer in this life. We all have bouts of joy.

Now think. Watch what happens.

Your thoughts have the power to ruin the most beautiful day. Your thoughts have the power to ruin your relationships. Your thoughts have the power to bring you to hell without you having to move an inch.

Likewise, your thoughts can bring you comfort. They can also build your strength. They can lighten the loads you carry, draw support from those around you, and inspire others to think more carefully as well.

A man's life is what his thoughts make of it.

—*Marcus Aurelius*

You have a choice.

It isn't always easy.

And it may totally offend you to read that.

The first time someone told me to fix my thoughts, I was fourteen and irate. I was lashing out and accusing everyone of a failure to accept me. My dad stepped in calmly and said, "Megan, you need to control your thoughts."

He was a well-meaning man. He wanted me to think differently. When he said, "Control your thoughts," however, the stream of thoughts accelerated and mobilized against him.

The thoughts were offensive—in meaning and effect. I let him know how he was to blame, how he was the bad actor, how he wanted me censored. My dad may have been a drunk and an antagonist, but he understood something about the mind. He told me to be quiet and left me alone.

It was in that quiet, on the floor of the kitchen where I'd melted down, that I heard and acknowledged thoughts for the first time. They came like a stampede, I crouched beneath them and listened: they told me to shout, to leave, to pity myself, to weigh all the injustices in my life and acknowledge that no one could possibly have it worse than me. One said, "Your dad doesn't love you."

That was the one that really got my attention.

It was patently false.

It was a thought that I caught and knew wasn't mine.

So, it was a matter of understanding the verb. My dad didn't want me to control my thoughts so much as he wanted me to listen to them. Objectively. To hear them. To witness them. To watch how they evolved and faded.

It is absolutely the case that I couldn't have controlled my thoughts at fourteen. Not then. But I could listen. And I could discover that they don't all require my attention. My mind needs me, but the thoughts don't. They simply come and go. I saw how thoughts teased and taunted to gain attention.

It was that one thought I noticed wasn't mine that convinced me that these thoughts are just berries on a bush. I don't need to pick every one, and I'll surely feel sick if I eat them all. I discovered how tempting and how dangerous they can be. Thoughts grow and overflow and sometimes look delicious.

I learned from my dad that I get to choose and that the choices I make dictate the way I engage with the world. From moment to moment, I can pluck and discard from an infinite supply of thoughts. I can also simply watch. The fruit may be inviting and distracting. Compelling and also empty.

Like every human being, my dad was flawed and perfect. He loved me deeply, without fail. Some fathers teach children to fish. Mine taught me the patience and discernment to harvest appropriate thoughts.

In my first mindful haul, I found the right thought to establish my suspicion in the whole thinking process: I am something other than the thinker. I am not my mind.

My mind wasn't even doing the thinking. My mind was simply harvesting from a familiar source: it was choosing thoughts based on a belief that I was alone and incomprehensible. My mind believed this because I wouldn't choose any thoughts that would allow a suspicion otherwise.

My mind wasn't as credible as it seemed.

A man is what he thinks about all day long.

—Ralph Waldo Emerson

Let's discover how we can all see more clearly what the mind is picking.

You Are Not the Mind

Here's a surprise party for you. Take a moment, get comfortable, and tune in to the mind. Let's see how it takes in the information around you.

What color are the walls? What smells are around? Is sound moving through? How does the chair feel?

Now put this book down, and really pay attention.

Notice how the mind takes this information in. We label the wall color, identify smells and sounds, determine whether the chair is comfortable or not, and shift in response.

Consider, for a moment, the difference between your wandering senses and your directed senses. When left to wander, they move about toward objects of sensation. Over there is a sweet smell! Over there is a noxious odor! Over there is a clown on a bicycle! Over there is a flashing light. Left to their wandering, the senses hop toward objects of perception. The mind receives the information from the senses and gives us certain conclusions in return.

These hopscotching senses bring us so much disparate information, we can often feel distracted and overwhelmed.

Now let's guide our senses. Please take a moment to direct your eyes toward a lovely object in the room. Now notice the texture of the wall. Please direct your smell to the air. What does your nose bring you? Listen, for a moment, to a single sound. Choose another and listen again. Close your eyes and feel the chair beneath you. Or the touch of air on your skin.

Sit with the information you gathered for a moment.

The mind receives the information, and we get a sense of our surroundings. Please make note: do your surroundings feel clearer and more comprehensive after your senses have been sent out to gather information for you?

This mind is a wonderful assistant to us. When left unattended, however, the mind can become unwieldy. It strays. It time travels and more. It wanders from past to present to fantasy in just a moment if we aren't careful to gently restrain it.

All the while we observe.

In the Katha Upanishad, we're offered a helpful metaphor to consider our approach to the mind. This body carrying you is likened to a chariot. The senses are the horses pulling it on the journey. The mind is the reins. How well do you know how to hold the reins?

And who, exactly, is holding them? We'll discuss this further in chapter five but for now, consider your identity as the driver. Realize for a moment whether you feel properly equipped to guide a team of five horses. Realize for a moment how you feel yourself holding the reins. And let's continue.

Take a look at a familiar object. Observe the process your mind undergoes to examine, label, and know it. You may become aware of stories unfolding. Watch them.

This is the mind with loose reins.

Some of us may have noticed the mind interpreting information, offering stories, and selecting various other thoughts to deepen the experience of the object. Little things like "That reminds me of the time Grandma Josephine burned the turkey." The mind took information and selected a thought in response. We watched all that.

We watched the mind.

If we watch the mind, what is the mind?

Not us.

We may have convinced ourselves otherwise because we love to get lost in the incessant activity of the mind. Or maybe, we tend to get a bit overwhelmed in people, places, thoughts, and emotions. The result of our sense of being overwhelmed is an overactive mind that doesn't leave much space for the realization of this simple fact: if we're observing the mind, we can't be the mind.

We only have to observe for a moment to discover just how much the mind has to say to us. It never stops talking, actually. As long as we let the reins loose, the senses run wild, and the mind follows. When others are talking, it keeps talking. You've probably noticed that you can sit through an entire conversation with someone and not hear a single word said. You only listened to your mind. It has so much to say, and it rarely expresses peace toward the moment.

Listen in for a minute. Notice all the stories the mind will tell you. It'll take you to the recent past, a distant memory, a potential future, a dream, an illusion. It'll tell you you're wrong, you're right, up is down, or everything is absurd. The mind is a chatterbox.

So what is our role?

We listen. We watch. We learn to hold the reins of the mind. When we learn to direct the mind, we quiet its chatter. In the resulting space, we can discover the true nature of ourselves and the world around us.

We'll consider later who that makes us.

For now simply become aware of who we are not. Set a timer occasionally. Start with five minutes or so. Observe the mind and its thoughts. Start to notice that they come and go with an impressive amplitude. See where they take you.[11]

---

[11] It's estimated that each of us hosts about 60,000 to 80,000 thoughts per day. Over 24 hours they come with a frequency of approximately 49 thoughts per minute.

The mind catches thoughts in response to whatever the senses catch. Let's shift metaphors to understand the mind's eccentricities. Think of the mind as a personal chef. The mind has access to whatever comes in fresh in the moment and may spice it up with a variety of stuff kept in the pantry.

Frequently the chef gets lazy and doesn't bother to harvest the moment. The chef insists on canned stuff from the past—old flavors, old, packaged ideas. Sometimes the chef insists on the same recipes. Over and over and over. Whatever comes in fresh starts to taste exactly like whatever came in before.

We don't even realize the possibility of a new flavor.

Familiar?

We all do this. We discover two years after moving into a home that the trim under the roof is actually blue. We realize that our neighbor shares our mother's name. We didn't ask the mind to pay attention, and the mind filled in the gaps with old flavors.

We ignore the moment; our minds wander. This is the nature of the mind. Please be gentle with it. Expecting it to behave otherwise is like demanding that an elephant ice-skate. It may be able to learn, but it's going to take some training.

We have zero consciousness of how richly served we are because the mind is so busy taking shortcuts and long ways around whatever is happening right now. It isn't the mind's fault. It's just its nature.

Approximately 70 percent of these thoughts are repetitive and negative. It's no wonder we sometimes feel anxious. There's so much noise going on persistently.

The fault is entirely with us. We forget to ask the mind to find the moment.

Let's see how it feels right now to find the moment.

Read this sentence and breathe in.

Read this sentence and breathe out.

Read this sentence and feel the breathing in.

Read this sentence and feel the breathing out.

Read this sentence and feel your body breathing again.

Read this sentence and feel the space surrounding your body.

Here you are. Every bit of life has arrived with you at this moment.

Pause. Be in the moment.

Pause.

Now notice how quickly the mind comes back to tell you its stories about what just happened.

Our minds eat and metabolize what our senses perceive. The nature of the senses is to find nourishment for us. Our sight offers food for the eyes, our smell gathers food for the nose, and our hearing brings music to the ears. The senses may run wild, gathering heaping basketfuls of experience to stimulate the mind. Notice, however, that even the most beautiful song will not register in the mind if we're otherwise distracted. A perfect rose may be sharing her scent, and we may neglect her completely if the mind is absorbed in something else.

Understanding this relationship between senses and mind helps us recognize the role we play in choosing the nourishment our senses deliver. Sometimes we may want to savor the wonder of the world.

Sometimes we may wish to sit quietly, satisfied. When the senses persistently run, neither experience is easy.

The senses can be still. It requires that we learn to focus the mind. We miss a hilarious joke or a beautiful sunset when we're totally captivated by something else; likewise, we can intentionally focus the mind, and the senses will follow.

Until we learn to do this, the senses will continue to hunt and gather. In response, our minds digest the sensory perception and come up with thoughts. The thoughts generate emotions and moods, all of which our senses will perceive and deliver to the mind. Our minds digest these emotions and moods as well, becoming receptive to additional thoughts.[12] We find ourselves in this eddy of experience. We spin around and around every experience without a moment to catch a breath and see what it really has to offer us.

Some of us may realize that our minds are persistently sketching our worldview and some of us may not.

This has happened to me. Personally I don't love the taste of broccoli. One time a friend made me a pizza. I do love pizza, and he put broccoli on the pizza. Left to its own reaction, my mind prioritized my aversion to broccoli over my delight with pizza. I immediately felt disappointment. I had to find some appreciation that would keep my mood content. I chose to be grateful that someone would make me food. And maybe pizza with broccoli could help me enjoy broccoli. (This didn't turn out to be the case.)

---

[12] It isn't only thoughts that create moods and emotions. Each can each initiate the others, as well as sensation in the body.

When we perceive something we don't like, it causes us to feel an emotion, which leads us to access thoughts that propel us into a pattern of aversion. We say, "I don't like it."

Guess what happens when we perceive it again?

If we aren't careful, our mood starts to shift. We can ruin our whole day because someone gives us broccoli. What was going to be a fun lunch is now broccoli with a side plate of emotions and thoughts. If we fail to attend to the emotions and thoughts, a foul mood is dessert.

So it goes. This is the mind, taking in and offering a view on reality.

But is it real?

You're the one who chooses how to experience the view.

Whatsoever things are true, whatsoever things are honest, whatsoever
things are just,
whatsoever things are pure, whatsoever things are lovely, whatsoever
things are of good report; if there be any virtue, and if there be any praise,
think on these things.
—Philippians 4:8

So what's real?

Our minds offer us a view of the world that's based on our patterns of perception. Becoming attentive to the mind, we may discover some of its views can be improved. Others could be scuttled. This is the beginning of mindfulness. We watch the mind to understand how we perceive the world. We have to decide how skillful we will be with our minds.

Perhaps you can imagine the mind as a super-high-quality instrument panel of engagement. Pretend it's the most robust dashboard you've ever seen. Sure, you can steer right or left, but you can also make yourself invisible or very large. You can time travel or head toward imaginary worlds.

Notice how tidy the controls of this highly sophisticated panel are?

If they're lousy with grease and dirt and the crumbs of everything you've ever consumed through your senses, how certain are you that these mechanisms are working well? Likewise, how much dexterity can you assert on those slimy controls?

If we don't touch them, the instrument panel stays on autopilot. It does its thing, and you go where it takes you. Occasionally some misfire occurs when all the coffee you spilled gets into the wires.

Thankfully, our minds are also resilient.

The Mind Can Be Used

Do you know this trick?

Look at the world. When you feel messy, do you perceive the world in great order? More likely, you're pretty sure it's a mess too. Or it may go like this: A friend is in chaos. You get involved in that chaos. Soon, you're in chaos too. And the whole world feels chaotic.

You may have noticed that we tend to become the way we perceive the world, and the world tends to become the way we perceive ourselves. When we're overwhelmed, the world is overwhelming. When we're joyful, the world grows alive with smiles. Likewise, when we scowl, the world is likely to scowl with us.

Go easy on yourself with this one. It's just training we've all had to help us belong. We've learned to be mirrors but we don't realize that the world also reflects us. Our perception is as magical as a quarter in your ear. It's a sleight of hand or, at least, a distraction successfully applied, so we feel like we fit into the world.

Who performs the trick? That's the mind. Or more precisely, the mind untended by you.

Let's use another metaphor.

Compare the untended mind to a toddler. It's entertaining and occasionally sweet, but if we don't watch carefully, we're in for a heap of trouble. These sweet, hilarious, totally selfish, and occasionally cruel beings are skillful explorers.

Everything is "mine," and they might kick you if you disagree.

Also, they are walking non sequiturs. What is interesting now is quickly replaced by the next distraction.

"What's that?"

"An obsidian rock...look how glassy..."

"What's that?"

"Another rock, but that one's..."

"What's that?"

"A cigarette butt...smoking isn't..."

"What's that?"

"A tractor...a stop sign...an abandoned shoe...trash." This is the mind without a guardian.

And when the mind has compiled enough data from the scene, it just replays old stories over and over. Like a toddler's repetitive conversations.

We've heard the story so many times, and we still don't know what it's about. We just know it goes on and on and loops when it's done. Or until new data comes to take the mind to another inquiry.

What's that?

It's just how we are. Me, you, and everyone we know.

If we leave our minds to their impulsive wanderings, they follow the senses and whatever patterns are most familiar to them.

Overwhelmed by an abundance of information from every direction, the mind can become anxious or agitated. It will try to control the input by growing immediately fond and attached to what it perceives, or it will cast aspersions and push the perceptions out. These likes and dislikes become the root of emotional responses, which affect our thoughts, our mood, and our behavior.

Our role is to pay attention. We learn to see how to overcome the mind's pattern of distraction by considering how our desires and aversions serve us.

The Mind Can Be Misused

If we examine these likes and dislikes, we start to see how efficiently they control us. Like stubborn, mindless gatekeepers, the mind's judgments guard us from the entry of new experiences and the expansion these experiences may offer. Guarded from growth, we begin to perish.

We don't let life in because we don't like the possibility of endangering ourselves with something we don't like. We don't let life out because we don't like the idea of losing what we have.

In other words, we prohibit change. Or we try to.

Change is inevitable. All we can do is influence its direction.

Change happens regardless of our attempts to stop it.

Change is the nature of life.

On one end of life, we are born; on the other we die. Every moment in between offers a series of births and deaths. This moment you have now will never return. The cells of our skin renew by dying and sloughing away. So it is with our minds. Our senses reach out to take in the world. New information replaces old. Ideally we direct the mind toward every fresh moment. We refresh the mind through new sensations.

If we don't, the mind sticks to what it has liked in the past. Our senses will still perceive what we don't, but our minds will ascribe a negative meaning to it. As skin grows rough or brittle when it does not renew, so too will the mind.

Here's what I love. What we perceive carries none of our judgment on its own. That is, the thing itself is quite neutral. So what if I don't like the taste of broccoli? Broccoli doesn't carry my distaste. Only *I* carry that.

Broccoli is a beautiful creation of the earth, and it serves some people well. It has no intention to harm me. You don't like snakes? Also a creature of the earth with no inherent interest in you. Averse to flying? Or guns? Or certain political opinions? Fine. These too—despite what the mind tells you—are just creations of this earth. Humans—also of the earth—made them. As such, they are just as beautifully in service to some as broccoli may be to others.

Say you don't like people, or a few in particular. Again, what if you realize the existence of everything as a neutrality? It's your take on the thing and not the thing itself that generates your defenses against it.

In fact, the things we dislike the most have the most to teach us. But more on that later. For now let's see how our preferences impact the way we use our minds. Or the way our minds play with us.

For instance, by playing a thought experiment. Consider the heartbreak of a mass shooting. What a deeply disturbing event that leads to enduring trauma in individuals and the community. It's not uncommon to hear, in the aftermath, facts and opinions about the perpetrator. We form our judgments.

Many of us go directly to abhorrence. The shooter is cast in the shadow of evil. We hate the evil. It's a way we reconcile ourselves with the incomprehensibility of the act. We may even say things like, "I hate this hate."

But let's see if we can look at this differently for a moment. Let's guide our minds to surrender a pattern of dislike, briefly, in order to contemplate the following.[13]

Someone who goes to a school with a weapon makes a poor decision. It's a decision that follows a series of poor decisions that are not all on that individual's tally card. This doesn't relieve that person of fault. Looking more deeply helps us understand the shooter's path. Our minds

---

[13] Please notice your resistance to this exercise. Please also remember, none of this is intended to suggest that violence is justified.

will defend against this, but what if you'd walked this path? Not for a mile, but your whole life? What if you'd done just the same thing?

A sixteen-year-old girl named Brenda Spencer, who shot into a San Diego elementary school in 1979, killed two adults and injured many children. When asked why she'd done it, she said, "I don't like Mondays. This livens up the day." We cringe.

Now pretend you've lived her life. Not for a moment, but for your entire life. You were born to this world as Brenda Spencer. As a young teenager, you shared a single mattress with your father. You lived in poverty. You were rarely attentive in school, but your family did nothing to intervene. You experienced undiagnosed epilepsy. School officials and juvenile probation suggested mental-health treatment, but your father would not allow it. Your father was told that you were suicidal. At Christmas he gave you a gun.

You may insist that you would never point that gun at an elementary school and do what Brenda did. And you, being you, probably wouldn't.

But if you were Brenda, you would.

Because she did.

Can you realize the horror of making her choice? Can you feel every impetus that motivated her toward her choice? This is what you can do from your perspective. You can feel, empathetically, what a different life you would be experiencing that would prompt you to take her actions.

Can you recognize that if you'd lived her life, you would have done the exact same thing? You would shoot into a school. You would have no regard for the trajectory of your life or the lives of others. You would feel that desperate.

Instead of disliking Brenda, we become Brenda. Now we might redirect our grief for her actions to the relief of suffering. We might look around and see how we can improve situations for others who may feel so much despair.

We might even recognize our role in the series of decisions that brought Brenda to her decision. We share in her reality, without regard for time or place. We share in the reality of suffering that creates more suffering. We also share in the reality of compassion that leads to greater understanding and relief.

This is when the mind's patterns move into defense mode.

No, no, no, it says. *I have no fault. I didn't even know Brenda; I might not have been alive at the time, and I would never do such a thing.*

Great. Thank goodness. What great fortune.

But if you'd lived every day of your life as Brenda, you would possess every aspect of her—the compilation of every decision and experience that brought her to that tragic choice. You would do what she did because she did it. This practice trains the mind to replace a pattern of defense with a pattern of compassion. You feel with others their mistakes, their hurt, the way they've hurt others. You feel the weight of their lives as your own.

With this practice, our minds expand. We move through our aversion to the suffering of life. We learn how to feel the suffering and journey beyond it.

Take a moment now to redirect the mind to another sadness. Consider how you play a role in a community that, however unintentionally or thoughtlessly, contributes to a reality that brings a man to beg on the corner.

See how your initial inclination is to mourn his position. We all want to help. We have a moment of feeling our hearts yearning to care. This is our moment of freedom.

Then, in a flash, the instinct is overwhelmed by a quick return to our patterns of separation. We go right back to thinking of ourselves and what would happen to us if we tried to help. Notice how the majority of times you've seen a man on the corner, you've ignored him. You didn't have time, money, or interest. We acted for ourselves instead of another. It isn't that we did nothing; we chose the act of ignoring.

Now see the times when you've been ignored by someone who didn't have time.

The patterns of someone else's separation conflicted with your need for connection. Just as the man on the corner's need for connection conflicted with your pattern of separation.

Have you ever wanted money and been denied it? Have you been judged for a behavior that was none of the judge's business? Have you been ignored?

The mind may suggest that the difference between you and the man on the corner is vast. The mind says this because the mind is trained to feel averse to his situation. The mind is trained to say no to that experience. It prefers to look away. This is the mind's patterned reaction to protect us. It doesn't want to be associated with all of the conditions of a reality that leads to that outcome.

And it may be the case that living on the street wouldn't be ideal for all of us. In our discernment, it may be that asking for money on the corner isn't our calling. Many of us are fortunate that those circumstances are not part of our path. The pertinent inquiry here is: Can we train the mind to see beyond its pattern of aversion, so we might acknowledge the man on the corner and our connection to him? Are we willing to learn from him about how to deepen our strength and compassion?

Look a little closer. This is where the mind erects its defenses.

The mind will resist by relying on patterns of preference, even to prevent the continuation of this thought experiment. It will give us reasons why. They'll be familiar. They're patterns.

If we frequently guard ourselves from fear or dislike the risk of new situations, the mind might caution that, unlike us, the man on the corner is dangerous and unworthy of further consideration. If we frequently protect ourselves by ruling out the sanity of others whom we don't understand, we may believe he's crazy. If we prefer to stay free of responsibility, we may call him a loser, an addict, a freeloader. If we tend to isolate ourselves in morality, we'll call him disrespectful.

The mind follows our patterns.

Listen to the mind and acknowledge its patterns.

Then look again.

That man on the corner has a body, as do we. He has to find it space to rest for a significant portion of the day, just like us. He has to feed it. He has to eliminate waste and will want a safe place to do so.

This man, like us, is the child of a mother and father. At certain points in his life, like us, he's felt the giddiness of excitement. At other points he's felt despondent. Just like us. He's experienced suffering and transient freedom from it. He wants to find comfort in life. So do we. We are not different. Behind and beyond all circumstances, we are the same.

Now consider a less troubling scenario. Imagine a wealthy prince. He has everything, including good looks and earnest manners. He's a good guy. A charming guy. He's such a good guy that we all get invited to his party. We don't know him, but we're invited.

Check out the mind's reaction to this possibility. Some part of it may say, "Cool." But a chorus may arise to pull us back. What's he getting at? What does he want from us? Maybe he doesn't have it all, if he has to invite us. Maybe he has horrible manners or cruel intentions.

Besides, what if it's dangerous? And, if not, what would we wear?

The mind can talk us out of an interesting possibility for nothing more than sartorial confusion.

Again, the mind protected us. It did the same thing to the prince as it did to the pauper. It sequestered us in patterned thoughts.

Like we did with the man on the corner, look at the prince. He too has a body with needs, many memories of wonder and anguish, an instinct about freedom and comfort. We wouldn't call his situation bad, but some of us kept ourselves from joining it as sheepishly as we backed away from the man on the corner. It's this good-versus-bad scenario that the mind loves.

This very same scenario keeps us from feeling a deep relationship with the world around us.

Every time the mind qualifies something, it separates it from everything else. We, as a result, feel separate.

Though we're not.

We are, as a matter of fact, so much the same: humans in a spiral of life. We expand and contract and come back around to do it again. Our bodies grow and decay. Our energy cycles. Our relationships wax and wane. When we see that we're the same, we can be compassionate. We can share stories. We share attention. We share love.

We Are Responsible for the Mind

We also share responsibility.

This notion needs a recast. We commonly believe that responsibility is a burden.

"Oh, life. What a chore."

As if our whole plight is this onerous responsibility to sweep up.

Now ask yourself: If not me…then who? Would you prefer to hand over the assignment?

We've heard friends and family let us know how they have no interest in taking responsibility for problems not of their making. We've heard ourselves refuse to take responsibility for trouble, whether we caused it or not. On the other hand, we've all probably placed ourselves in a position to accept blame for a wrong because we sensed someone needed to do it.

So often, we believe responsibility means fault. Depending on the style of person we are, we might stand tall and accept it or slump away to reject the unbearable weight of our world.

Set the mind to another task for a moment. What if responsibility is what it says? We can respond. This perspective is kindly described by modern yogi Sadhguru. He says: "Responsibility simply means your *ability to respond.* If you decide, 'I am responsible,' you will have the ability to respond. If you decide, 'I am not responsible,' you will not have the ability to respond. It is as simple as that. All it requires is for you to realize that you are responsible for all that you are and all that you are not, all that may happen to you and all that may not happen to you."

Responsibility is not simply taking on burdens, accepting blame, or living in guilt. Responsibility means accepting our power of response. This power is our means of engagement with the universe. It means we become present to every experience, no matter what's happening. It acknowledges every moment as a unique opportunity to become aware and to contribute.

The world around us conspires to invite us into cooperation. Our response dictates the manner of our attendance.

Are you responsible for the rain? You may say no because your mind is patterned by a limited use of the word *responsibility*. Pause for a second and I'll ask again.

When it rains, do you have the power to respond? Of course you do.

So what do you choose? Do you resent every raindrop because you forgot an umbrella? Do you hide in a hallway waiting for it to pass? Do you make your merry way home, stomping every puddle you find? You're responsible at every moment. Every moment is all you have, so choose wisely how you participate.

This is where our minds shiver.

It isn't that our minds can't perceive this present moment; in fact, the data that our minds receive from our senses only arrives in the present. There is no other time. Indeed, there is no other space. We are creatures truly invested in this space in time. It is infinite and expansive and only right now.

What do we do with all this infinite space of now? We constrain ourselves to illusions of the past and future. We give safe harbor to fantasies that no longer exist because we're so well trained in review and concern.

We either lament the past for its departure or apprehend the coming of the future. Only rarely do we situate ourselves in this space of now.

Yoga with Words

Let's be in the moment together.

Read the following words aloud: *I am.*

Read these words aloud again: *I am.*

Feel who, what, and how you are. Watch how quickly you want to identify yourself based on notions of the past or present. Instead, allow yourself to notice what you are now.

Your body is probably sitting or reclining. Your breath is coming or going. You are engaged in the act of being you.

Read these words: *This is.*

Look around and see what is. Not how you'd like it or how it was. Just everything around you, perfectly as it is. Notice how it cannot be any other way than it is right now. It will change and is in the process of doing so, but right now, it is.

Read these words aloud: *I love this moment.*

Feel that. Notice what comes up from the past and future to persuade you otherwise. Or, if nothing arises, simply love this moment.

Where Is Your Mind?

We may label the present to distinguish it from what's gone and what's to come, but there is no other space in time in which we operate. We are creatures of now. We forget because our minds love to time travel, neglecting all the fresh data in favor of memory and anticipation.

Well, the past is gone, and the future never comes. Concepts about either are based on references acquired and applied religiously both backward and forward. Our experience of either is a fantasy that falls like a shadow over our present moment.

We might lose a love. Our minds busy themselves endlessly with regrets about past behavior or anxieties about future uncertainty. Unfortunately, without appropriate conversations with the mind, these ideas come to nothing. We'll likely behave exactly as we always have because a mind so focused on the past and future always neglects a better response to right now. Our obsession with the past and future simply trains the mind to exist in these shadowlands rather than the brilliant space of now.

The only frame in which we have any ability to engage is the brilliant space of now. The present moment. A letter written to our future selves will reach our hands in a moment yet to come, but it's comfortably accepted as the present when we arrive in it. The writing of the letter will have happened in a past we can't touch or alter. We have—only and always—now.

We discover this more readily when we pay attention. When we become aware that we make the decisions to be everything we are and everything we aren't, we experience the power of responsibility. We discover that we were and are the one who has the power to respond in every moment. All that is coming will come; if we stand comfortably in the moment and observe its arrival, we decide how to respond.

This is responsibility.

What is it, then, that is preventing us from being truly responsible? Why must we choose between being heroes, martyrs, victims, or bystanders when situations arise? Do we truly believe this wonderful world is only capable of being good or bad, liked or hated, for us or against us?

What if we participate instead of casting judgment? What if we respond instead of react?

When we discipline our minds to become responsible, we emerge from the shadowlands and become present in the space of now.

I asked a group of US veterans to tell me about reaction. They all answered similarly: it's quick; it's reflex; it's programmed; it's without thought.

One said, "It's how you survive."

I asked them about response. They took their time with the answer.

That's a true response. A response is considered. It's thoughtful instead of programmed. It takes a moment. It requires a pause. While a reaction may help us survive in urgent situations, a response gives us a means to thrive in life.

So why don't we respond?

What is it about responding that makes it such an effort in our daily lives? Mindless patterns don't serve us well in most situations. They provide convenience and efficiency but not necessarily a friendly relationship with ourselves and others. They may be comfortable, but they may not promote our comfort with the great abundance of experience that life offers.

For example, notice how often your reaction comes flying back at you. Your angry reaction provokes anger. Your careless reaction results in another careless act. Our reaction sets other reactions loose. A chain reaction binds the whole world.

Maybe this sounds hyperbolic.

Consider the angry reaction for a moment. Maybe someone is disrespectful at a store. You feel upset and react in anger. In other words, disrespect turns into anger; one person's misstep turns into two people's anger. You tell the story to a friend, and she becomes frustrated that you didn't behave differently. Now two people's anger has morphed into anger *and* frustration. Your friend then talks to a delivery driver while still frustrated. The delivery driver feels disrespected by her and is then rude to his next customer.

A chain reaction of emotional turmoil continues to move through us all.

Which brings us back to influencing the direction of change.

With thanks to all the saints and sages who have come and gone, I offer you a lesson that is most effectively taught by life itself.

Change happens.

It's the nature of life. As we begin responding instead of reacting, we guide the direction the change follows. This requires a decision and a whole lot of practice.

We practice finding the moment first. We practice being in the moment. As we learn to linger in it, we realize it expands. Our ability to respond has space to develop. Reactions no longer feel appropriate.

Yoga with the Mind

Let's consider reactions and responses.

Someone steps in front of you in line at the store. You feel anger arising.

You feel the injustice of losing your hard-earned position. This minor injustice morphs into a generalized anxiety that you are not doing enough, and now you're worried that you don't have enough money to pay for groceries that someone wants to sell at such a high price.

Now your heart is racing; you're mean to the cashier, who makes less money than you do and only wanted to know if you needed a bag. Suddenly you're disappointed in this grocery adventure, and you anticipate the traffic in the parking lot. (You'll probably scratch your car door when you get to the parking lot.)

I'm sorry, my friend. That was a reaction gone awry.

Your uncontrolled mind did that.

Here's another option.

This morning you decide "I'm good for whatever this day delivers." You head to the store. The girl cuts in line, and you start to feel the injustice but remember your promise. "I'm good."

You smile at her instead. You ask about her day. The girl apologizes and says she's spaced out because she had an odd experience at work, and her boss is mad. You say nice things because you've been there.

Now the cashier loves you, and you get a free bag and smiles all around. The girl invites you to a party over the weekend that her boss is giving. He's actually a prince, and it's in his castle. She says, "Don't worry about what to wear. Just wear jeans." Now you're awesome, and you're heading to a prince's party.

New pattern developing! That's a mind you're guiding.

Watching the Mind

By no means should you think that one good hoorah at the market will turn into a lifetime habit. We have to work at our new patterns.

We commit to remaining cool both in the morning *and* when a provocation occurs. We recommit to being cool in the moment that we discover we aren't. We acknowledge the patterned reaction and choose to cultivate its opposite. If we feel frustrated, we deliberately redirect our minds toward a different response. Love will do. Joy is good. If the mind moves toward envy, we can shift the mind toward gratitude.

It's a practice. It requires effort. It can feel like heavy lifting, so we return to our breath. We pay attention to the feeling of a deep, centering breath. We pay attention to the feeling of our feet on the ground. We devote and do our best to stay consistent. We forgive ourselves, gently review our errors, and recommit to practicing our cool.

We commit and remember, in our own ways, to do it.

This is a practice of recognizing that we are not our minds. We are not our minds.

This is a practice of watching our minds. As we watch our minds, we experience how distinct our minds are from us.

Our minds are instruments. They are exceedingly robust, plastic, helpful, and efficient…when well-tended. If not, they are distracted chatterboxes overly dependent on past experiences and future fears. They dare not tread in the moment.

The practice of watching the mind allows us to get to know it. As we familiarize ourselves with it, we discover how to befriend it. We are the custodians of the mind: caretakers and guardians. Our relationship with our minds can be kind and gentle, but it must be conscientious. It's for us to ensure they're used properly. It's for us to know when to listen to their noise and when to disregard what they want us to hear. It's for us to keep our minds well.

To cultivate a friendly relationship with the mind, we have to be engaged with its various traits. This means allowing for awe when our minds astound us. Also to laugh kindly when they amuse us. Can we forgive the mind when it wanders to distraction or gives in to pattern? Can we gently remind it of our commitment to be in the moment?

The strain many of us feel in our relationship with the mind is rooted in something we've forgotten. We forgot how to see beyond the mind. When we decide to watch the mind, we see again.

Playful Swami Rama, an Indian yogi, explains it like this: "For the ignorant there is misery everywhere. The moment a student realizes his essential nature, the darkness of ignorance is dispelled, but before that the individual mind travels to the groove of self-created misery and thus projects the belief that there is misery everywhere. In reality, this universe is like a great poem of joy, a beautiful song, and a unique work of art."

He calls it ignorance. The word in Sanskrit is *avidya*. A not seeing. A forgetting to see.

Forgetting to see beyond the mind, we allow the mind to follow patterned grooves of likes and dislikes.

What if it isn't only our experiences creating these grooves? Aren't we also influenced by our mother's likes and dislikes, our family's likes and dislikes? Even the preferences of the zeitgeist? And possibly the zeitgeist that preceded ours?

When we remember to see, in each moment, we become capable of responding to events. As we become friendly keepers of the mind, we learn how to invite the mind to rest from its persistent travel and simply see where we've arrived.

We come home.

We discover its comfort in a world constantly rocked by every kind of weather.

Be assured: the weather will continue. You, however, will see through the clouds to the clear sky above. From this place we watch the weather come and go. We choose how we respond to whatever the conditions bring.

Our patterns took time to deepen their grooves. And they'll take time to replace with new ones. So, patience, Cool Breeze. We'll all get there in our unique ways. The truth is there's nothing to accomplish. Practice watching the mind in every moment. Forgive yourself when you forget. Recommit. Offer your attention to every moment as it comes and let yourself experience the joy awaiting you.

How to Nurture Our Minds

So, what is it about these patterns that make them so strong in the face of new possibilities?

I'll share a story with you.

A friend has an esteemed position at a well-regarded company.

Everyone around him says, "You're amazing." He loves to hear that.

He also hates his job. He feels miserable a lot of the time. He likes the money but can't find fulfillment. He's on antidepressants and antianxiety medication, often wondering why he has to remain dejected when he should be feeling as amazing as everyone claims he is.

I asked him once, "How would you feel if you were laid off from your high-paying job?"

He answered, "Oh my God, that would be awesome!"

He won't quit his job; he won't even admit to most people that he doesn't like doing it. He complains and waits for others to tell him how good he has it. For short periods he lets that bolster him. Unfortunately, when someone's praise is the source of our strength, we form a dependency on that someone.

It doesn't matter who that someone is. If we need the approval, we'll be dependent on anyone willing to give it.

If you look to others for fulfillment, you will never truly be fulfilled.

—*Lao Tzu*

So, what's going on here?

To put it plainly, fear is going on.

My friend's mind is patterned to maintain an impressive identity.[14]

My friend would say the same. He knows he's afraid. He knows he wants to look like a guy with the good fortune to be at a well-regarded company. And he's had a few jobs at other well-regarded companies. But he keeps following a pattern. He goes out and finds a great new job that he despises.

Could it be that he has also forgotten to see and has grown miserable as a result?

As we discussed above, forgetting to see is a limitation. It isn't a life sentence.

It's a dark veil over a bright light—easily removed when we realize the veil is our patterns.

Or more appropriate to those of us who are a bit nerdier: We think we're seeing the world as it is, but we've got grease on our glasses. We can't see clearly because haven't cleaned our glasses. What we see is the smudge of all the experiences we've had—our solid education, our good jobs, our ambitions to do more.

---

[14] We'll discuss identities in the following chapters.

Old wisdom suggests that our inability to see is the source of our ego, our fear, and our insistence on categorizing the world into things we like and things we don't.

When we don't see clearly, we're right to be afraid. Our mind can't bear going beyond our patterns because it doesn't have any assurance of stability in the unknown. A pattern of pretending to be someone else leaves the mind resistant to being you.

If we aren't who we are, we have a hard time discovering our potential. We believe we can't access our infinite potential.

We tacitly accept a limited potential.

Getting into the world is important. But our training is paltry.

As we venture forth, we must also venture within. We must remember how to see. We must learn how to be.

Consider a tree.

As often as I can, I head out into forests to sit with our original teachers. What I learn from them is simply this: Be. Just be. Walt Whitman wrote about trees like this: "What suggestions of imperturbability and *being*, as against the human trait of mere *seeming*. Then the qualities, almost emotional, palpably artistic, heroic, of a tree; so innocent and harmless, yet so savage. It *is*, yet says nothing."

A tree doesn't pick up and move because it isn't its nature to do so. It doesn't worry about limitations but always grows toward the light. Likewise, it holds its ground.

And water flows clear, only colored by the path it takes.

Rocks hold still for long periods of time and allow change to take its effect.

And light always finds its way in.

To nurture the mind, we offer it the quiet guidance that comes from seeing beyond it. We see nature; we recognize harmony even in the chaos.

The truth is one; sages call it by various names.

—Rig Veda

Life is that. How can you ever feel satisfied following the techniques and guidance of another? If you attempt to live the life of someone else, you're bound to be miserable. Like my friend with the amazing job. He's living the life that everyone else thinks is ideal. His heart disagrees, and he doesn't know how to follow it. His truth is seeking to live through him. As soon as he looks for his truth, he'll feel the gift of his life.

Let us settle in, then, and become friendly keepers of our minds. Even if they wander and spiral, become uncertain or dull, let us tend to them with kind discipline. As we do, our bond will strengthen. We will know how to use the mind well.

There is only one way to know the Self, and that is to realize it yourself.

—Kena Upanishad

Yoga with a Friendly Mind

Here's a practice to move toward greater cooperation with the mind. It's so simple and can serve us for a lifetime. At its heart it's a concentration exercise. But it will also help you refine your sensory awareness and your powers of acceptance.

Sit quietly and comfortably. As you breathe, become aware of the condition of your body in the moment. Notice also the condition of your breath. Make a nice commitment to yourself: *I am attentive and curious; I do this practice to come home to myself.*

Become aware that you live in your body. Be aware that you reside in a physical existence and from this place you watch your interactions with the world around you. Sense the ground beneath you. Sense the moisture in your body. Sense the heat in you. Sense the feeling of air on your skin. Sense the space around you and within you.

Notice the breath.

Now become aware that the mind is offering an abundance of thoughts in relation to these experiences.

Watch them arise, grow, move, fade. Remain passive, neutral, equanimous. If you find yourself judging the thoughts, observe this with a simple statement: *I am judging this thought instead of observing it.* If you find yourself following a thought, simply come back to your point of observation and forgive the mind for wandering.

I like to say this: *Oh dear mind, I've let you run off again. Please return, so I can watch what comes and goes.*

And then I watch. Without judgment. With pure love.

As you watch, begin to notice a space developing between every thought.

And say thank you. To the abundant capacity of the mind to experience this world. To the world for offering you an experience. To the way you're remembering how to see beyond the mind.

Wisdom to Bring Home...

- You are not your mind. The mind is one of the many instruments we use in life to enhance our experience, but it is not who we are.
- We can learn more about our minds by observing them. As we watch our minds, we discover how much they love to wander. What we call deficient attention is simply the mind in its natural state responding to stimulus.
- It is our responsibility to work with the mind just as it is our responsibility to care for the body. Working with the mind involves learning how to recognize our patterns or storing information, our reactions to stimulus, and the ways the mind limits us.
- As we learn to work with our minds, we become more adept at caring for them. We learn to see what the moment offers rather than react to the thousands of thoughts that tell us stories beyond the moment.

To continue contemplating this mind, please see the study guide at the end. The practices presented in this chapter reappear for your consideration. Sit with them. Be with them.

4. What Are You Doing?

Knowing others is intelligence; knowing yourself is true wisdom.

—Lao Tzu

You are not the creator of the world. You are a fortunate inhabitant.

We're Doing Too Much

Consider this bit of mental high jinks. We pretend to be very busy while concurrently suspecting we're not doing enough. It's the stuff of comedy. And it stymies us.

It's also totally true.

You've heard these lines, or you've said them: "I'm so busy. I'm not keeping up with demands, and I have no time for myself."

Some of us may truly worship our busyness. Others are devoted to feeling obligated. And then there's those of us who fanatically believe no one can replace us; if we don't do the task, no one else will.

We're convinced that we're busy and indispensable. Is it the case that the rat race can't release a single rat to a bit of rest? Or even all the rats?

Are we looking to prolong the rat race or care for the rats?[15]

Everyone's schedule is full, time is fleeting, and we barely keep pace with requirements. Most of us truly believe this. Quite a few of us also believe we're expected to do everything we do. We may feel very close to breaking and buckle anytime another straw lands on our back.

We may believe this is just how it is.

And that's definitely true.

At least until you decide otherwise.

You're in Your Own Way

If you're ready for the truth about all that activity of yours, here it is. (If you aren't ready, skip a few paragraphs and come back later.) You're spinning your wheels and going nowhere. The going nowhere issue isn't really an issue. Going nowhere is fine actually. You can see the whole world from the space where you are.

> *Everything, Everything in existence, does point to God.*
> —Hafez

It's the spinning of the wheels that's keeping you from knowing this.

This may be a fascinating contemplation for you: How do you feel about the moment you're in? Do you enjoy it? Would you prefer it was

---

[15] If rats are troubling, please forgive me. I had a pet rat as a kid. His name was Rat. He was a lazy and fat rat, most at home on my shoulders. One of my guardian angels. What a loving creature. Just like you and me.

different? Do you accept certain parts but wish other parts could be razed by a bulldozer? Do you believe you have the power to change it? Do you long to drive the bulldozer right into this moment and somehow make it suit your better sensibilities?

Now ask yourself: Why would my sensibilities, as young as they are, trump the sensibilities of the thirteen-billion-year-old entity that has expanded into the life I know right now? The present moment in this entity's existence is what manifests as your form. Is it possible that your juvenile judgments and cloudy misperceptions of the moment block your engagement with this ancient entity?

What do you really know about this ancient being?

In other words, how friendly are you with life itself?

This life we share moves ever lifeward. We're small but essential players passing through a few precious moments. From this perspective, what would it be like to honor the lifeward journey and our roles in it? How would it feel to celebrate the extremely unlikely chance of our arrival in this space of now? After all, it's in this space of now where you and I exist.

Our limited view of the present moment is like a bouncer at the end of the velvet rope. As he selects from the crowd of the unified whole, he shapes a much diminished reality for us. We may think we're curating our experience, but we're actually imposing barriers. In this paltry, deficient version of what life actually offers, we find ourselves unhappy, dissatisfied, bored, angry, and maybe even jealous of some other party. We blame the experiences and demand that the bouncer further narrow his criteria. Soon enough he stops letting anyone in. And we wonder why we're lonely.

Likewise, please consider our eagerness to constantly qualify, categorize, and critique every moment before we allow it entry. Isn't this a close relative of that woman who talks through the movie, letting you know what's good, bad, believable, or not? If she would hush for a moment, we might start appreciating the show.

The moment you've found, right now, is a miracle. It is the aggregate result of every moment of our entire existence plus every life in all of creation and the evolution of life itself.

Whoa. You made it.

This moment is way bigger and richer and more complicated than anything you could conceive. I promise. And you're perfectly placed to be in it.

You didn't make this moment. You're simply experiencing it. You can block it and find yourself in a reduced and vague state. You can judge it and miss its wonder. Or you can invite it in and play with the whole of it in every component you discover.

Then you realize the miracle of the moment.

Look around you. It's a select group of people who can construct the setting you inhabit. Look more closely. Who do you know who makes the glass? The wood? Who created the land on which you rest? The clouds passing overhead?

This isn't a demand that you honor some celestial God but merely look around and realize the simple fact of your status. You are not the creator of the world. You are a fortunate inhabitant. You may have built your house, but you didn't make the wood. You may even have grown the trees, but you didn't create the DNA and embed it in the seed that initiated the growth of the tiny sapling that eventually gathered the stability to be harvested and used to frame your house. You don't have that capability.

If you aren't convinced, look at your own self. Look at your hand. Could you make one of those? How about your liver? Please write me a letter and explain to me how you might create and command the function of your liver throughout the next twenty-four-hour period. Please be sure to include if you could do this while maintaining all other life function and luxuries like entertainment, sex, and hopscotching.

The lives given to us are overwhelmingly complex. None of us could direct our bodies and minds to do the work they do automatically. If we had to control every one of our functions, we would have precious little ability to wander malls or hug redwood trees. And yet, somehow, we each have the hubris to groan over pain, weight, mood, and stress, even as we load ourselves up with inappropriate food, activity, company, and opinions. We do this to ourselves. We expect the organs of our body and the energy of our minds to see us through. We do very little to cooperate with their efforts.

And when we suffer, we feel as though an injustice has been done. We're so confused by the world of form that we think we're meant to take control of it. As in any relationship, your attempts to control what you cannot delivers you directly to resentment. We resent the suffering because we tried so hard to be persuasive with life. We want something different. We want the sun to rise differently. We want the weather to shift. Our desire that everything become different is the cause of our suffering. Which is the greater challenge: to suffer your habitual judgments and desires or to practice reverence for the ancient entity of life and your existence in it?

At this moment, regardless of your relationship to it, the mechanisms within your body are breathing for you, converting glucose to energy, translating light into vision. Take a moment to imagine if you had to consciously orchestrate these activities. Imagine having to do them all at once. Remember that hectic schedule of yours? You'd be dead before you could establish a new relationship with the next moment.

Which is now.

Yoga with the Moment

Here's a practice to become connected to the moment.

Sit comfortably, or even lie down if you're sure you won't fall asleep.

Now tune your senses in, one by one, to everything around you. Awaken to your surroundings.

First, notice the ground beneath you. Feel its stability and support. Now turn your attention toward the scents that the earth provides. No need to try to find smells. Just notice what smells are available to you.

Feel into the qualities of water within you. You may notice the moisture in your eyes, nose, mouth. Become aware of taste simply by checking in with your tongue.

Now find light by opening your eyes as you gently inhale and closing them as you gently exhale. No need to control or strain your breathing. Simply notice the light beyond you and within you.

Become aware of the feeling of air on your skin. Notice that the surface of your skin is as much a bridge as a barrier to the space that surrounds you. Finally, become aware of the sense of spaciousness surrounding you. Hear any sounds and do so without classification or identification. Simply listen.

Spend a few moments now experiencing the moment as a whole, a compilation created by your sense of smell, taste, sight, touch, and hearing. See if you can allow your senses to share information with your mind without any interference. If a loud noise or offensive smell arises, allow it without judgment. If you feel uncomfortable, allow it, and move if you must. Welcome all sensation if you can. I like to say these words: *Oh, hi, you're here too. Thank you for being here.* Choose your own words to allow all sensation to simply be with you.

Spend about five minutes a day with this exercise and notice how your perception of activity begins to shift.

Doing or Trying to Control?

Here's the thing about doing. So many of us think we're supposed to keep the world under our thumb. We work hard pretending that we have our lives "under control." The pretense is absurd. We have no more control over our lives than we have the means to burst a supernova. To paraphrase my teacher's teacher T. K. V. Desikachar, it's better we learn to influence the direction of change than pretend we can arrest change.

But isn't this what so many of us do? For a living? I spent a few years as a lawyer. Sometimes, I would end up with cases that basically boiled down to a client's rage at change. He didn't want to find a new job. She didn't want to accept that a mistake could not be undone. Often the best I could do was secure a little money to compensate someone for the fact of change. It never satisfied anyone. Maybe it made the process of moving along a little easier, but many clients accepted it with a bit of resignation. They just wished things could have held steady in some pattern that suited their sensibilities better. Even though nothing holds steady forever.

I have a friend who works as an engineer. He spends his days working up systems to hold off the natural wear of water flowing through pipes. Thank goodness for him and others who keep our infrastructure sound. Eventually water will win. It's one of the great destroyers, and it will eventually do its job. All my friend can do is influence the rate at which it softens up and erodes whatever carries it. If he tries to do more, he's going to frustrate himself again and again.

Which brings us back to all the doing. It's in the way.

The peace we're all looking for is readily available in every moment to every person. The issue is not what we need to do to acquire it but what we can stop doing to give ourselves a chance to experience every moment fully.

To undo all we do, we must understand why we do it. We must realize what we think we can control and determine if we have any chance of success.

(Most of the time, chances are slim.)

What Energy Creates You?

Have you ever performed a budget analysis of your energy? Most of us review our finances from time to time. When was the last time you did an accounting of your energy?

Acquainting yourself with energy doesn't require an advanced degree in unicorn husbandry. We start simply. We notice how we feel.

Are we low or high? Are we sluggish or spinning? Slightly electric or slightly soggy?

Energy serves as the building block of our existence as physical entities. It surrounds us at every moment, flowing in and out with every breath…at the very least.

Energy accumulates in and around us, balancing us as we share and receive kindness, love, and compassion. Likewise, we've all experienced the deflating, destabilizing sensation of energies withdrawn, whether by death, distance, or choice.

Yoga with Energy

Let's take a moment to consider our relationship with energy.

The elegant and ancient system of Ayurveda, a sister science of yoga, offers a useful framework for our self-analysis.[16] By asking us to consider our preferences and traits, it helps us to identify the way energy moves in us.

Please answer for yourself the following questions.

---

[16] To explore this complex and profound science of well-being, please look for the teachings of Dr. Vasant Lad, Dr. David Frawley, or Dr. Robert Svoboda. These three masterful teachers offer credible and accessible information on the topic.

1. Are you...?
    A. a bit slow to start but sure to finish
    B. actively ready for whatever project comes your way
    C. curious about everything but committed to very little
2. Do you like to...
    A. sit around
    B. keep intellectually busy
    C. stay in constant motion
3. Do you prefer...
    A. lots of friends
    B. only the right friends
    C. friends who come and go
4. Would you choose...
    A. to admire and collect art
    B. to critique art
    C. to make art
5. Are you...?
    A. slow to learn and slow to forget
    B. curious and ready to learn more
    C. quick to learn and quick to forget
6. Do you eat...
    A. too much and when you don't feel hungry
    B. so, you don't get angry
    C. occasionally, when you remember
7. Do you...
    A. comfort others
    B. intimidate others
    C. play with others
8. Would you rather...
    A. ignore conflict
    B. win arguments
    C. let things pass
9. If someone hurts you, do you...
    A. hold a grudge
    B. maintain a justified resentment
    C. forget there was ever an issue

Now consider your answers. Tally up your As, Bs, and Cs. It is absolutely normal to have a predominance of one or two. Some folks will have an even distribution.

Part two of this practice is to think a bit imaginatively. Ayurveda suggests that energy moves through you as it does in nature. You are a creature of nature.

In Ayurveda every person is said to be a composite of the five elements of nature: space, air, fire, water, and earth. The elements are evolutes or manifestations of essential life conditions: activity, stability, and consciousness. Think of it like this: life vibrates. Slow down a vibration, and you find the rise, the fall, and the space between them. Like breath itself. We inhale and expand, exhale and contract, and there's a space between each expansion and contraction in which we simply are.

All of life is created by the interweaving of these life conditions, and every experience is born of the shifting dominance of one or more of them. For example, if you feel weighted down by a challenging conversation, you are sensing an overwhelming feeling of stability. If you feel enraged by a bad act or distracted by pain, you're encountering a surge of the active force. Maybe you can think of the harmony and calm you feel while listening to a beautiful piece of music. This would be the clarity of the conscious force.

Every form in the universe is said to be made of all three, vibrating at various frequencies. As a creature of nature, you are a realization of these frequencies. You're a unique vibration of energy. You're a tapestry that takes its shape through the elements born of the three primary forces. Your energy manifested through a beautiful composition of earth, water, fire, air, and space.

Returning to the results of our quiz…

Lots of as suggest an earthy, watery person. This person may be a bit heavier in the body, with energy that moves somewhat slowly. Stagnation can happen; laziness can happen; depression can happen. These are the folks who give great hugs and know how to comfort others, often with food.

Lots of Bs suggest a watery, fiery person. This person may be a strong leader, prone to anger, and quick-witted. Because of that wit and that heat, these folks know exactly how to hurt someone. They may intimidate others, but they get their work done.

Lots of Cs suggest an airy, spacy person. This person is usually thin, highly creative, very good at brainstorming, and not always certain to execute the plan. While these folks may not prove the most reliable, they always know how to set things in motion. This is an innovator but not someone to hold to a schedule.

What Are Your Frequencies?

If you find yourself quite sedentary or a slow mover, this can indicate a bit of earthy energy. Most earthy folks will not be surprised by this. They know they love to rest. They're also adept at hiding away when they don't want to confront change. They may hide their emotions, their ideas, and their truth from themselves and others in order to maintain stability—even if the stability isn't working.

Perhaps you feel entirely opposite. When stability isn't working for you, you're quick to overthrow it. Or maybe it is working for you; you may still enjoy the stimulation of upheaval. This is like air. Airy people are runners, escape artists, and travelers. They move through relationships, cities, and jobs as readily as the breeze. They're quick and happy to recognize themselves as playmates of the wind because they've heard often that they need to sit still, stop fidgeting, and keep focused. All of this is a little foreign to them. Movement is intrinsic to their being, but it can also be used to avoid a better understanding of what will soothe them.

As they read this, fiery folks will have already identified the fire within them. They may, however, have points to raise in debate. These are the strategists, the planners, the warriors. They use their sharp and lucid minds to see through every obstacle toward a solution. They have a tendency toward control; when their ability to control conflicts with the natural order of things, they can become angry. They are, quite likely, already looking up Ayurveda to learn how to better use it.

Creatives? They whip things around like the air. Rational, science minds? They are keen and penetrating, like fire. Slow to learn and slow to forget? These are comfortable, deliberate earth people. Intimidating? Fire. Prone to holding grudges? Earth. Eccentric and slightly unpredictable? Air.

None of this is meant to pigeonhole you but simply to give you an interesting framework for considering the energies that move you through life. When you perceive a challenge, do you look to escape, to fight, or to hide? These energies help us understand our tendencies and how we use them in our interactions with others and ourselves.

We can see these energies in ourselves, no matter the composition. Think of yourself in the morning. We are slowly awakening, perhaps a bit stiff and heavy, like the earth. By midday we are active, getting our chores done. By the late afternoon, we may find ourselves a bit scattered but also ready to move. We may hit on some interesting new ideas.

When we see ourselves as these vibrations and influenced by these vibrations, we get a sense of how we might be in or out of rhythm. For example, a very earthy person might get uncomfortable if asked to travel frequently. Likewise, a decent amount of movement may be helpful, though not always welcome, to counteract heaviness.

An airy, creative type might not enjoy confrontation as much as someone who has a strong fire element, but this person may find surprising ways to whip around the conflict. An earthy type might want to eat more than required, whereas a fire type might get angry when food isn't available on time. Meanwhile, an airy type could forget about food completely.

These energetic stories help us see ourselves more clearly and understand how we might not honor our energies well. When we recognize our energies, we can begin to free ourselves from patterns holding us in. We can also learn to thrive in their balance. For someone grounded, coming to a sense of well-being and balance will require different techniques, diets, and lifestyles than it will for someone of an air or fire nature.

We've made it this far in life, and for this, let's be grateful. As we progress, let's recognize that our energetic tendencies are guideposts toward home. Perhaps we've long used these patterns in reaction to challenge and found that they provoke more anxiety, anger, and despair. When we acknowledge and understand our energies, we learn to optimize them in harmony with nature. We're the ones in these bodies. We're the ones being moved in this energy. We're the one privileged to hear life calling us toward balance.

As the last part of the above exercise, consider what habits you have that might challenge your natural energies and what habits make them a little strong. Notice how your energetic tendencies keep you stuck in detrimental patterns and how these patterns prevent you from choosing wisely to be in accord with nature.

Perhaps you noticed you're pretty airy—ideally dancing, quick to laugh, and rarely on time. You may have habits, however, that put you into extreme movement. You might not like to stop at the end of the day. You might not like to stick around people. When you do stop, you feel anxious, like you're missing life. You can't stop your thoughts for even a moment to consider how you might relieve your pain, so you just push through it.

Perhaps you are quite clear that your fire is strong, and you're in a friendship with someone who keeps telling you what to do. You may notice yourself becoming more frequently angry than you like. Or you find yourself disgruntled and stymied by the bad decisions of work superiors, and they aren't hearing your suggestions for improvement. You may find yourself feeling frustration that morphs into persistent, inflammatory joint pain or migraines.

Or you are earthy but, for various reasons, are being pulled in all directions by work, family, and/or friends. You want to be a solid, reliable person for everyone, but you're starting to feel overburdened. You take to the couch for rest, and you no longer wish to get up. You eat more and often what you know will only make you feel heavier.

Of course, understand that we are all made up of everything. We are all composites, and we are all perfectly imperfect. You might be able to choose from wiser alternatives that will bring your energies into balance. You might be overwhelmed by the very idea of this.

Rest your head.

Simply consider, for now, what are your self-care routines? And how well do they complement the elemental composition of you? So often, an airy person will try to keep moving when a little quiet would be more soothing. Likewise, a fiery person may take on more work just at the point that they've burned themselves out. Our earthy friends will resist any movement or change at exactly the moment when movement and change are required.

How might you complement your natural energies so they can move more freely through and around you while receiving the support of nature's other elements?

This is our life's work, truly. Our privilege is to learn how to operate as beings of energy in an energetic world. Our great fortune is to learn how to live with life. When we do, life thrills to live in us.

We aren't given owner's manuals at the start of our life, but we learn as we go.

Let me share a story. This one is about me.

The third time I went on a personal retreat was entirely different. On previous adventures, I'd done everything I normally would. I squeezed in time to run, to write, to do additional yoga practices, to hike, to explore, to talk on the phone, to socialize, to complain about retreat meals.[17] In other words, I kept really busy. More often than not, I was late for the actual instruction the retreat had to offer. But I prioritized my patterns of activity. I wouldn't let them go.

---

[17] So many people on retreat love to complain about retreat meals. Since there's limited access to the news on retreat, the quality of the meals always seems to become the main topic for debate. Which is amazing because someone is actually making it and serving it, and that someone isn't usually you.

On my third retreat, I did my best to maintain my status quo. I had my running shoes, my projects, my intentions to do everything I needed to do. On the third day of 14, during a 90-minute break for lunch, I took off for a run. It was beautiful land, protected by redwoods and embraced by fog. I took an unknown trail. About 25 minutes into the run, I realized I'd crossed a property line. I also realized I was trailblazing. Finding my way back would be tricky, so I decided to continue forward. Somehow, I believed that persistent motion would bring me back where I needed to be. The land descended into a valley, and I continued. One foot in front of the other. Another 15 minutes or so, and I was imagining who would be in the search party. I took one more step and tumbled.

I rolled. And I laughed. My idea of persevering had been commandeered by the universe, and I ended up face-first in mud and what I was sure was poison oak. Then I cried. I sobbed. I wailed.

Then I just sat. I sat at the bottom of the valley and saw for the first time how the redwoods formed in families. I saw how the hills used their shade and mulch to grow moss and fern and tiny irises. A deer appeared, and I understood how the cushion of redwood needles silenced us both. I closed my eyes and decided, finally, to just be still.

I stayed there for a while. I rested. I listened to the hum of beetles and the chides of chipmunks. When the light changed, I decided to try my way back before dark arrived. I asked the trees for guidance. And I walked. So slowly. About two hours later, just as the sun set, I arrived at the retreat center.

I was ecstatic.

This ecstasy lived separately from the relief of a safe return. The ecstasy lived in the discovery of stillness. It lived, and I knew it lived in me. I would know it whenever I remembered that my natural instinct to move could be met with rest. I would know it when I surrendered to conditions, just as they are, rather than trying to mold them into a reality I preferred.

This was when I truly understood how to quiet my airy nature and soothe my fire. This was the moment when the earth came for me and held me quiet.

I didn't always have to run. I could be still.

Wisdom to Bring Home...

- We are beings of energy. When we use most of our energy keeping ourselves in motion, it's difficult to feel into and appreciate the nature of our energy.
- Learning about our energy and its cycles helps us better understand how we engage with our days, our people, and ourselves. How we live in this world is totally up to us, regardless of what the world decides to do.
- We have the means and ability to engage in activities and routines that will complement our energetic tendencies, so these tendencies don't guide us into persistent, detrimental patterns.

- Working with our energetic cycles requires that we forfeit old patterns in favor of learning to be with ourselves anew. Ideally in every moment.

To continue contemplating your activities, please see the study guide at the end. The practices presented in this chapter reappear for your consideration. Sit with them. Be you with them.

5. How Are You Doing?

It is a bit embarrassing to have been concerned with the human problem

all one's life and find at the end that one has no more to offer by way of

advice than 'try to be a little kinder.'

—*Aldous Huxley*

A sturdy and effective practice in kindness is to accept ourselves, mistakes and all.

Energy on the Move

Having assessed your own energies a bit, you might be curious about the way you can work with them. How can you influence the way energy moves in and through you?

While there is infinite knowledge available to all of us addressing the principles and pragmatics of working with our energetic tendencies, I'm going to focus fairly broadly on the essentials.[18]

You'll recognize these core lessons immediately and might even realize that their very simplicity is part of the reason they're so quickly left in the dust along our journeys. While they may not be the stuff of scientific inquiry or technological advancement, they enable an enduring

---

[18] Here's another little plug to inquire more deeply into the beautiful, living science of Ayurveda. A good Ayurvedic practitioner can help you determine appropriate modifications to your diet and lifestyle and much more. My intention here is to kindle the fire of transformation that your guides will nurture. Onward!

foundation for success in any endeavor. This grandiose statement is intended to include the greatest adventure of all: life.

Consider the attitude you take toward a blue-sky day off. You wake up, you have no plans, and the day seems as full of potential as the sky itself. Feel the momentum building as you simply imagine such a day.

Now consider the attitude you take toward that day when your schedule is packed through and through with appointments you'd rather not keep. The whole day is dentists, doctors, traffic, meetings with grumpy coworkers, and then you have to fold all the laundry.[19] Maybe you feel how closed down you become just thinking of the burdensome day ahead.

We all do this to ourselves. We have attitudes that set our energies into motion. These energies surge ahead of us and create the dynamic we'll encounter at each step. Under the blue sky, we see our smile returned by strangers. As we race from meeting to meeting, we see our misery reflected in the posture of those who don't even lift their heads to greet us. We rarely stop to realize that *we* put the energy in motion. So how do we prefer to proceed?

Feel How You Share

Let's feel a little bit. Call to mind a memory of a really pleasant time. You were laughing, loving, surrounded by good friends or maybe completely alone and content. Take a moment to let the memory expand for you. Focus on the colors you see, the sounds you might recall, and

---

[19] This says more about me than you. You know you. Any one of the above is fine. Personally, for my peace of mind, I do my best not to schedule all of the above on a single day.

any elements of nature or community around you. Now check out the feeling of the memory. What do you feel in this moment as you remember this pleasant time?

See if you can sit for a moment, feeling that pleasant time now, and notice. Do you feel lighter in your shoulders? Is your mouth smiling gently? Did your face relax?

Now consider. Is there someone in your life who might benefit from feeling these sweet sensations? Maybe you have a friend going through a rough patch. Would you be willing to share these sensations if you could?

You can.

For now just send a little thought toward your friend: *I give you these sweet sensations. I want you to feel better, and these sensations felt good to me, so I'm sharing them.*

For now, that's enough. We'll do more in a bit. Let's explore what else we share.

Remember the last time you became angry.

Recall the surge of energy that sought and maybe found an outlet in a raised voice, a physical gesture, or even a trembling of the limbs. If you directed your anger toward someone, you may have noticed that its release provoked a chain reaction; the energy you aimed toward someone may have provoked an arising of energy in that person. Maybe that individual volleyed the energy in anger as well or maybe not.

It's conceivable that the energy of that anger continues to ripple around the world and through it; energy never fades.

It travels and transforms through the channels it follows. As it lands here and there on various creatures, it may rebound in anger, or it may be shifted into love, depending on the condition of the next recipient. Energy takes our spin and carries it along.

Energy itself is neutral. The spin we put on it endures until it meets another force. This is the inertia of emotion. If I send out anger, it continues as anger until it meets an opposing force. Let's say it finds love. It will shift. We can't rely on anyone else to create the shift we'd like the world to experience. We're the ones who create every shift. If we're skillful, we're the ones who create send out love regardless of the conditions that reach us.

We decide how what kind of spin we'd like to apply on the energy moving in and around us.

As energy travels, it undergoes various reactions with the energy it meets.

Anger, for example, thrives on disgust, envy, and greed. It weakens in the presence of joy, and it's remedied by love.

Sadness is alleviated by hope, gratitude and love. Courage wanes in fear but can be amplified by anger or love. We will rise to an injustice to protect a dear friend and also when we can no longer tolerate abuse.

As we consider our impact on energy, we weave a response from the various restraints of the sutra. We may even ask ourselves before we speak or share, *Is this kind, true, generous, moderate, and appreciative?* If the first principle isn't met, we adjust our intentions. If the first principle isn't met, we don't bother to share.

Envision yourself as a power plant. As a human, you are in the business of converting resources into attention and activity. Energy that flows into you is converted into energy that flows out of you. Your attention flows into power lines you've established toward various neighborhoods; these neighborhoods may include your lover, family, work, pets, hobbies, spiritual pursuits. Scoping out the quantity of your lines and the quality of your transmissions is a good way to get a sense of your reliability as a power conductor.

Sometimes we don't realize how certain lines seem to trail off into a dead zone. You may call these dead zones by proper names (think: social media outlets or the friend who always depletes you), or you may acknowledge them as certain habits (think: engaging in mindless screen time, debating useless topics with your partner, or reading entertainment news).

Whatever they may be, it's a worthwhile exercise to consider whether this is how we'd like to channel our energy. It's also interesting to note who or what our energy serves as we direct it toward the dead zones. If it serves us, honestly, great. If not, it may be time to take down those wires.

This means we have to learn some skills.

Principles of sharing

In the *Yoga Sutra of Patanjali*, an ancient, practical guide to unifying our experience of life as body, mind, energy, and spirit, we're instructed to cultivate positive thoughts in response to negative thoughts.[20]

We come across this guidance in the midst of an introduction to the preliminary steps to yoga itself. Believe it or not, the first requirements

---

[20] The word *sutra* means a stitch. Like suture. It's worthwhile to remember that a single stitch is important, but we want to remember how a single stitch is strengthened by what has been sewn before and after. Likewise, we can appreciate how one unraveling stitch can ruin a beautiful tapestry.

of yoga are not stretchy pants and a mat. The first steps ask us to look carefully at our behavior.[21]

Yoga, among other things, means union. It is the process and practice we undertake to find our connection with the whole of life, ourselves included. To become one with the whole, we have to practice. What we're practicing is mind training and behavioral modification. To turn negative thoughts into positive ones, we first need to observe our behavior. Trust me, you're not the only one who stumbles over the way you do things.

Let's look at how we behave. Or how we might control our behavior to become a little more graceful.

To discover union with the whole, the Yoga Sutra advises us to first (and forever) practice with kindness, honesty, generosity, moderation, and gratitude for what we have.[22] These practices are considered restraints. In other words, we're meant to witness our impulses to do their opposite and make the necessary adjustments. That means these restraints are both the means of changing our behavior and the result of changing our behavior.

These principles are meant to keep us out of patterns that might hurt ourselves or others. Consider how well you keep to these practices as you do what you do: Are you kind? Are you honest? Do you take what

---

[21] For more on the limbs of yoga, read The Yoga Sutra of Patanjali at chapter two, starting at verse twenty-nine through the end.

[22] Strident scholars will shudder, but that's okay. I'm playing with the translations a bit to give us a positive means of working with them. The restraints are nonviolence, truthfulness, nonstealing, celibacy, and noncovetousness. I've found that working with the negatives tends to make me focus on the idea meant to be canceled. I prefer to work with the positive aspect as this sets my mind directly to task. Try out both for yourself. Become a strident scholar of you.

isn't yours to take? Are you moderate in your actions? Do you covet the belongings of others instead of appreciating what you have?

When I teach these concepts, students love to raise objections. They argue it's impossible to follow these principles all the time.

"Super!" I say. "Make all the mistakes you like but learn from them."

When we want to hit a target and we miss, we adjust our aim. Walking the path of failure is our journey to success. Failure is the guide we all share, but many of us refuse to hear its wisdom. If we choose to listen, we strengthen our commitment to behaving well every time we misstep.

See for yourself.

If you choose to focus on truthfulness, you will spend a day noting a few silly fabrications, a couple omissions, and maybe an impulse to tell a real whopper of a lie. Because you were watching, the whopper didn't come out. You opted otherwise, and truthfulness became a little more established in you. It's said that our diligent practice with truthfulness makes everything we say come to be.

(How could it be otherwise?)

When you decide to become respectful in all matters, not stealing others' ideas, time, or belongings, you may notice how frequently you pilfer here and there from the world around you. We're meant to share everything, but an attitude of respect means that we seek consent before we make a grab and show appreciation for what we gather. When we commit to this generosity, we can anticipate that all treasures will find us.

(Isn't it the case that acknowledging someone's help brings us greater reward?)

Our moderate behavior and our appreciation of who we are, what we own, the way things are...well...

These are the behavioral restraints that turn our ambitions a little upside down. We've been brought up in a world that educated us to do what we're told, to work hard, to rise to the top, to strive for more, to push ourselves, to compete, and to win.

These two restraints gently suggest that we take a look at how we do this.

I have a friend in sales. Let's call him Henry. Henry's very good at sales and he's done well for himself. He works for a family business that recruited him young. While he had different visions for himself, his family encouraged him to succeed with them. So he did. And twenty years into his career, at forty-five, Henry felt completely numb from the moment he left for work until he returned home in the late evening. For many years he drank because it masked the contrasting emotions that slapped him across the face at the end of every numb day. He felt disappointment, yearning, anxiety, frustration, resentment, despair, and he preferred to feel nothing. Drinking gave him the means to remain numb.

When he stopped drinking, he felt again. And because he didn't know what he was feeling, he sought help. With guidance, he discovered how to become moderate and grateful.

And he realized his error. He had to feel if he wanted to learn how to change. He realized that his success in sales was also one of his greatest failures. He'd done well for his family, and he'd gained many skills; his failure was refusing to be grateful for what it had taught him. He'd been unhappy because no matter how much income he'd generated for himself or his family, he'd never known satisfaction. He tried to find it in cars, a home, girlfriends, adventures, until he stopped looking entirely. That was when Henry went numb.

He knew what he'd done wrong. He'd neglected himself. He'd lied to himself. He'd taken a role that his family had given him instead of creating one for himself. And he'd worked as hard as he could to make the role fit him instead of honoring the truth.

Henry eventually opened his own little store. He laughs at himself for remaining in sales. But he also laughs at how much he loves what he's selling and whom he's selling to. Most importantly, he loves who *he* is and how he keeps finding more and more to love.

We may ask ourselves if we're really having an experience of union with the whole world if we're competing with every part of it to stake our little claim. After all, we're part of the whole world. Why would we need to claim any of it? Every bit of life is us, in service to every bit of life. Just as our hands hold our fingers and our fingers hold our hands. A single drop of water is at home in the immense Pacific Ocean. We are, at once, life and everything in it.

So can we all be a bit more moderate? Can we choose to accept that the destination is in the path itself? Can we appreciate and say thank you to the path for every twist and turn that takes us home? The approval we seek through status and possessions is available in our honest pursuit of our heart's mission.

We discover this mission by accepting ourselves, mistakes and all, with honesty, generosity, moderation, and appreciation. Most importantly, we accept ourselves with an attitude of kindness.

We are, constantly, all of us, making small messes. Let's not cry over all of them. Let's smile, laugh, and be friendly toward ourselves and everyone else.

Let's be kind and share kindness.

It's simple, and it's the great imperative for all of us.

Live Each Moment in Kindness

Three things in life are important. The first is to be kind. The second is to be kind. The third is to be kind.

—Henry James

We must be kind. It is the first restraint in the Yoga Sutra, and it's been reiterated by teachers through time in all traditions. *Do unto others as you would have them do unto you; be compassionate; the highest form of wisdom is kindness.* Recall your first teachers' insistence on it. And how much you appreciate it when you find it.

Kindness is more important than wisdom, and the recognition of this is the beginning of wisdom.

—Aesop

Kindness is the mechanism by which we find our way to joy, peace, and love. It's also the means by which we share it. We want our possessions, people, food, status, and professions because we mistakenly believe they'll bring us joy, peace, and love.

And for a moment, they do.

And then they change.

And we think we've lost our joy, our peace, and our love.

Through the consistent exercise of kindness, we're assured that our joy, peace, and love endures. Kindness brings us home to them. We realize they are always waiting for us.

A sturdy and effective practice in kindness is to accept ourselves, mistakes and all. Henry found his way when he chose to become friendly with himself. He acknowledged his mistakes, honored his skills, and transformed himself by applying both to the task of transformation. He heard his heart's call through the kindness he gave to himself. He learned to be kind. He healed his mind by attending to his heart.

We all have the means to conduct ourselves this way.

May we be kind to ourselves and one another as we figure it out.

This attitude, directed toward ourselves and in all directions, gives us all a friendly space to listen to the call of our hearts. And to heal what needs mending.

Yoga with Kindness

Please take a moment to review the kindness you've extended over the last twenty-four hours.

Please be kind to yourself as you make note. Include even the simplest act. A door held open. A small smile toward a stranger. A pause to allow someone to pass.

Now notice the spaces that could have used your kindness. It's okay if you didn't give it. Just notice. Maybe you saw a scowl on a cashier's face. Maybe you saw a mother struggling with her kids. Maybe it was you, feeling low.

Even if you missed the opportunity earlier, you have the opportunity now. While we can never go back in time, we always heal through the present moment.

Take a moment to choose a few responses you could have offered in the spaces that wanted kindness.

Watch yourself offering your kindness.

Share your kindness and watch how it spreads beyond you.

Feel your kindness growing through the ripples you created.

As energy conductors, we hold great power. What if we set an intention for the energy we expend? Let's say we choose kindness. We commit to acting with kindness, regardless of the circumstance.

Feel for a moment the strength required to make this commitment.

Feel for a moment how your experience of life will shift as you prioritize kindness. Feel the softness available for you.

Feel the acceptance. Feel the curiosity. Feel the joy.

Kindness sets in motion further kindness.

You must be the change you wish to see in the world.
—Mahatma Gandhi

As we feel, so goes our energy.

We do our best. We will sometimes fail. Next time we'll fail better and continue on our journey with greater understanding. We'll err and correct our course. We'll engage in the feedback loop. We'll understand that ever little mishap is a gift to teach and eventually delight us.

This is a practice of consistent and unconditional love—toward ourselves and others—for the good of all creatures. That's big love. And it's not just possible for each of us; it's our highest potential.

It doesn't mean we won't make mistakes. It means we intend to avoid future suffering—whether generated in ourselves or others—and we pay careful attention to the ways we fail in our intention.

This isn't an easy practice. Some days simply remembering it will be our greatest success. Still we make the choice. We do our best and acknowledge every idea and belief that gets in the way of our love. These are the obstacles.

The only way to progress through our practice is to acknowledge and dissolve the obstacles that keep us from gaining ground.

This means at every breath we recall our presence. At every breath we remember our existence. We feel the hesitation keeping us from loving completely.

When we manage this, we can choose peace over violence, honesty over lying, generosity over stealing, moderation over indulgence, gratitude over desire. Sometimes we may not know immediately what choice to make to uphold these values. In these circumstances we might simply choose to pay close attention. By remaining engaged, we invite the moment itself to guide us. We simply choose to be. That decision demonstrates our respect for life and its treasures more than any action we can ever take.

Yoga with Obstacles

A useful practice is to make a commitment every morning to love everything. Although this may seem like a practice in loving, the challenge is actually to strengthen our discernment.[23] To love everything, we need to know how to choose wisely.

Take a moment to see how an obstacle has appeared on your path lately. Consider what has kept you from deeply loving every moment you've experienced in the last day. As you do this, remember you're not alone with your obstacles. We all have them, and we all have the responsibility of learning how to dissolve them.

Maybe you judge everyone you meet. Judging others is a surefire technique to ensure our own suspicion that everyone is judging you. We find ourselves vulnerable to embarrassment, guilt, shame, fear that someone is going to realize our weaknesses.

Maybe you keep telling lies. Our dishonesty often leaves us with a sense of instability and shame. Our hearts know the world is all right the

---

[23] Truly, we don't require practice in loving. It's who we are. We may be sheltered by so many obstacles that we've forgotten but under all the rubble, there's the love.

way it is, but our lies insist on making it otherwise. We've all done it. We tell a lie and gently excuse ourselves with an insistence to our conscience that it was really nothing. But we still feel the sting.

Maybe you feel insecure in your job or relationship. This insecurity can bleed into other experiences and lead to an overall sense of distrust in the way things are. You may even find camaraderie with others when you complain about your work or partner, but it doesn't really feel like fulfilling friendship.

Maybe you're going so hard in your activities that you can't remember how to have fun. Alternatively, maybe you're feeling dull. You can't even remember what fun feels like. Sometimes we compensate for these imbalances by settling more deeply into them. When we go hard, we feel like the way out has to be just as hard. Likewise, if we're dull, we may just give into the couch. We make patterned choices that deepen the pattern itself. And we wonder why we keep feeling pain and discomfort.

Maybe you're just feeling like you can't win. Your progress is slipping, and you feel like quitting. Sometimes we feel disappointed when we start to compare ourselves with others. We start thinking we aren't succeeding if we don't measure up to the standards of others. We forget to see how much we've learned, how well we've recovered from challenges, and how *our* standards have improved because of *our* hard work.

As you look toward your day, you may discover that every single obstacle is an opportunity to make a difficult choice. We can choose to feel limited by our behaviors and feel the challenge of them, or we can choose to change our behaviors and feel the challenge of the work. We have the privilege of getting to choose wisely.

Based on your observations, choose one of the following mantras, or shape one to suit you. Invite the mantra to become your guide to sharing love.

Today, I am kind. Today, kindness guides me.

Today, I am honest. Today, honesty guides me.

Today, I am generous. Today, generosity guides me.

Today, I am balanced. Today, balance guides me.

Today, I am grateful. Today, gratitude guides me.

Now take a seat and examine your breath. Feel the movement of your inhale and your exhale in the body. Expand your awareness beyond your breath to the guidance you've chosen.

As you inhale, silently say the first part of the mantra to yourself.

As you exhale, silently say the second part of the mantra to yourself.

See how it feels to make this commitment. At the end of the day, notice how your responses to the day improved due to your commitment. Notice when you failed to follow the guidance you chose. Become aware of the thoughts, emotions, or judgments that steered you away from your commitment.

Affirm to yourself: *I have a choice at every moment. I will choose wisely.*

Wisdom to Bring Home...

- We are, all of us, energy converters. We influence the quality of energy in us, around us, and everywhere by sharing it. We can choose to influence it with kind and positive thoughts and watch the effects on ourselves and the world around us.
- Practicing kindness, honesty, generosity, moderation, and gratitude gives us a means to observe how our behaviors shape the way we see the world.
- When we train our behavior in kindness, honesty, generosity, balance, and gratitude, we access positive responses to our negative thoughts and beliefs.
- Committing to kindness gives us a new pattern to replace tired practices of resentment, intolerance, and anger.
- It's our responsibility to work with our energy to benefit ourselves and others. This includes learning to respond to those obstacles appropriately so our love is unobstructed.
- How we choose to respond to every moment is up to us. Life is full of challenges, but we can choose the response that will promote greater ease. We must practice choosing wisely.

To continue contemplating your activities, please see the study guide at the end. The practices presented in this chapter reappear for your enjoyment. Sit with them. Be kind with them.

6. How Are You Being?

Living, there is no happiness in that. Living: carrying one's painful self

through the world.

But being, being is happiness.

Being: Becoming a fountain, a fountain on which the universe falls like

warm rain.

—Milan Kundera

Now we have a sense for the decision, courage, and conviction it takes to liberate that bare nature.

You Are a Composition

Take a moment to notice yourself. Look at what you're wearing, how you're seated, how it feels to notice yourself.

This *you* who you're seeing is a beautiful composition.

You are composed of myriad experiences—each one essential, informative, and perfect.

Those experiences settle in us as players—each one called to perform at various times based on their purpose and strength. These players wear their various costumes. Our awareness of these players may be limited. As we turn our attention toward them, however, we recognize them completely. We are these players. These players are aspects of us.

We may observe, sometimes, the arrival of a child who wants to explore. We may see a teenager seeking rebellion and independence. In response, we may witness the arrival of a stern figure of order—a cop, supervisor, or parent. Sometimes we are the vigilante demanding justice. Sometimes we are the judge casting judgment.

We may appear as clown, healer, hermit, wanderer.

We are a composition. We are not always intentional in the way we arrange ourselves, but we are patterned.

You Are a Pattern

Whatever it is that we're presently up to, it's likely the manner we're doing it is patterned. We're sitting in a way that we normally sit. We're enjoying a snack we frequently enjoy. Around us is a room that represents, in various ways, the patterns of our movement, taste, comfort, and relationship with money.

To be brief, we're being us. You're being you: you-ing.

I'm being me: me-ing.

We aren't exactly sure how we're doing it. Sometimes we aren't even sure it's allowed.

So we follow a few ideas that have worked for us, here and there, then largely forget that there's a you and a me beneath the experience of the act of you-ing and me-ing.

In general we're following patterns put to use in moments we survived or moments in which we thrived.

Take note: those moments are in the past.

We saw in the last chapter how we forget about now. We also forget we have options about how we can be now.

The patterns we follow formed in the past. For various reasons, including safety and efficiency, they become our trench. They give us our manner of belief, movement, and reaction. We stay in the trench because it's easy. Creating a new way of being—deciding to simply be—requires that we climb out of the trench and navigate on our own.

Many of us prefer to live in the trenches.

Constantly. Usually mindlessly.

When we start to observe our trench, it's pretty humorous.

Also, instructive.

Why do I wear jeans? Because they let me play rough when I was eleven.

Why do I enjoy cheese? Because it was a luxury available at other people's houses when I was a kid. (Thank you to those who nourished me when I didn't have the means to nourish myself.)

Why do I leave the airport before anyone can pick me up? Because, at 13, I put myself on a bus from the airport when no one was there to get me. Sure, it was a little sad but more importantly the memory is one of total freedom. I loved finding my way home alone.

Patterns develop and carry us until the point we chose to do otherwise.

Let's remember how our patterns demonstrate our survival. Also, they show us the ways we've learned and evolved. From this perspective, we can cultivate gratitude for what we've experienced and overcome. Patterns save our lives, and then they complicate them. We survive; we learn; we keep up the patterns until the moment we decide to navigate beyond the trenches. We usually maintain our patterns right up to the point when life conspires to show us that the *status quo* just won't work any longer. Rarely do we evolve any sooner.

We can be grateful for this perfect timing as well.

For example, my airport pattern changed one night when I left the airport and got a phone call from a friend looking for me at the curb.

He said, "Well, I guess I'll head home and put my jammies back on."

I realized in that mildly shameful moment that the pattern I'd followed was well past its expiration date. I had friends who would collect me. I could rely on them. Plus, I have freedom whenever I want it; a solo trip from the airport isn't necessary. This overripe pattern had inconvenienced me, my friend, and our friendship.[24]

We have our funny patterns.

You have funny patterns too. Look at those simple things you do and consider why you do them. Sometimes it's silly. Sometimes it's sad. Occasionally it's horrifying. Frequently it's sweet.

Truly, our ways want to be quite ephemeral. As in, they want to fade with the conditions that prompt them. Our ways want to dissolve like the sunset, leaving us to be. But we hold on. We've shaped ourselves in the mold of a firework that exploded many summers ago. Or a snowflake that melted last winter. These shapes don't always serve the current season.

---

[24] My friend was kind and understanding when I explained what I'd learned from the experience. He even made a point of offering a ride the next time I traveled. Our patterns often give way to deeper connections if we're willing to relinquish them.

We are meant to shift and transform.

Like how a spring dries up in summer, leaves change in autumn, snow falls in winter and creates a new spring—processes of change are meant to take their course. Instead our patterns try to stall us. They have us pretending like we can resist change.

Sometimes, when justifying our actions, we even say, "This is who I am."

As if the things we do are the definition of who we really are. Our tasks, opinions, thoughts, and other random activities do not create us as beings. You can understand how an opposite belief might cause us apprehension and anxiety. If we have to do things to keep being, we certainly don't want to stop doing.

All we have to do is allow ourselves to be. We recognize our patterns and prepare ourselves to relinquish them.

To which we reply quickly, "But I worked so hard to become who I am."

We are perpetually becoming. Whether we force it or not.

We are all persistently unfolding. We are leaves unfolding and flowers in bloom. The best action we can take is to surface and appreciate the patterns that stall or trouble our process of opening. These are the obstacles we keep finding on our path. This is what keeps us from navigating in freedom.

The next time you find yourself stuck in the trenches, encourage yourself. Remind yourself that it only takes one new step to move toward emerging.

To emerge, find the step that leads within.

What comes in through the gate is not family treasure.

—Chinese proverb

We follow our patterns so effectively that we forget how we even acquired them. We don't perceive the process, just as we don't notice moment to moment the unfurling of a new leaf, the growth of our hair, or the accumulation of items in the garage.

We have certain ideas, behaviors, and habits that we wear like clothes. Indeed, we can't even fathom what we would do without them. Be naked?

The answer is yes.

Clothes off, everyone.

Or be free as you wish. No pressure.

Being naked is a decent metaphor to remind us that we aren't looking to define ourselves through our wardrobe. We are not the costumes we wear. What if we shift our efforts toward a quiet, unencumbered inquiry into the gold awaiting us beneath the surface? What if we look for the diamonds within?

We can inquire deeply. We can rise from our patterned reactions to old experiences. We can choose our response to experience and maintain our freedom from moment to moment.

Consider how tightly you hold on to fading moments you loved; also, feel the persistent push and pout we all offer those apprehensions and challenges we'd rather not face.

The act of gripping or rejecting essentially amounts to the same thing: behaviors that define us. Behaviors that also confine us.

As we change our interaction with the world from mindless reaction to considered response, we perceive a higher-quality connection with life around us. We climb out of the trenches, and we tune into what is. We no longer experience the world from the patterns that taught us what to see in it. Our behaviors shift as we connect to life itself instead of the apprehension of what life has been or could be.

In connection, in tune, in appreciation, we feel the freedom of love.

In the meantime it's common that we find ourselves captivated or even slightly aggravated by our conduct. We trip on our reactions. Often.

We've been trained to call this, with all compassion for the awkwardness of the experience, self-consciousness.

In its colloquial sense, it's a pretty paradoxical term. It usually means we aren't conscious at all of who we really are.

Let's say our friend Amy is known to be self-conscious. She fidgets, won't speak up, regrets every action, and does her best to avoid attention. The fact is, she isn't paying much attention to herself. Sure, she's not *comfortable* with herself but that's not consciousness. Her consciousness is invested elsewhere. She's paying attention to everything around her and observing how it reflects her discomfort. Instead of observing herself, Amy is overwhelmed by a paralysis of will. She's looking in every direction to keep from looking within a true awareness of who she is. She's not exerting her willpower toward a single, vital choice: to simply *be*. The choice to be—to exist, full of grace just as we are—feels unapproachable to her.

What binds us in self-consciousness?

A sense of expectation.

No matter the source, we tend to mold ourselves into the shape of what's expected, just as water takes the shape of its vessel. We pour ourselves into these expectations and can't remember the way we actually flow. Often, we can't even remember where we discovered the expectation.

In our self-consciousness, we forget how to flow into the authentic contours of the "self" who lives within.

Imagine a set of Russian dolls, one opening to another, all adorned in their costumes. The naked, authentic "self"—the true self—who lives within us is cradled deeply at the center. We shed one recognizable version of ourselves and find another and then another. Our true self is hidden under the layers of who we've become to meet the conditions of our evolving lives. We are, all of us, ready to be mined from our source.

Self-consciousness is, in fact, a confirmation that we have no consciousness of our true self. One is blind to oneself.

Self-consciousness, in its quest to meet expectations, becomes an obstacle to authenticity.

Consciousness, on the other hand, is a means to liberation. We become free and flowing in connection.

I have a friend—John—who spent twenty years in a difficult marriage, working the same job he once loved but had outgrown. He would go to gatherings and stand alone, making himself completely unapproachable. He was generous with his wife though not kind to her. He was vigilant with his child but not understanding. He'd lost his sense of how to share himself with others. He knew the following about himself: husband, father, worker. He knew he was doing none of the above well, but they were the clothes he expected himself to wear.

When I first asked him to recall his deeper, true self, he scoffed. "I don't have depth," he said. "I just do what I'm supposed to do."

"Who is this part of you who says you have no depth?" I asked. "What role does he play?"

That was when my friend started to see himself as a whole lot of rock housing a rich deposit. Deep in his core, he found his precious, naked self. That was when John started to mine his resources.

I asked him to consider who he would be without his wife. Would he disappear?

Who would he be without his son?

Who would he be without his profession?

He recognized that he would still be. Beneath the doing, beneath the expectations, he could simply *be*.

Now, when he considers his actions or new opportunities or awkward situations, he reminds himself, *why not let my true self experience this*?

The self that we all are—the naked self—is who we realize as we journey with open eyes. We discover what it feels like to unfold into wholeness.

We're more than the clothes we wear; we're more than the roles we play; we're more than the stories we're performing.

Let's not limit ourselves to these parts. Or even to their compilation.

Let's do the work to integrate and become whole. To become holy, even. Otherwise so much is missing. We feel our deficiency in the holes.

We seek partners and pals to fill in the gaps. Our partners and our pals will never fill a you-shaped hole.

These folks, bless them, are simply representatives of ideas we find soothing or exciting or attractive. They show us what we're missing, but they can't be the replacement. Not in the long run, anyway.

We may touch their arms and delight in the feel of their skin. But the touch itself is our experience. And if they too delight in the touch, our perception of their delight is our experience as well. The wonder of the connection is in the experience of shared delight. We may finally see ourselves mirrored in their pleasure, but it is our pleasure that we feel.

This is how we come to consciousness. We realize that we are. We share the world, certainly, and through these connections, we learn more about who we are. We realize that we are not limited by the thoughts, judgments, and opinions that we may use to uphold our identities. These are the confines of the trenches.

Let's climb out of the trenches rather than demanding that others climb in with us.

Our Patterns Limit Us

I promise you: we're absolutely perfect when we're absolutely naked.

When we let go of every expectation we've claimed or wanted to claim, we realize we exist with a greater buoyancy. We aren't weighed down; we simply float in being.

Consider how challenging it is to float with clothes on.

As we float in being, we grow comfortable with our naked self. You might like to call it soul, spirit, essence. Or you might not. It doesn't really matter what we call it because it can't really be named. It's simply an awareness in rhythm with every transient moment. It is tranquil, established, at rest in the meandering we perceive in all directions. We float.

Contrast this with that old self-consciousness we recall from adolescence...or last week.

Recall the sinking vulnerability and the discomfort in our own skin. We've all been there. Well done, and I'm sorry for all of our suffering. Look at it this way: if we use the awkwardness to become aware of the particular odd seams and ill fit of our costumes, we're well on the way to finding our way beyond it.

We're on our way to standing comfortably naked.

Imagine standing in all our bare glory.

Now we feel it: the reluctance, vulnerability, and evolving liberation. When we shed the weight we carry, all the trappings of the roles we try to maintain, we encounter a lightness in being. All our seriousness and gripping holds us captive, isolating us from our laughter, our kindness, and our mercy.

Now we have a sense for the decision, courage, and conviction it takes to liberate that bare nature.

This is what it takes to climb out of our trenches.

We might take a moment to consider Eve in a new light.

Genesis teaches us the parable of the garden. We took on the burden of the fig leaf when we bought into the idea that our intellects would supersede our wisdom. This is not to say that we should heave our intellects onto the compost pile where Eve's apple core rots. Instead, we have to learn how to use the intellect.

The intellect is a sharp knife. When wielded with skill, it helps us carve into the feast of our insight. It helps us walk our paths with discernment.

If we use it well, it aids our journey back to the garden, back home. And as we return to our nature, we don't bother with fig leaves anymore.

Naked will do.

The old wisdom traditions caution us frequently to be vigilant to the grandstanding of the intellect. Its sharp edge, used in darkness, used without understanding, cuts us. We blame it on anyone who blindly bumps us. Assured in its power, the intellect resists a confrontation with its own patterns. This, however, is exactly where it must be applied.

The truest form of renunciation is a release of all that creation did not give us. That is, all the clothes we wear to help us feel like someone.

For the mere scholar who knows not the Self, his separateness becomes

fear itself.

—*Taittiriya Upanishad*

Yoga with Our Players

Here's a little exercise for you. Please take a moment to respond to the following thoughts.

Describe the qualities of your ego.

Describe the qualities of your intellect.

Describe the qualities of your identity.

Now contemplate these ideas of yourself and notice how they're different players in the same story. We can think of them as actors in the story of you.

Also notice how your resistance to the word *ego* is probably slightly greater than it is toward the words *intellect* and *identity*. Maybe you were a little more reluctant to consider your ego's contributions. We tend to have a certain notion about the ego being a bit of a stage hog. Our concern with the ego often allows it to grandstand.

Let's watch your identity for a moment. Here's the player who defines your walk, your glide, your stomp, and stumble? Here's the player who is most easily recognized by others as you.

Now let your intellect play a role. Here's the player who helps us see the opinions and judgments driving our story. The intellect is the player who motivates us to laugh and cry, to understand our motivations and to question if they're right.

Now cast the ego in a role. Watch the ego mediate between the world around it and the world within. The ego creates our story's conflict by drawing lines of ownership. The lines are often drawn a bit tightly to make our story distinct and unique. Ego creates our drama. We may think the ego only wants a blockbuster story that everyone loves but it really just wants to keep us safe and steady. Ego may do this by broadcasting our story to billions or keeping it in the shadows.

When ego is taught that steadiness and safety are assured, it will become an important player in nurturing our connections.

All three words—*intellect, identity, ego*—come together to tell our stories to others.

But who wants to put on a show?

Fortunately, these players also give us access to deeper connection and union with the world around us. First, we have to acknowledge the show. Then we can direct them otherwise.

This is our responsibility.

Acknowledge the Show

Let's imagine that the show is called our personality.

We see our qualities of behavior in a kinder light when we think of them playing together as our personality. *Identity* on its own can seem a little bland or colorless. *Intellect* is a word that symbolizes an aspect of self that we celebrate. *Ego* carries the zing of old squabbles, bad choices, and the therapist's office.

Personality is the entertainment we offer. In Latin, the word *persona* means mask. We wear these masks as we play our life roles. We can learn how to remove them.

We must be aware as we do… our personality instinctively protects itself. Personality is smart that way. It's also restrictive.

Thankfully, the personality respects a clever plan. The clever plan is to use our story wisely and find strength in the dissolution of our boundaries. Then, we start to explore.

As always, the show goes on.

The Boundaries of our Composition

Here's the razor's edge of our personality: we yearn to belong, but we establish ourselves as intractably separate.

It's our show. We want the credit. We also want the applause.

This blade exerts a pressure on us. We want to connect, to collaborate, to love. And yet we believe we're meant to conform ourselves to our own story.

We believe we are this, while everything else is that. We believe we're meant to perform but not connect.

This sense of idiosyncrasy prompts us to claim a domain. We draw boundaries and create defenses to uphold them. We say, "I am this" and "I am not that," and whatever it is that we are or aren't sets up a border that limits experiences and others from joining us.

The truth is: we are so much. We are a little bit of this when we are that. We are also that when we are this. We are everything, in fact.[25] We live our lives as individuals, pretending to be alone. When we realize we are undivided from the whole, we become as new as a sunrise and just as bright. We shine with everything.

Fortunately that brilliance begins within. In all of us, there is a guiding light that directs us toward coexistence and sharing. We may not see it that way. But it's there.

---

[25] All the players are showing us just a glimpse. The "I am" beyond them is infinitely expansive and whole. Our exploration is to acknowledge and welcome our players and their patterns. We invite them to come home with us.

169

We know we're born alone and die alone. And yet something in us compels us to dream of existence beyond this finite, mortal realm.

We inhabit and maintain our personality's story. And yet we consistently invite others to join us, to find comfort in us, to accept our help, support, love, jokes, opinions, and all the treasures we've accumulated. When our story is threatened by their presence, we ask them to leave and fight them when they don't.

We live our lives as individuals, but somehow we can't stand the possibility of standing alone.

We demand respect for individuality. And yet we take a defensive position against other individuals doing what we ask.

What a puzzle. What a complex tribe we are.

This conundrum is what the old wisdom of the Vedas baldly calls our ignorance.

We just don't know. We don't know what we don't know. We don't know much more than we do.

And how is not this the most reprehensible ignorance, to think that one

knows what one does not know?

—Socrates

Socrates would advise that we make peace with our not knowing. Only in the wonder of not knowing do we begin to learn.

From the perspective of widening our experience of life, this ignorance—our strident individuality—is an obstacle. If we prepare our personality to float in the fluidity of wonder instead of defending our battery of knowledge, our commitment to our story will diminish. We'll take down our borders so we can travel toward all that we don't know. We'll join a bigger story. And it will delight us.

We don't know so much.

In this illusion of separateness—in the uncomfortable confinement of our story—we estrange ourselves from the shared reality of our existence. It's okay. Our personality has been educated to do this. We can develop our clever plan to introduce the personality to that greater story.

Learning to resolve our ignorance enables us to support and nurture each other in the process of life. We come and go together with gifts we're all meant to share with each other. We limit ourselves and others because we are fundamentally mistaken about the reasons for our peculiarities. We are not meant to defend them; we are meant to delight in the sharing of them.

How else are we going to learn this life?

We learn to live. We live to learn. We all feel unique, and we are. To an extent.

On the other hand, we all come into life born of mothers and fathers who are present or absent to the extent they choose. We all harbor desire and aversion. We all appreciate love and fall into traps of hate, greed, envy, laziness. We all hurt sometimes. And we all recover sometimes. This is our shared experience. And it's awe-inspiring when we share it with each other.

I have a friend who sometimes forgets that his story of work and mortgage and pain and love and confusion and a certain forlorn happiness while watching the sun set is just as particular to him as it is to everyone else. When he's reminded that the mundane events of his life are commonly experienced by others, he finds solace. He realizes he isn't alone. This comfort, however, prompts him to solicit the misery of others. He'll ask about their suffering and pile his on top of theirs.

He collects misery. When he accumulates too much, he starts wondering about the quality and purpose of his friendships.

Thanks to his developing awareness, he realizes what he's done eventually. At that point he reminds himself that the connection he really wants is forged in joy, not misery. He does his best, like all of us.

He remembers more and more regularly to tell stories of happiness and encourage his friends to do the same. He remembers that these stories are refreshing and nourishing. In these shared experiences is the camaraderie of life.

Our personality's story of self, however, frequently overrides these worthwhile commonalities. We recognize them when we see them, but like my friend, we soon forget because our patterns dictate a belief in being who we're supposed to be instead of who we really are.

We believe we're meant to be successful, wealthy, famous, wise. We believe we should be parents of perfect children who live peacefully in a perfectly modest mansion. We believe we should be perfect partners to perfect partners with perfect cars, clothes, and community standing.

We find ourselves so frequently disappointed.[26]

The personality gorges on these upsets.

---

[26] We don't remember that we are, and everyone is, perfect, even as we shift and evolve into what remains perfect.

Consider the news. It capitalizes on this belief system. It delivers disappointments, failures, conflicts, and fights as information. We consume it hungrily. We bond in the misery. Our common enemy— regardless of the issue—is a fear that we'll never create a perfect life. We may blame it on someone else. Sometimes we blame ourselves. We unite in blame, disenchanted and disempowered.

Well, we all do it. Why blame anyone at all?

Our only error was the decision to feed on the misery. We ate the bad news, and it metabolized into the fuel of pain or self-loathing. Sometimes we eat s

o much that we can't even move under the weight of it.

An ignorant person is inclined to blame others for his own misfortune.

To blame oneself is proof of progress. But the wise man never has to

blame another or himself.

—Epictetus

You, and everything, define perfection.

What if we realized that everything, as it is, is absolutely perfect? What if we saw the upsets to what we believe, big or small, as contributions to an already perfect whole? After all, whatever is inherently perfect will remain perfect even with a bit of perfection removed.

And if you're laughing at the possibility of perfection, look around, and become aware of the marvelous ways this life of ours has sustained us. You, me, and everyone we know made it to an existence so unlikely that to take any stance other than awe is an admission that you aren't paying attention.

Some of us may protest and call to mind some sadness, fights, accidents, and abuses.

I'm sorry these happened, but we made it through and are in the process of making it beyond.

Every day the sun rises. We don't make that happen and our story doesn't influence it in the least. The sun rises perfectly. Every day that we awaken is a day deserving of respect and admiration.

Some of us may feel like no one respects us; if that's you, make a decision to respect what this world has to offer you. Watch how things change.

If you feel like you've never been admired, share your admiration for the skills of a friend or the virtues of a stranger. Observe what happens.

If you establish respect for the magic of every spontaneous moment—arising in the buzz of bees, the laugh of kids, the drone of traffic, and the milk that spills over the countertop—your interest in respect and acknowledgment will make way for simple gratitude.

You are a part of all this. All of this is part of you. We are all experiencing this wonder together. You are what you respect. You are what astounds you.

Or you can keep protesting and demanding attention without noticing the gifts scattered at your feet.

Many of us guard perfection as though it can be diminished. We barricade ourselves in our story, in the form of family struggle, community strife, international conflict. You see how alike we are in our peculiar ways? We all seek to protect the borders, no matter what form they're defining. We forget how to connect; we regret our solitude. We are prisoners of our own stories.

Let's break them down.

The personality believes itself separate; the separation is the cause of our suffering.

We want friends, lovers, community. We want togetherness. And then we become afraid of the vulnerability required to maintain it.

As we consider our paths home, we've got to shed the ideas that hold us in fear. We've got to shed the ideas we maintain to keep us from experiencing fear. We've got to get naked.

Let's commit to easing our path at every step. Let's invite others to join.

Remember, regardless of how elaborate your trench system has become, you can take one step to emerge. And then another.

So let's emerge. To ourselves and others. Let's put our personality to task with a clever plan to explore bigger stories. Let's use it to understand what we've put in place to protect us and evaluate whether it continues to serve us.

Let's become open to all experiences, welcoming them as guests to show us what life has to offer. We don't have to invite every guest to stay for three weeks. But tea and a chat will bring us more delight than we thought possible.

Thank You to Our Patterns

Consider your morning routines, your habits of hygiene.

Consider how these patterns morph into the form of our reality.

Maybe we go to work at 8:30 a.m. and sit in traffic. Maybe we scoot home at 5:00 p.m. and then line up outside restaurants that everyone else likes too. We pay premiums for certain kinds of shelter, certain kinds of shoes, certain kinds of phones. We live in areas we are patterned to like. We are sweet in our similarities.

Now look at the partners we choose. The way we eat. The way we talk to strangers or don't. The way we anticipate the day or don't. The way we appreciate our lives. Or don't.

These are our patterns.

Notice the efficiency of these repetitions. Notice also how we may be a little obsessive about our habits.

In a society that endeavors to pathologize so much behavior, we may even have contended with the rigor of compulsion or the trial of addiction. We may even have been medicated for it. Interesting to consider whether the medication does anything to break our patterns. While helpful in so many ways, sometimes our use of medication reduces our awareness of sensations we don't want to feel. We can do the same things again and again, but we don't feel it. We know we're acting against our benefit but it's okay because we feel it less.

These personalities are obedient. They're behaving as trained. The training, once we become aware of our patterns, is up to us.

These patterns serve us. Daily. Hour by hour even.

We use patterns to get by. They benefit us in some way for some period of time. They help us learn, develop our functions, or provide us relief. Over time the habits may strengthen even as their function diminishes. Sometimes our habits get bigger than we are. We may even believe our patterns are who we are.

They are simply a means. They shift with the power of our will.

What a relief to remember that patterns are just part of the organic mechanism that we are.

They grow in response to the actions we take and the feedback we get. We may have decided to cultivate some of them; others may have taken root without our conscious knowledge. Either way, these patterns of ours are responsive to us. Which means we have a direct channel to communicate with them. Our patterns will be responsive to our decisions.

A friend of mine is a young man diagnosed with ADHD. He told me early in our friendship that he had no control over his attention. I asked him to notice how he'd made a choice to believe that idea. I asked him to notice how much focus he'd given to the idea. He told me that his memories of childhood are mostly about his teachers' frustration and his mom's quest to find him help. He told me about his medications, his therapy, his shame that he couldn't control himself.

I asked him to realize how much attention and thought he'd given his youthful inability to pay attention over the course of his life. He realized that he had greater power than he thought. He understood the pattern was old. He knew how to pay attention; he'd simply been trained to pay attention to his distraction.

I have another friend frustrated by weight gain. She said she can't control her food intake. When I asked about her eating habits, she said that she doesn't feel hunger because her partner loves to bring her food throughout the day. She said she doesn't want to hurt his feelings by saying no so she eats it all. I asked her to observe the ways she *was* actually controlling her food by taking in more than she wanted, as a loving gesture to her partner.

She saw the issue immediately and found the courage to begin a discussion with her partner that included thank you and no, thank you.

These folks were in their trenches. They mistook their perspective for the way of the world. They felt out of control, but they were simply in patterns. They took one step to emerge. And then another. They realized their patterns could change.

Our perspective is just one more pattern. As we climb from the trench, we may realize it no longer applies. At one point it did. It enabled safety, comfort, attention. But a perspective can become its own beast with too much attention. Taming the beast seems beyond our control, but the beast is our creation.

It's nothing more than our own behavior pretending to be bigger than we are.

I ask you: If we can't control our behavior, who can? We live in an outsourcing culture. We look to doctors, therapists, call centers to fix our problems. We believe they know our inner workings better than we do. Consequently we limit our experience of personal exploration.

It may be that these folks—friends, lovers, or family—can provide valuable guidance. They offer valuable reflection for our consideration.

But pretending they know us better than we do is total delusion and self-defeating. You know you.

If you don't, you are the best-placed person to get to know you. Look at your friends, lovers, or family and get a sense of you. But don't expect them to tell you who and how you are. This is your job. A belief otherwise is simply a pattern you've held. It's a pattern that protects you from all the emotions that rise to the surface as we get to know ourselves.

Underneath these patterns we stand vulnerable.

I have lived on the lip

of insanity, wanting to know reasons,

knocking on a door. It opens.

I've been knocking from the inside!

—Rumi

The thing is, our vulnerability is precisely what allows us to become intimate with ourselves. We've got to be willing to move into this vulnerability.

This is where intimacy with others becomes possible.

The pattern of our thoughts, moods, and behaviors are just layer after layer of costumes we wear to protect us from the elements. Frequently we dress for the elements that have already passed.

My friend Marie recently shared with me her sleep patterns. She'd been feeling quite fatigued and was considering sleeping pills. She related how she woke up every morning at 1:00 a.m., a time when she would feed her infant son. However, Marie's son was no longer an infant; he'd just become engaged and lived in another city.

Marie felt nostalgia for the togetherness she shared with her baby boy in the peace of the deep night so long ago. As the feedings became unnecessary, she still enjoyed the quiet and solitude of the hour. The quiet and solitude, however, had become available in daylight hours after her son left for college.

Regardless, Marie's pattern still woke her every morning at 1:00 a.m.

The sweetest thing about this pattern was her surprise when she realized there hadn't been a single night in twenty-seven years when she'd slept through the night.

What a vigilant and adoring mother.

As soon as she acknowledged the connection, her pattern started to shift.[27] She awoke but didn't leave her bed. Instead she said a prayer for her son and lulled herself back to sleep with a breathing exercise. Soon she stopped waking up. Her prayers for her son moved to the morning and so did her yoga practice.

Marie's pattern was important at one point in her life. Thanks to her strong maternal commitment, her son grew up to be a productive and intelligent young man. While he outgrew the pattern of midnight feeding, Marie didn't. She may have had her reasons to continue it, but the reasons eventually gave out. The pattern didn't serve her. She finally gauged that she needed additional sleep.

It was a good instinct. You may think it was long in coming but think again. It was her instinct that guided her. It was her self-awareness, and that means it came at just the right time. She even admitted that her husband had asked her to change her habits at some point in her son's

---

[27] It's good news that awareness is a substantial remedy for patterns that no longer work.

childhood, but his suggestion irked her. She didn't see her actions as anything that needed a fix.

Let's all ask ourselves the question: What thing do I do, again and again, that just doesn't serve me anymore?

And then say thank you. It served you once. And now, maybe it doesn't.

We all have something. Do you go to bed too late? Do you eat too much? Do you make promises you know you won't keep? Or run chronically late? Whatever habit you have, various forces in your life assisted you in its development.

This, I think, is one of the kindest thoughts you can apply to yourself. Our habits had a function at one point. Maybe we went to bed late to get through our studies. Maybe we eat too much because food meant love in our childhood homes.

Maybe we run late to protect ourselves socially.

Among my family, for example, tardiness is expected. (My sister would exclude herself, but she's probably the only one.) And while it may not be appreciated that everyone of us will arrive fifteen minutes late, it's never a surprise. It's usually a joke. As I grew into adulthood, I realized my relationship with time had roots in these childhood periods of waiting.

One of the great consistencies in my childhood was being the last to arrive and the last to leave. I was the kid on the sidewalk after everyone had been picked up. I was the kid at the birthday party who helped clean up after everyone left. I was the kid who knew the school office and its staff.

Arriving late meant developing a tolerance for jumping in cold. I learned to say I'm here, get the scoop quickly, and settle in as if I'd planned the whole entry. Leaving late meant finding ways not to be a bother. I'd either pitch in with household chores or cut out with everyone else and hide down the street. Somewhere down the road, I'd stand idly, kicking my toes against weeds. I'd read. I'd count cars. I'd talk to bugs in the cracks of sidewalk.

In the days before cell phones, daydreaming was the universal distraction. Letting a kid wait somewhere wasn't such an offense in the parenting game. Sometimes an adult would check in but not frequently. When I recall small me sitting on sidewalks, I'm fairly certain I appeared confident that wherever I was exactly where I should be.

This was an important lesson. Wherever I am is good. And eventually I'll be somewhere else.

Now let's check in on that little girl a little more grown up.

In my early twenties, I was always late. For school, for work, for dates, for everything. And then I got serious about a few things.

School lectures were not to be missed; the information was profound to me. Work too demanded my presence; I enjoyed the ways I could contribute to the course of the day by arriving early. So I changed my habits. Or my preferences changed my habits. It wasn't as intentional as it was imperative. My ambition required it.

Among friends I remained as late as ever. Always flush with apologies but not excuses, I would announce myself quickly, jump in, and play along with whatever. I was good at leaving early too. Just up and out. No fuss; no muss. I never lost friends or lovers over it; if I had, maybe my preferences would have adapted again. The need never arose.

Until later. It was a big moment when a mentor asked if I could please be on time for a gathering. I laughed and said, "Maybe, but don't worry. I'll catch up when I get there."

He said, "You deserve better."

In those three words, I got it. I was holding a piece of life at arm's distance. In that piece of life, what was on offer? The joyful moment of reconnection with friends. The sweet recognition that we'd experienced change. The chance to discover someone new whose path was intersecting with mine.

I could do better; I could learn; I could experience more of what life had on offer—if it was awkward at first, even better. And if I arrived on time, I wouldn't have to catch up. In fact, I wouldn't have to be any kind of spectacle at all. I could just *be* there.

And it hit me: the thought of just *being* at the start of any sort of social gathering provoked panic.

What the hell would I talk about in that horrible period when people just mill about? What kind of conversations would be expected of me? And could I be patient through whatever logistical housekeeping was underway? I realized in a moment: I'm horrible at fluff. Not only horrible, but I judged it. I found it tedious. In the judgment, I was holding myself separate from all its gifts. I was missing too much experience and too much growth by insisting on an old pattern.

It was in that moment that I watched the old pattern evaporate. Not only did I have no reason to be late; I also had every reason to be on time. I had a new experience of life to discover. Wonder isn't isolated to vacations and art. Those few minutes of timeliness would be a foreign land; why would I deny myself the opportunity to explore it?

I said thank you to the many things tardiness taught me. I opened myself up to the lessons of timeliness. I also offered forgiveness—to my mom and myself—for the inconveniences we caused.

This is a long explanation of a short realization followed by an occasionally frustrating, occasionally surprising, and diligently thoughtful process.

This is pattern change.

We see the pattern; we take a step to emerge; we work (sometimes incredibly hard) to keep taking steps toward a new, expansive way. The pattern lasts as long as it needs to. It serves a purpose until it doesn't. We're fortunate to realize it on our own. We're even more fortunate when someone who cares has the courage and compassion to help us identify it in a way that won't offend us. Our greatest treasure is in our ability to respond appropriately, without defense, with an open heart and mind. At that point we say thank you to the pattern, initiate the change, and heal ourselves of the hurt it may have caused.

How Do Our Players Play?

Let's return to the guidance of the Katha Upanishad for its perspective on our engagement with pattern change—more commonly known as life.

We're advised to imagine our body as a chariot pulled by a team of horses that represents our ever-seeking senses. The mind is the reins.

If the reins of the mind are too loose, the senses are out of control.

Our personality, the driver, settles into familiar routes. To be a truly effective driver, however, we have to be willing to take new paths. The familiar routes are the trenches. If we can be freed from our patterns, we'll thrive on the open roads.

But not until we know how to drive. We must learn how to handle the reins of the mind. If we don't, our life journey becomes a ride so wild we wish we could jump off. We have to hold the reins steadily and with ease—not too tightly but with ample room to experience the terrain ahead.

We want to see the world, hear the world, taste it, feel it, smell it. But we don't necessarily need to be so overwhelmed by constant stimulation that we don't even realize what it is we're sensing. We don't want the chariot overturned or the reins overstrained by the persistence of the horses.

How do we pursue a comfortable and interesting journey?

Consider how you hold the reins of your senses. Do you grip? Do you let go? Do you trust your navigation or progress through fits and starts? And what happens when the passenger has something to say? Do you listen to and act on your passenger's guidance?

Wait. Who the heck is the passenger? When did we pick the passenger up? And do we know our passenger's destination?

These questions arise again and again as we befriend every other dimension of ourselves. Put another way, we start wondering just who is befriending these dimensions.

We've acknowledged we aren't the body, and we've come to appreciate how it's constantly changing. We feel our energy shifting and can observe our monkey minds hopping here and there. Even the personality is in constant flux as it performs our story.

Once we were students. Then we were workers. Then we were parents or spouses or single or sick.

All these qualities come and go. The passenger stays along for the ride.

Who is the passenger?

The passenger is you. Or, You…with a capital Y.

The passenger is that abiding presence who's been observing every turn and bounce of the journey. And the passenger is going wherever we decide. The passenger watches.

The passenger is the reason for cruising around in the first place. We may spend most of our lives ignoring its presence, but it doesn't mind. The passenger is along for the ride and committed to the experience, wherever we wander. The passenger watches, waits, enjoys every rocky path and smooth side road we choose. Sometimes we'll hear a whisper and shiver to realize its import.

That's the passenger. You. That's your unchanging awareness.

Take a breath and settle in for a moment. This is a good time to pull in the reins, slow down the horses, focus on your position, rest.

We've come to understand that we exist in these bodies, but we aren't them. They change every day, but something in us remains consistent. We see we've got fickle minds that sometimes help and sometimes hinder. With training, we learn how to direct them, rather than letting them direct us. We realize the precious gift of our minds as tools of recognition, integration, and efficiency.

And now we've encountered the personality who maintains the patterns. At various points in our lives, for various reasons, our patterns change. Maybe because we change them or maybe because the world makes them untenable if we want to survive or remain comfortable. Our patterns become the story we present to the world.

Meanwhile the passenger watches. The passenger enjoys the show.

From this perspective, you can see how your patterns define your interaction with what's to come. A well-developed pattern of patience will allow for distractions on the journey without resentment. On the other hand, persistent impatience reacts to any obstacle with a marked intolerance. Usually followed by an exasperated *Why?*

In that one little question, the anxious source of the impatience pattern ties tighter knots in this pattern. The trench grows deeper.

Every "why" is evidence of an intolerance for things as they are. This isn't to say that things won't or shouldn't change but rather to remind all of us that whatever happened already did. A pattern of suspicion that you could do it all better fuels impatience for the way that things happen. Things happen. If you'd like things to happen differently, do the work to change the way you perceive them.

Get out of the trench.

Likewise, if your pattern is to approach the world with curiosity, with loose but well-tended reins on the senses, consider the ample information that will come to you. Or the information you'll miss if you don't give space to the senses.

If your pattern is confusion, guess how your world will appear? If your pattern is mistrust, consider your world. Our patterns not only direct our behavior; they define our story.

The cycle persists.

Yoga with the Will

Let's explore our will. Are you willing to be aware of the ways you cultivate joy?

As you breathe, become aware of the condition of your body in the moment. Notice also the condition of your breath. Become aware of the activity in the mind. Are your thoughts erratic or focused? Are you consumed with one or two ideas, worries, thoughts, or is the mind bouncing from subject to subject?

Now make a commitment to yourself: *I am attentive and curious; I do this practice to come home to myself.*

Consider the events of your day.

Ask yourself: *Did I remain joyful and peaceful throughout the day?* If you did not, ask yourself why you chose to let go of joy or peace.

You may hear yourself responding: "It wasn't *my* fault." Acknowledge the message and notice that a decision to surrender joy and peace is a choice you don't have to make. You have other choices.

To maintain your peace, you must have the will to choose for yourself.

Even if someone else does something you don't like, what can you do in response that you do? What will cultivate and sustain joy and peace in a moment that challenges joy and peace? What can you do to choose your joy and peace in the moment of provocation?

How can you create that pattern?

What Power Do You Really Have?

The practice here requires that you remember this important and essential lesson: you only control yourself.

Our personality prefers that we believe otherwise.

It doesn't even matter that the way you react to situations may upset you. The personality will always seek to maintain the status quo, unless you choose otherwise.

Just like every other driver on the road, the personality likes to look around and blame conditions. Maybe it's politics, your job, your home; maybe it's that other personality near you—your lover, your boss, you brother.

The personality prefers to be scot-free of blame. Consider this: Are you willing to be responsible for the attitude you take toward life? Recognizing this potential threatens our lifelong allegiance to fear, unhappiness, guilt, or shame. Without these habitual attitudes, we aren't sure who we are or how to present ourselves.

If we take responsibility for the way we experience this life, we discover that we're the ones creating the world around us. We turn a certain attitude toward the world, and it reflects us. Our life becomes what we give it.

If you grumble, the world grumbles with you. If you smile, it will smile back.

Most of us are afraid of life because we've ceded our power to everyone else. In other words, if the world is grumbling, we don't realize we don't have to grumble along. We become unhappy because we don't like what life is giving us. We become ashamed because what life is giving us causes us discomfort. We are guilty because we've placed ourselves in competition with life, and it continues to give us only what we offer.

These are all patterns of interaction. Very human. Efficient until they aren't.

It's possible to choose otherwise. It's possible to realize an alternative world, but we must have a will to implement our vision. In other words, we must offer the vision we have to the world around us.

If you want to be happy, offer happiness.

If you want kindness, offer kindness.

If you prefer to live in love, share love.

To make a reasonable offer, it's necessary to trust ourselves. How anyone chooses to react to us is irrelevant so long as our attitude toward the world reflects the vision we have for it. If we want forgiveness and compassion, we are that. If we want peace, we are that. Strongly that.

Our vision requires our will. No one else has this responsibility.

We're the ones required to imagine the world we wish to see. Trying to take someone else's vision as our own can have us feeling trapped or inadequate. Someone imposing their vision on us may feel burdensome.

Sometimes we start to believe in someone else's vision just to confirm stories we believe of our unworthiness or doubt. Our vision is clouded by an incorrect view.

We want to feel good in our lives and to fulfill a vision, but we believe we don't deserve it. Why?

From infancy we've been instructed to change our nature. We've been taught to distrust our instincts. We've been educated to believe ourselves unworthy because we are mostly taught about what we do wrong.

We're rarely commended for the many things we do right, like loving our neighbors, offering assistance, giving a hug, and smiling at strangers.

These choices count. And we could all use a certificate or two celebrating our frequent displays of humanity. Because we all do it. We just forget to acknowledge others and ourselves.

If we loosen our grip on judging what's wrong, we make space for something different. It doesn't matter whether a situation is pleasant or unpleasant. When we make space, we discover a certain peace. We don't even have to create it. It simply exists where we choose to release judgment.

To remember that space is available, we train our personalities to pause. The driver has to learn how to slow down.

In the face of provocation, we pause. We take a breath. We feel our feet. We create a moment and guide our intellect toward spaciousness. Our response is then rooted in the joy and peace that reside there.

This means we must be prepared to meet the challenge. This means we establish the power of our will and commitment to remember our choice. This means we practice our protocols for finding the space to change our patterns. We practice breathing. We practice feeling our feet. We back off from reaction and make room for a response that upholds our vision for the world.

Yoga with Space

Let's explore how we make space.

Here's an inquiry for you.

Imagine yourself standing on the sidewalk. A car goes by, and someone yells.

Be honest: What's your reaction? Do you yell back? Do you think they're yelling at you? Do you believe they should behave better? Do you laugh at their good time? Do you simply stand?

How we react to these unintentional provocations tells us a lot about our patterns. When we're stimulated by a sudden event, we can choose to make space before we offer our response. In that space we often realize no response is necessary.

Our patterns thrive when we forget to make space for another option.

So, we breathe and remember to find space in this moment. This is how we come to be. We remember that the likelihood of our existence is so minimal. We see that those around us are just as fortunate to exist. This is enough to make us precious and worthwhile. There is nothing we need to accumulate or deliver to prove our worth. Nor is there anything that anyone else needs to do to justify their purpose.

Being is enough. Be fully as you are. And remember that you are a precious life in a wondrous world. This is enough and will fulfill you for your entire life if you allow it.

Now how do you respond to the yelling and screaming?

Everyone, including you, is truly doing the best they can.

Everyone will experience a life that, occasionally, delivers horror and awe. Will you guide yourself to make space for the error and the wonder? For the shits and the giggles? For all of it?

Wisdom to Bring Home...

- We are patterned beings. This serves us in many beneficial ways and also serves to trip us up. Some patterns manifest as behaviors that arise in response to certain familiar stressors or challenges. We can inquire into the source of these patterns and often find their origin in response to situations that overwhelmed us in childhood.

- We are not often aware of our patterns until they threaten our peace. Even then we may not choose to alter them until we are just as overwhelmed by them in our present condition as we were as children.

- Patterns often become uncomfortable because they restrain us in a certain state when all other conditions have changed.

- These patterns identify us, and we identify ourselves with them. They shape our personalities. We are not simply these personalities. The personality is one more wonderful dimension of our existence, and we can learn to use it skillfully. Our attempts to maintain, protect, and assert our stories exhaust us and lead us into conflict with others.

Our skill at employing the beneficial aspects of our personalities empowers us.

- We are responsible for tending to our personalities and learning to choose wisely those aspects that serve our purpose.

To continue contemplating your personality, please see the study guide at the end. The practices presented in this chapter reappear for your consideration. Sit with them. Be you with them.

7. How Are You Guided?

When the play, it may be the tragedy, of life is over, the spectator goes his way. It was a kind of fiction, a work of the imagination only, so far as he was concerned. This doubleness may easily make us poor neighbors and friends sometimes.

—Henry David Thoreau

If you're handy with it, the personality is a ridiculously good tool. Handled without skill, it will cut you up.

A Ready Personality Respects Guidance

We saw above that the impulse to change a pattern may come about because something in us gently kicks our bum.

Or someone else does.

Sometimes, and this can be a real bummer, it isn't an instinct or a friend, but a very complicated series of events. Sometimes the bum-kicking isn't gentle or friendly. Sometimes it feels more like the finishing blow.

We've all been there.

If you're familiar with inertia, you remember that things set in motion tend to continue that way. Likewise, things at rest keep resting.

Your patterns are like that. It takes a bump to jar them from their cycles. It takes a mindful step.

The amount of force required to change the course of your patterns is totally up to you. It depends on you, the degree of your readiness and the energy of your effort. You can ask yourself: What does it take to drop-kick me beyond the intractability of my identity?

The way life goes, we can rest assured we will all find a few desperate moments in which we'll be required to seek help. It's possible, however, to train ourselves to remember that desperation isn't always necessary. We can choose other options without urgency pressing on us.

In the last chapter, I mentioned the road-tripping metaphor from the Katha Upanishad.

Here's the verse.

Know the Self as the lord of the chariot,

The body as the chariot itself,

The discriminating intellect as

The charioteer, and the mind as the reins.

The senses, say the wise, are the horses;

Selfish desires are the roads they travel.

The personality is the driver of the chariot. The naked self is the passenger. More importantly, that naked self holds the map.

The naked self may not be choosing the route, but it knows the terrain. It's ready for whatever ride you choose, but perhaps you've been lucky enough to notice once or twice that tap on the shoulder that startles you to remembering your destination. Thank you, naked self. The tap may be gentle or bone-rattling; it's always calibrated to you and your willingness and receptivity to feeling it.

Our naked self is invested in the purpose of our journey. It doesn't mind that we lose our way sometimes, but it will always encourage us back to our path.

The means of its encouragement are not always comprehensible to us, especially if we aren't paying attention.

So who is this naked self, exactly?

I took a deep breath and listened to the old brag of my heart. I am, I am, I

am.

—*Sylvia Plath*

As we discussed in the previous chapter, we can call it soul or true nature. We can call it Spirit.

If you bristle at the word, please take note that the Latin root of *spirit* is *spirare*. Meaning "to breathe." It's your primary fuel in this life. Both essential and eternal in this life of yours, it connects you with everything that's ever been. Every inhale is new life. Every exhale is a return.

Every inhale nourishes you. Every exhale is a surrender.

As you breathe, you may like to feel the impact of our human tradition of uniting breath and spirit. Our many ancestors found in their breath what we also discover: vitality, energy, and a relationship to the eternal.

*The Lord is the Spirit, and where the Spirit of the Lord is, there is
freedom. And we, who with unveiled faces all reflect that glory, are being
transformed.*
—*2 Corinthians 3:17–18*

The Greek term for *spirit* is *pneuma*, also described as the breath of
life or the divine breath. Among the Stoic philosophers, pneuma is the
essence of the cosmos, uniting the human soul with the life-giving
principle of the creator. Among the Hebrews, *ruah* describes breath,
wind, and spirit. It is a principle of animation more than a thing. It
describes physical breath, the words that ride on breath, the emotions
that move through us, and mental activity.

Not Christian or Jew or Muslim, not Hindu,
Buddhist, sufi, or zen. Not any religion

or cultural system. I am not from the East
or the West, not out of the ocean or up

from the ground, not natural or ethereal, not
composed of elements at all. I do not exist,

am not an entity in this world or the next,
did not descend from Adam or Eve or any

origin story. My place is placeless, a trace

of the traceless. Neither body or soul.

I belong to the beloved, have seen the two

worlds as one and that one call to and know,

first, last, outer, inner, only that

breath breathing human being.

—Rumi

And perhaps Lao Tzu also recognized the breath breathing all of us and returning us—consistently, persistently—to everything that is and has been when he wrote the following:

There was something formless and perfect before the universe was born. It is serene. Empty. Solitary. Unchanging. Infinite. Eternally present.

It is the mother of the universe.

For lack of a better name, I call it the Tao.

It flows through all things, inside and outside, and returns to the origin of all things.

The breath is what flows through each of us and returns us to each other. My breath will be yours one day. Regardless of our distance from each other, we are connected as one in the spirit of the breath.

While I stood there I saw more than I can tell. And I understood more than I saw; for I was seeing in a sacred manner the shape of all things in the spirit, and the shape of all shapes as they must live together like one being....And I saw that it was holy.

—*Black Elk*

Thank goodness for our every breath.

Thank goodness for our spirit. May it guide us.

The Guidance of Spirit

As you read above, the *lord of the chariot* is often translated as *Self* with the big *S*. Its very existence is the honorific of you: You. When you see the Self in another, you may feel the reverence that would be demonstrated by an old school formality: Thou.

Depending on your particular brand of semantics, you can think of the spirit as your soul, your nature, your essence.

It's the existence of you that remains unchanging in a changing world. The essence of you that somehow makes you recognizable to an elementary school friend after fifty years. Also that essence that continues to feel what it is to live this life, even after your life has taken you through various physical versions, different careers, new opinions, and complete perspective conversions.

The girl raised a Catholic who spent time at a kibbutz before converting to goddess worship is still of the same essence. Her wild ride may have created new patterns of yearning, perspective, behavior—new modes of navigation—but the passenger is still going along for the adventure.

The spirit is always cruising along, experiencing it all without liking or disliking a thing. The spirit is in it for every experience we encounter in life.

But it's not always quiet. Sometimes spirit has a point of direction. A truly decent road buddy, it won't resent you for ignoring its guidance. It also won't get proud when you listen in. Spirit's cool either way.

At this point you may be realizing that you've had at least a few interactions with this dimension of you. Thank this dimension of you for every glimpse, moment of knowing, and gut instinct that suggested you take that lucky left turn when you were intending to head straight toward danger or crisis. Thank you, spirit.

Most of us wouldn't have an interest in a book like this if we hadn't experienced something similar. Truly, most of us wouldn't have survived to this point without these occasional admonitions because the spirit is that part of us who gently steers us away from harm or into safety when our patterns fail.

It is that wise voice that offers insight every once in a while. Or more frequently, if we begin to listen carefully.

Sometimes we shut it down. We may even become afraid of what it's trying to teach us.

Sometimes we realize the importance of its counsel.

Our spirit shares guidance so we can recognize truth and realize power. Our spirit inspires us to become conscious of what is real, what is not, and how we navigate between the two. Spirit helps us dissolve our delusions, if we're prepared to listen.

So how do we ask the driver to pay attention to the passenger?

First, we find a moment of quiet.

In the quiet we listen.

Which is basically like learning that the best way to become a concert violinist is to play the violin in concerts.

If we knew what to do, we'd be doing it. This is where we stumble. People think quiet is easy to access. In silence we notice the loudest of noisemakers: our minds.

This becomes our struggle as we journey toward the sacred space of home.

We want to use our minds to experience silence; our minds are the instruments by which all the stimulus of the external world finds its expression in us. We want to use our personalities to train our minds; our personalities are uncertain we can or should make that effort.

The question therefore becomes: Can the mind experience the world without our personalities insisting on its patterns? Will we allow ourselves to see without the veil of what we know, believe, and prefer?

How do we allow this?

How do we ask our patterns of perception to rest so we can rest in the clarity of silence?

We've seen how our patterns form from the stories of our life. These stories may be memories, past friendships and loves, beliefs, comparisons, chance encounters, trials, accomplishments and failures.

Now think of yourself motoring through life. Our perspectives are colored by the residue that remains on our windshield as we go. All this residue of the journey obscures our ability to see the present moment clearly.

Now consider how our personalities and our spirits interrelate. Let's explore.[28]

I like to think of these two as bosom buddies. Even literally. The old teachers say they reside in the cave of the heart together.

Let's say Peter is the personality and Stan is the spirit.

Peter has the likes and dislikes and tries to get more of what he likes and less of what he doesn't. Stan is the one who smiles and nods, knowing that Peter's going to do what Peter's going to do. Stan has tasted the sweet and the bitter and knows life in both.

Peter, active and ambitious, likes to go places and do things.

Stan is accepting and tolerant; he has a compass and knows how to use it.

Together they're a great pair. Peter, the whippersnapper— ambitious, precocious, fallible—and Stan, the steady sweetheart.

---

[28] As I mentioned early on, this isn't meant to be some sort of pop psychological treatise. This is an offering of teachings that have guided me and friends in spirit for millennia. Which means, we're dealing with ideas that predate our friends in the modern psychological field. This is what I like to call old school. And this isn't the place to go on and on about its impact on modern psychology, but I'll mention quickly that well-being has long been a subject of inquiry for humanity, and we are wise to appreciate the thousands of years' worth of personal experimentation and discovery that predates modern psychology. Look at the work of William James, Carl Jung, Virginia Satir. Truth is truth, and there are friends from every age who speak it.

Everyone loves them both. Lots of folks in the neighborhood aren't sure Stan would do anything without Peter. They also see Peter as the kid with promise. Stan just seems…well…a little disinclined to go anywhere on his own.

And it's sort of true. But not really. Both Peter and Stan are fine.

But they'll do really well if they work together.

Over time Peter will gather knowledge, a family, property, and whatever status he works to claim. And Stan, well, he'll look on. An admiring friend and a trustworthy guide through Peter's ruts. Stan offers a steady ear, good counsel, and space for Peter to make his choices. When they are estranged, Stan is still present and available. Peter, however, may not always feel the treasure of his support and counsel.

These two aren't exactly foils in the literary sense. At their best, they are complements and cooperatives. When at their worst, Peter runs the show, Stan's ignored, and Peter feels alone.

While a lot of spiritual business may advise a dissolution of the ego, kicking Peter to the curb isn't necessary or even recommended. Indeed, it seems clear the work of our life is to sort through the roles and patterns of the personality so the stirrings of our spirit can be heard clearly.

If you're hellbent on enlightenment, you'll eventually contend with Peter in just the right way. And it may be a raucous confrontation. Nevertheless, Peter will not disappear. Rather, he'll understand his role and apply himself to the task of coming home.

That's when you'll discover that the enlightenment you seek is only present in your every enlightened deed. It is Peter in action, following Stan's perfect lead.

For many of us, allowing the personality to acknowledge and own its myriad parts and patterns is a relief. Not easily achieved, but a relief nonetheless. We become integrated and whole.

As we've seen, the parts and their patterns work. Until they don't.

What if we become aware that we simply are...spirit? Every adjective we place after *I am* represents a part, a pattern, a role we play. We play the role again and again. What if we apply the personality to understanding the purpose of every role we play? What if we release the roles and simply choose to be?

The Many Parts of Personality

Personality is a vulnerable friend. This friend is often uncertain and skeptical when new possibilities arise.

A retired lawyer once approached me to ask whether meditation would be a suitable practice for him. I asked him if he was ready to learn new ways to work with his mind. His immediate response was "I spent my whole life working with my mind; I want to meditate so I don't have to do anything."

I asked him if he was ready to learn to do nothing.

His next response was "It doesn't seem like there's much to learn about that."

I told him he was partly right and asked if he wanted to experience what might be helpful.

His response was "I don't want to have to do anything."

We can appreciate his honesty.

This man's personality, at that moment, wasn't inclined to explore. His spirit prompted his questions, but the roles he'd played for years deterred him from a new avenue of inquiry.

For all of us, explorations of the unknown can be particularly worrisome. When we approach darkness, we don't know what we'll find. In difficult situations our personalities react according to patterns already in place. Depending on the challenge before us, we may perform in ways we know are totally inappropriate. Still we perform.

It's helpful to appreciate the many parts required of us to enact our stories. Our personalities are constantly shifting with every plot twist of our story. New characters emerge and develop. Old characters reprise their roles. The story may start to feel like it's repeating, depending on our awareness of who's on the stage.

Until we get to know these parts and to welcome them home, they'll enter the scene... even when they aren't welcome.

Feel it for yourself. Think of a time in the recent past when you saw yourself behaving in a manner you didn't anticipate. This can happen in arguments with a lover or sibling. We may see it come at the end of a long day, when we're fatigued and hungry. Sometimes a simple sentence can set us off.

Watch how you behaved. Did you experience and perform anger? Maybe you needed to escape and watched yourself shut down in the face of conflict. Some of us may find that we take on a part who becomes highly rational in the face of emotion, so he doesn't have to feel the weight of the experience.

We all have our parts, and some of them appear with frequency.

Some of our parts may overact and embarrass us. These may be familiar to us though still uncomfortable. They play roles to maintain a status quo, to keep us safe, to tell us we're unworthy or worthy, to avoid or attack, or simply to assert.

Some of our parts may be quite foreign to our consciousness but recognizable from our past. These are our young ones who behave immaturely because they've been isolated and exiled at various times in our childhood or youth. In troubling times they reappear to enact roles that can cause even greater drama. These parts feel childish. They may present rage, demand impossible justice, blame others, or collapse in confused tantrums.

These special parts appear when we confront a situation that resembles the period of their origination. We can think of these special parts as members of our personal tribe of heroes. Every superhero has a unique origin story. Learning their origin story will help us call these parts home. Unfortunately their arrival usually takes so much of our attention that we fail to consider what called them to the stage.

An example: We're in a store, looking at various objects. We pick one up, and the shopkeeper asks us kindly not to touch anything on that shelf. She notes that there's a sign, but we failed to see it. We find ourselves in a state of agitation, shaking and embarrassed. As we sit in our embarrassment, we become nauseous, annoyed, maybe even angry. We leave the store feeling terrible, listening to thoughts telling us that the attendant behaved inappropriately. Outside we remain shaken and uncomfortable. We tell our friends that we'll never return to the store.

What we don't realize is that the experience of agitation, nausea, and trembling is all ours. It doesn't happen inside the store; it happens inside *us*. So when we left the store, our discomfort came right along with us.

To leave the discomfort behind, we might look at our behavior and discover the reasons for it.

In this example we're in the midst of a performance by one of our parts who arrived on cue when we were reprimanded. As we begin to look into this character's origin story, we might recall the way our father often became angry when we played with his tools. He may have yelled, and we may have felt embarrassed, nervous, and vulnerable.

The origin story isn't always tragic or dramatic. It's simply a lingering pattern of our young selves trying to make everything okay. Maybe we ran from our fathers. Maybe we became angry that our father didn't try to console us.

When we notice we've become immature, we can use this awareness to recognize that a part from the past has returned. Unless we learn how to make the peace this part seeks, we can count on its return whenever similar trouble arises.

Returning to our discomfort in the store, we may console ourselves in the present moment the way we wished our fathers had. We may even offer our thanks to our fathers for doing the best they could. Finally, we could commit to sharing our belongings a bit more freely with others.

Our Parts in Exile

Why do these parts of us hide away? The same reason they play their role in the first place.

Our personality demands roles that, ultimately, it believes will guarantee our safety in the status quo. Sometimes, as we develop and evolve, there are roles that helped us survive that become less effective for the identity's aim.

As we grow and change, we hide certain aspects of ourselves so we can keep living.

Still those parts exist. In their exile they remain intact, young, and stuck. When they return, they come back expecting the situation they left. Our new developments, new learning, new patterns of behavior have not reached them.

Maybe we had a tumultuous childhood that we left in the dust. We've been serene for years. Or at least free from the old stories. And then the day comes. It can be the smallest trigger or a great tragedy. It doesn't matter. When an exile returns, we find ourselves reverting to reactions in the exile's bag of tricks. The tumult returns via our own performance.

The exile comes back as though the whole world had stalled since its last performance.

To understand our exiles, we've got to be willing to welcome them home. This means looking compassionately at our wounds. The children we were may have grown into adults, but many of their disappointments are still painful. We may not feel the pain daily, but we may in certain circumstances.

Establishing care for our exiles puts us in touch with the important work they did for us in our past. These parts gave us protection. They defended us in times when someone else could not or did not. As we befriend our young, wounded parts and welcome them home, we may remember beautiful, disgusting, ugly, horrifying, and difficult experiences we've survived.

Thank you to these young ones for giving us the means to move through. Now we can care for them by showing how we've continued to establish safety in our lives. This is the work of the personality and the spirit together.

Sometimes an exile enters the scene without any discernible provocation. It's just time. What if we ask our identity to say thank you for the return, as destabilizing as it may be in the short term?

Consider the alternatives. How much alcohol is consumed in the effort to ignore old players? How much pain and shame is experienced as we burden relationships with exiles we're unwilling to bring home? How many conflicts do we start because we revert to old patterns that our new friends and lovers can't comprehend?

When our exiled parts are invited home and made welcome, our personalities evolve. We grow more accepting and grateful for the myriad ways we've been resilient throughout our lives.

Our personalities are like raw gemstones, cut by the elements, cracked by pressure and growing stronger. When we find a gem, we know that every flaw will refract the light in a unique way. We admire the way time has etched the stories of challenge into every rock. We are wise to look carefully. We are no different.

Our many exiled parts comprise the beautiful texture of our precious hearts. We can learn about them by observing our patterns of protection, defense, and escape, as well as our patterns of connection, expression, and play. With training, we can appreciate how every defense and every love has an origin story. They developed at an important time and place. We'll realize we can become grateful for these patterns and invite them all home. The ways we once saved ourselves from destruction can destroy us or become a path to healing.

We have the power to transform every moment of our past into a perfect present moment.

Thankfully our personality will delight in this transformation. We have only to make the choice. And to make it again and again.

We teach our personality to follow the guidance of spirit. Spirit wants all the exiles to come home.

They are our reminders of the ways we've yet to heal.

Bless them.

So how do we support ourselves as we look into the darkness? As we encounter our exiles?

We tread carefully and compassionately. We are honest with ourselves, and we ask important questions. We enlist the support of guides and friends. We say, "I'm ready." When we're ready, the journey advances.

The Question of Personality

This may be the most challenging part of your journey. First, as we invite our exiles home—each and every exiled part of you—we may very well hear our personality protest. "But I *am* home."

The personality is a master at using defenses to justify patterns in play. The personality wants security in the way things have been. It wants the security of ordering the world for itself. It separates us from the way things really are. It divides us from our true selves.

From its position we establish the form of the separation and then rationalize the form. When I assert, "I'm a teacher," I establish myself as someone different than nonteachers. In this assertion, it becomes far too easy to create boundaries separating myself from others. My personality has created an us-versus-them situation that it can use to justify any experience that may serve its sense of separation.

This is not to say that the role of a teacher isn't important and worthwhile. Simply that it isn't the only, or even most important, role I play.

When I distinguish myself in this way, I lose sight of the connection I have to nonteachers. I limit myself. I prioritize separation over our inherent unity.

To a bee, both the dandelion and the sage offer nectar.

See the world as your self.

Have faith in the way things are.

Love the world as your self,

then you can care for all things.

—Lao Tzu

For survival purposes, our personalities aren't inherently fans of change. As a result we often use our sense of separation to disregard the suggestions or opinions of others who aren't like us. We may even choose to be highly offended by the ideas of people who we hold apart.

You know what I mean, right?

Consider my friend the engineer. He's very good at finding solutions to problems. When he was asked to design a fix for a problematic groundwater issue, he worked diligently and succeeded. During this process he cooperated with many engineers and technicians and listened carefully to their feedback to accomplish the task.

When he was asked by his family, however, to spend more time laughing on weekends with them, he was at a loss. He didn't want to take their suggestion. He couldn't even see the problem. For him, that meant no solution. They kept pushing, and he retreated further away. Finally he realized, fatigued by the conflict, that he was choosing to see them as adversaries to his interests. He was seeing them as beings unlike him. They weren't engineers like he was. They weren't as rational. They weren't as serious as he was.

When he realized the lines he'd drawn, he knew immediately his mistake. He didn't want his family to be engineers or rational or serious with him. He wanted them to be his family. He didn't want to keep his family on the outside. He decided to see them as a *part* of him, rather than as apart from him. That's when he came up with all kinds of solutions to their need for more weekend fun.

Our personality often likes to say no. That's a useful tool of the personality to maintain its integrity. It likes to be right.

It likes to maintain the story.

Recall what we learned: the personality strives to save our position and keep us steady.

You say, "Maybe we turn left and avoid traffic." And I say, "I was already going to."

Sometimes the personality feels diminished by anyone with counsel.

Sometimes we even pay money to disregard advice. Someone gives us challenging guidance; we pay an expert to contradict the advice. We want to be able to say, "I already knew this," "I knew better," or "I knew that was wrong."

You may have noticed that when lots of information or advice is offered to you, a voice within responds with some version of "No."

Whether it comes out as a straight refusal, a hemming and hawing doubt, or even a polite rejection, it amounts to the same. The offer is suspect. Some part of our personality believes it knows better.

Those of you in sales know this deeply. The work to be done in sales has less to do with the product and more to do with appealing to the personality of the potential buyer. If you validate the personality, you probably make a sale. If you don't bother to validate your customer, check out whether you're happy for the salesman who does. The personality will likely offer you a few thoughts to disregard the technique he used to make his sale.

Likewise, any new or challenging request is often met with a voice that says, in some manner, "Why?"

This can be the personality's favorite response to anything it doesn't understand, that may be a menace to its existence.

Let's be ruthlessly honest with ourselves. When we ask *why*, we may actually be seeking the answer to "How?" *How are we supposed to do that*, wonders the personality. *How is this happening to me? How am I going to solve this?*

We don't really want the reason or purpose. We want a process that will meet our pattern or give us a new one.

How is about process.

How does one act follow another act? How does matter interact with other matter? Writ large, how do we as material beings interact with other material beings? How do our roles and patterns define our experience as these beings? How do we choose differently?

Why can be philosophical, but many philosophers turn to the issue of *how* when *why* becomes unwieldy.

And it always does.

Why?

Or rather, how?

> *Don't explain your philosophy. Embody it.*
> —*Epictetus*

Because in the personality's maintenance of our stories, it is disinclined to say, "I don't know."

Listen up! This wisdom is worth the repetition. The amount we don't know far exceeds what we do. What I don't know could fill a galaxy of libraries. And the equation gets more and more lopsided as I live deeply with everything that is. I know far less now than I ever have.

The *why* is an ongoing personal inquiry. Any answer I find will always evolve as I continue to live. Otherwise, the reason for my existence would be complete and so would my experience of life.

Thank goodness it continues. May it linger for all of us, to just the perfect length. May every day be a new experience. When we're no longer capable of savoring new experiences, may someone throw dirt on us all.

The answer to *why* is always conditioned on the experience and perspective of the person asked.

The answer to *why*, at its best, is a story of purpose and creation.

We are not the creators of each awesome sunrise and sunset, though we may forget. We struggle when asked to contemplate the purpose of it all because we don't know. We can get angry, maudlin, or dismissive about our ignorance. We may say the *why* is for science. Some will say it's for religion. Some will say it's unknowable. Some of us may choose a stance that says, "It doesn't matter."

The funny thing about these positions? Each faces 180 degrees away from the target.

These positions are pure Peter. Stan knows everything matters. Our spirit may not articulate the *why*, but when we tune into the miracle of our existence, we realize our purpose matters.

Everything matters.

Why is for self-discovery. *Why* is not to avoid existence but to join it, sharing our mission with every moment.

The question is not "Why me?"

Ask instead, "Why is this for me?"

If we back away from our quest to understand purpose, we reject the gift of existence. We reject the potential of our precious existence, and in so doing, we limit ourselves as we live our lives. We don't realize we are beings with the special purpose to be.

Let's move toward being instead of acting.

The truth is, our every *why* is the grand *why*. How we interpret the grandiosity is up to us.

May I suggest that we allow for lightness as we contemplate our mission?

Please be sure that you don't forget *how* to dance as you ask *why* you dance. Also that you remember to love. And sit quietly.

It's in the quiet that we can hear spirit guiding us toward our purpose. In the quiet we learn to appreciate that *why* is for each of us to discover. You can do it as surely as I can.

It's important to note that any instinct we have to meddle in the *why* of others is an interference. You stick with your *why*, and I'll work with mine. When we're both inclined, we can chat over tea.

Unless we are asked to weigh in, the purpose of others is none of our business. Even when asked, we do a better service by holding hands than handing out reasons to others.

Why?

Because everything matters.

Here's the sweet thing. When we start asking *why* instead of *how*, we're taking a bold step on the path. It may originate in subversion, much like the persistent questions of a four-year-old. But like the child's *why*, our *why* is also meant to resolve in a black hole. It's fine, sometimes, to acknowledge mystery itself. We can't explore it if we don't.

Under all this sunlight, we resist the dark. When we move bravely into the dark, we discover the brilliance of faith.

Mystery and manifestations arise from the same source.

This source is called darkness.

Darkness within darkness.

The gateway to all understanding.

—Lao Tzu

Of course, even after asking, we may not want mysteries to unfold.

The Personality Comes Home

When some aspect of my personality asks the purpose of anything, I like to answer: "To know myself in this moment."

Another way of putting it?

Let's be at home. Let's bring the whole universe home with us.

With this response, my personality is soothed.

It doesn't resist kindness. It appreciates that it has an agenda to implement. Together we set about learning about all that appears in this life. Emotions that burble up. Moods that arise. The behaviors that start up when we aren't mindful. The space that arises when we are.

Sometimes we take a turn that clearly wanders off the path, and sometimes it's like an express gondola to another peak. No matter, and no big deal. Every adventure provides insights that are well worth the bumps along the way. It just depends on the expediency we seek.

We have consciousness in this life. Long may it endure. Let's put it to use.

May the work we do build on the work we've done before. May we remember this so we don't repeat all the mistakes again. This is how we realize we're forging our path home.

This consideration is a part of the process of learning our purpose. This is how we discover our own *why*.

These days everyone wants a study.

If I say a study measured a bunch of meditating monks and found their brain waves were superhuman, does this mean you should be a monk? Or that you should meditate occasionally? Or that you shouldn't bother because you don't have sixteen free hours for it daily or access to an alkaline, vegetarian diet and austerities that would require a couple of garage sales and a divorce? Would this be appropriate for you?

It depends on you. What do you know about you?

If I say a study determined that fifty-five of one hundred people reduced their pain with yoga, will yoga reduce your pain? Again, it depends. Who taught them? Can you go to that teacher? And what was up with the other forty-five people? Who are you more like? The fifty-five whose pain diminished or the forty-five whose pain remained? What will work for you?

Only you can discover the answer.

And yet the personality may insist on seeking the answers externally.

We study; we may even promote; but we have no inkling about how it may or may not work for us. We collectively quest for evidence-based practices and proof, but we ignore the evidence of our experience and the proof apparent in the quality of it. At least until we get fed up.

That's when we're ready. That's when guidance will come to us.

We are the only ones who can prove our well-being. We're also the only ones who can truly attend to it so let's feel inspired to do so. Let's study ourselves.

When we're ready, the teachers appear.

A theological student once stopped me as I walked my dog.

He asked, "Do you believe the Bible supports the concept of God as mother?"

I said, excited by such an amazing question at the park, "Absolutely."

He said, surprised I think by my enthusiasm, "Oh, um, can you prove it?"

I said, "Well, I see you." He blinked. I asked, "Is my experience enough?"

He looked at his Bible and hesitated. He said, "But do you believe the Bible offers you eternal life?"

I said, "I have eternal life. And so do you."[29]

He said, "Do you have proof?"

I said, "My faith." He smiled. I said, "That's been my experience."

My theological friend backed away without another word.

Like he'd hit an electric fence.

---

[29] I admit, this was probably more fun from my perspective than his. I love that kid with his Bible. And I always keep him in my prayers.

I don't think my proof satisfied him. Nor should it have. Because it's my faith. It isn't his.

But maybe the interaction will inspire him to come home. Maybe he'll find his own experience someday, and it will confirm his faith. Maybe he'll realize he's walking his own path, and it's dotted with guideposts, and poems, and people, and lovely scenery to deepen his own experience. No one else will host, direct, or control his path, but the whole world conspires to offer its support once he makes himself available to it.

Which is when we honor our invitation to come home. It comes at a moment of readiness. The readiness is the first point of transformation. Change will happen regardless of our readiness. Our transformation requires our attention and will.

This is a distinction the personality will honor. There is work to do. There is effort to be made.

The question is not how to set the goal but how to set the conditions. The sharp tools of the personality are meant for this project.

When properly used, these are the instruments of our discernment. They choose efficiencies and protocols that work with our particular patterns, whatever state they may be in. They also recognize the potential of players and patterns being employed to release others. These are worthy functions of our mindful personality.

If we're handy with it, our personality is a ridiculously good tool.

Handled without skill, it will cut us up.

In the Tao Te Ching, Lao Tzu writes, "Care what other people think and you will always be their prisoner."

The thoughts of others are none of our business. The more we cater to their estimation of us, the more we restrain ourselves to please them. We do the restraining. More often than not, they aren't pleased.

The thoughts we host, on the other hand, will tell us how our personality has established itself.

Yoga with Personality

Let's play with our masks.

Please get comfortable. Be with your breath for a moment and notice how it moves through you.

With each inhale, feel these words: *I am spirit.*

With each exhale, feel these words: *I play a role.*

Be with these ideas for about ten to twelve breaths.

Now notice that there's a voice in your head.

Notice that it's incessant and always has something to say about you, your actions, your decisions, your future, your past. It may also have a lot to say about everyone and everything around you. Notice that it won't always be kind.

You may hear thoughts like "Ugh, he always does that" or "Will she ever learn?" or "That's not my problem" or "Gosh, this is a terrible neighborhood."

That's the voice of your identity, judging, defending, separating.

It rambles, oblivious to any of the quiet magical moments of things like hummingbirds and baby smiles. It goes on and on. It tells you what you like and dislike, how you are, how you aren't, how bad things are, how great things are, how much you have to do. Seriously, it's exhausting.

Now I'd like you to notice what this voice says about you.

It's decent odds this voice of yours has worse things to say than anything anyone else could muster. After all, you know yourself better than they do.

These things you hear essentially are a ceaseless monologue of thoughts you've gathered. These thoughts are a great defense against the judgment you anticipate from others.

You stand in the throes of critical self-judgment while being afraid and imprisoned by a perception of judgment from others. And the truth is: you're perfect.

All this judgment distracts from your true mission of learning to love to yourself, without condition.

So, listen to the monologue of thoughts again and interrupt it. Just for a moment: *I hear you, and we're okay right now. Let's know this moment.*

Watch what happens.

If it argues with you or offers resistance, repeat the line.

I hear you, and we're okay right now. Let's know this moment.

When you get to the space where your body takes a deep breath, you've made a little progress. At that point offer your personality an intention to establish a new pattern.

From here on out, you might suggest, *what other people think of us is none of our business.*

Watch the patterns arise to tell you why this might be wrong and apply the original sentence again: *I hear you, and we're okay right now.*

As your new pattern establishes itself, set about watching the personality quiet down. It has a new agenda.

In the stillness notice how you occasionally hear the quiet breath of guidance from some place deeper. Notice how this sound guidance is always there for you. Notice how this guidance supports your kind reminders to remain present to the moment. Enjoy spirit.

You may also become aware of other players appearing. Perhaps a teenager dismissing this exercise. Perhaps a supervisor who wants to shut it down as a waste of time. Welcome these players. They are aspects of your personality coming forward to indicate places ready for healing.

As you welcome them home, the voice of spirit will enliven. Your sacred space at home will be infused with your spirit's wisdom.

When you become comfortable hosting a bit of silence, you'll start to cherish the wisdom that sings in the quiet. You'll also find yourself able to tune into the wisdom resonating in everything around you.

It's all here for you.

All of life is awaiting your decision to connect.

Wisdom to Bring Home...

- Spirit rides along with you. Spirit is innate—intact and a dimension of yourself to befriend.
- Spirit is always guiding you, and you've listened from time to time. You can listen more.
- It is the many roles of your personality that most frequently insist you do not listen. The personality can be trained to pay attention. As we integrate our many roles into our whole, we are better able to recognize the benefit of our spirit's guidance.
- We can work with our personality by writing *I am...*followed by all the many roles we claim. Then ask each of these roles how it relates and responds to the spirit. Invite these roles to engage with the spirit. Notice how this may change the way we act.
- As we work with our personality, it is most important that we prioritize the way we feel toward ourselves and not what others think of us.

To continue contemplating personality and spirit, please see the study guide at the end. The practices presented in this chapter reappear for Peter. Sit with them. Call upon Stan. Be you with them.

8. What's in the Way?

No matter what you are doing, keep the undercurrent of happiness.

Learn to be secretly happy within your heart in spite of all circumstances.

—Paramahansa Yogananda

We react to the transience of everything by trying to hold it steady. For as long as we can. We soon can't.

The Path Has Shadows

Now is as good a time as any to acknowledge that many of our best intentions are waylaid by the uprising of obstacles along our path.

Please accept this consolation hug from me. We've all experienced it.

Depending on the temperament of our intellect, we may blame others for it or the government or God or humanity in general. Here's some fodder for your consideration: every obstacle you perceive is actually a part of your path. Whatever interruption it offers is imperative for your growth and evolution.

I had a friend who once said, "I blame the sun." He said it made him too hot to deal with any of the horrible things going on in the world. I asked him why he didn't cool off in the shadows. He groaned. I asked him how else he would deal with the heat he felt. He understood and started to take some time for himself.

I like to think of all the bumps and ruts and barriers that pop up as shadowy reminders of my simple-minded misunder-standing. These obstacles ask me to acknowledge that I have to pay attention; they are the great guides along the way.

They fuel our torch of insight.

They turn up when I'm not remembering that things come and go, that life doesn't need my control, that the ways things are will only improve through my change of attitude toward them. When I forget, I stumble a little. I do my best not to fall down completely. (That's not to say I haven't.) So when I trip, I'm delighted. Here is something I'm meant to learn.

Then I take a look at the shape of the shadow to understand how I might proceed.

Our shadows are tailor-made by impressive agents of chaos within us that love to block the light illuminating our path.

Sometimes a little; sometimes a lot.

These provocateurs demand that we rediscover our light by placing us in the dark. Or in shadow.

When the light grows dim, we lose our way, become distracted, or even end our wandering entirely. We may just stop and sit in the dark for a while. Without the light of our wisdom, without remembering the nature of things, we suffer. Those agents of chaos then go about finding ways to challenge us further.

This is when we wonder, "How much more am I supposed to take?" Or, as my friend's grandmother would cry, shaking her fist, "God, why are you punishing me?"

Fortunately what blocks the light and fuels the light is the same. It's our responsibility to learn how to transform our challenges into our torch's fuel.

In the Yoga Sutras, there are five provocateurs well trained in casting shadows on our path.[30] They know perfectly and precisely how to limit our visibility as we journey. Some call these poisons or even enemies, which is understandable. Please make note: these agents of chaos are employed by us. We're responsible for hiring them, even if we had no idea we were recruiting.

Let's agree, however, that this doesn't mean we're meant to sink into the funk of victimhood. We're okay. Remember, we enlisted these agents. We must learn to deal with our staff.

We improve when we make friends with those we call enemies. We learn to appreciate them, invite them for tea, listen to what they have for us. We don't necessarily have to ask them to move in with us. We can allow their visits and recognize the wisdom they leave behind when they depart.

When it comes to these provocateurs, let's remember that we can't find an antidote without understanding the poison. If I refuse to study the poison, the consequences of any contact with it are certain.

---

[30] Read the complete text in the Yoga Sutra of Patanjali, at verses 3–15 of Chapter 2. What I call the *provocateurs* are the kleshas, commonly translated as afflictions, or troubles that impede our progress. They are ignorance, egoism, attachment, aversion, and uncertainty in our physical life.

Those who do not observe the movements of their own minds must of

necessity be unhappy.

—*Marcus Aurelius*

Let's look squarely at the provocateurs and the troubling shadows they cast over us.

Like most trouble, what we find often leads to other hidden messes. Also, it's fair to anticipate that these agents of chaos are often in cahoots.

Agent Ignorance

Please feel comfortable for a moment. Please know you're perfect. And allow me to introduce you to agent ignorance.

The way the Yoga Sutra explains ignorance is to baldly state we have no idea who we are.

More kindly put, we've forgotten our true nature. This ignorance is the source of every other provocateur that will befuddle us.

Take another moment. You've made it this far.

The constant activity of our bodies, minds, and the world around us is overwhelming. We react to the transience of everything by trying to hold it steady. For as long as we can. We soon can't. We try so hard to control what seems to demand our attention that we forget our own power to turn our attention within. What is within is constant, eternal, and joyful.

Ignorance, say the sages, is the creation space for every obstacle. When we realize ourselves as infinite, eternal beings engaged in a finite, limited world, obstacles to our progress will stop popping up everywhere.

In the meantime we stumble from time to time.

Agent Ego

Motivated by this clumsiness, the next agent of chaos persuades us that the way we stumble is who we are. It is the agent of ego. This provocateur conspires with our ignorance, so we're dealing with an issue of mistaken identity.

In other words, if we don't know who we are, we may as well be what we keep doing.

We've seen how our personality is comprised of all the roles we play. We have habits and tendencies that prompt behaviors. We have patterns of wanting our way. We think we are what we do. We end up trapped, persuaded that what we experience and how we experience it is actually who we are. We think we are our stories. It can feel so heavy.

In Sanskrit the word used to describe these patterns is *karma*. We may be familiar with this term as some form of universal mechanism of punishment, but it means something much more comprehensive.

Karma means action. It is that code in us built on every action we've ever taken. Every behavior begets another behavior. Every act incurs a reaction. When we throw a stone, there is a ripple. Our disregard for the consequences of our actions leads us directly into actions that may seem to have a callous disregard for us. But karma isn't necessarily punitive. It is the effect of whatever you've caused. We find ourselves burdened by the weight of our actions when we don't consider how much they may weigh before we put them into action.

> *Every moment and every event of every man's life on earth plants*
>
> *something in his soul.*
>
> *—Thomas Merton*

Resolving or remediating karma requires our mindful attention. We must become aware of why we're choosing to act and what we're aiming to create with our action.

Karma is a reminder to pay attention to our actions so their resulting ripples are the change we wish to see in the world, instead of a load we cannot bear.

> *The Self takes on a body with desires,*
>
> *Attachments, and delusions, and is*
>
> *Born again and again in new bodies*
>
> *To work out the karma of former lives.*
>
> *—Shvetashvatara Upanishad*

We don't know how to escape our stories. We believe we're the body, the mind, and their actions. The personality can't fathom who we would be offstage.

"I'm angry," "I'm hungry," "I'm sad," or "I'm a father, engineer, doctor, student…"

"I'm a white woman…a black man…a philanthropist…a fighter."

These are the roles we choose to maintain our separation. They are the roles of our personality, suited to our unique process of working through our karma. Our gratitude for the roles—seeing precisely how they give us a means to find unity beyond the separation—empowers us to release our attachments and confusions that trouble us. We find our way to our true self, to spirit.

Every passing condition offers perspective as we flow through life. What we are is the entity watching. Who we are is the *I am* before the role begins and after the role expires.

Finding our way beyond this shadow requires we acknowledge the constant change inherent in every bit of life. We ask ourselves, "If I see the constant change, who am I?" As we begin to see ourselves as the witness, we realize that the body and the mind are instruments we use, not entities we are. We may hide behind them, crafting personae from their attributes, but we are constantly within, observing.

Even the conditions of body, gender, and sexuality that seem so unchanging and identifying to us are simply conditions of this life. They're costumes… clothing we wear to present ourselves in the world. This isn't to disregard their powerful lessons of perspective. Our stories develop and evolve with their help. We are in these costumes to learn from them. They're suited to the roles we're meant to play as we discover who we really are. But these costumes are not us. They are conditions that pass with our bodies.

Spirit endures.

Agent Preference

You may have noticed that every person you've ever met has a list of things he or she likes and dislikes. You may also have noticed this in yourself.

Go ahead and take a moment. Become aware of what you like. And how you share this information. Now notice what you don't like. And how often you let others know what you don't like. You grumble and groan, just like all of us.

Our desires may become a deep longing. Our dislikes can become dreadful aversions. At the root they are the same. We have preferences. We want something; we don't want something. Either way the *something* is getting our energy instead of ourselves.

We are partial. Our partiality causes us to suffer.

We order our whole world around these preferences. Most of our likes and dislikes confirm the mistaken identity we assert. From a tender age, we're informed that these preferences are appropriate and even markers of our education, morality, goodness. We are schooled to believe our efforts to divide an indivisible world will somehow prove our merit.

So, we like or dislike places, people, objects, events, symbols, history, politics. All the while we never stop to consider how these likes and dislikes are benefiting or troubling us.

When people see some things as beautiful, other things become ugly.

When people see some things as good, other things become bad.

—Lao Tzu

233

These two provocateurs—desire and aversion—are two sides of the preference coin. When you want something so badly, you turn from a host of other possibilities. Likewise, your dislike establishes a strong desire to keep it away from you. Of course, desire doesn't stop at simple wanting, nor does aversion limit itself to turning away.

Desire, when strong, can manifest as lust, greed, anxiety, and even pride.

We might want the presence of another in our lives so badly that we begin to turn that person into a prize or a means of gratification. We might crave money so much that we take it from others. We might crave perfection so desperately that we grow nervous with every interaction, anticipating what we might do wrong. Or, having achieved a certain recognition or status, we might arrest further development in our lives. We become that guy that did that thing. We remain the homecoming queen. We never let ourselves move along. Our former pleasure defines us and holds us hostage from new possibilities.

While desire may be a decent entertainer, desire's twin—aversion, resistance, dislike—is skillful in the art of deception. We have a harder time releasing what we don't like because we've developed so many effective ways of pushing our aversions away. While we understand that we may not need everything we desire, our aversions may not feel so dispensable. We often feel our aversions are keeping us safe, principled, or on the right team. We sometimes maintain a belief that allowing those things we dislike to exist supports their existence.

In fact, those things we dislike rarely have any clue or care that we have feelings toward them.

We're the ones who suffer the aversion.

We don't realize the energy savings we could reap were we to change our perspective.

Instead of spending our energy on the rejection of objects, people, and ideas, we can use our energy to say thank you to what we have. We can offer gratitude to those people, creatures, and systems in our life who offer us support. We can give our compassion to those who suffer as we do.

This is a simple but very effective means of learning how to let go of our preferences. The world may not give you what you want, but it will always deliver exactly what you need to learn, grow, and become a great player at life.

If we insist on maintaining our preferences and demand the world give us only what we want, we soon discover that our aversion strengthens into annoyance, anger, or even behavior that causes harm to another. The physical and emotional effects are so strongly felt in us that we often intensify the experience as we attempt to stop feeling them.

A friend once said to me that she was so frustrated by her anger that she hated herself. Her whole body held tight the power of her aversion to her own behavior. I asked her to consider who suffered the turbulence of that emotion. She said, "My kids, my husband."

She was upset because she felt like she wasn't giving the best of herself to her family. And she was right. There is no doubt that our emotions ripple beyond us. But when we host them, we are the source of the ripple.

I asked her, "Who else has to feel this wave you're creating?"

She said, crying, "I hurt all over." Her shoulders, neck, and jaw softened as she said it.

Physical pain is as common a response to strong aversions as it is the source of our aversions. We guard against the intrusion so steadfastly that our muscles ache and our joints stiffen.

When the pain settles in, we want so badly to see it depart.

We've all seen this kind of dysfunctional relationship before. The more we push our pains away—whatever their source—the more they stake their claim on us. They will continue to gain power. Our defenses continue to mount.

You may have noticed that some aversions develop as a result of exposure to the actions of others. We decide, "I do not like that behavior." Or, perhaps more often, "I do not like that person."

We build up a resistance, and when we see that behavior again, we find ourselves resentful for the repetition. After all, we guarded ourselves against it. Even worse, our dislikes persist far beyond the circumstances that provoked them. We host the sensations of the unpleasant experience far beyond the end of the experience itself. It's a bit like refusing to shower after falling into mud. We keep ourselves dirty.

A better option is to recognize that we all make mistakes and that we all do the best we can. That simple idea washes us clean of the muck. With this understanding, we no longer need to stand guard and defend against all the things we don't like. Instead, we can offer ourselves compassion. We may not have even realized we were covered in all that mud. We may not have realized we could clean ourselves off.

To contend with these provocateurs, we must learn to welcome them. When we open ourselves to our desires, we often see we may not benefit from all that's required to obtain them. When we confront our dislikes, we feel the walls we build to keep them out.

We become prisoners of our desires and our aversions. We can free ourselves of both.

Agent Death

Perhaps the most daunting, and certainly most insistent, agent of chaos we must get to know is agent death. To be clear, it is not death who is our provocateur. Rather, it's our fear of its looming presence.

The grim reaper taunts us all. Not one of us will get out of this alive.[31]

You must face annihilation over and over again to find what is indestructible in yourself.

—Pema Chodron

Our fear of death is both logical and progressive. In our ignorance, we believe we have control over the way things are. We don't know who we are, so we give ourselves roles. We don't like our roles, so we cling to preferences. Finally, we worry and grip harder because we know it can all be taken from us.

Death, as an absolute certainty, is the one thing that resists our attempts to control the world. We may do okay in our efforts to control. Death, eventually, will overcome our efforts.

---

[31] This doesn't mean the end. Consider how many experiences of change have led you to greater growth and expansion. Consider how many experiences of loss have brought you wonderful new potential. Indeed, impermanence is a great blessing when we shift our perspective to enjoy the view.

May death be patient and collect us gently.

Our universal fear of the end is well represented in our shared perception that death is the stealth robber of life. Our collective will seeks to survive. We aren't keen to embrace death, even when we intellectually acknowledge its inevitability. So what if it's the beautiful complement to birth? Most of us prefer to keep our distance.

In the Yoga Sutra, not much is said about this provocateur. It is enough to acknowledge that we all experience a fear of death, but we can wonder. We hold tightly to life, and we all change consistently throughout. Our tendency to cling to life will linger until we become aware of and experienced in what remains when our bodies pass.

I'm a fan of preparing for death.

I cannot escape death, but at least I can escape the fear of it.

—Epictetus

I also pray that we thrive into perfect ripeness before we're plucked from the vine.[32]

Everyone we know will die.[33] Acknowledging this, feel for a moment your compassion. We will all lose someone we love, someone who has

---

[32] A beautiful mantra known as the Mahamrityunjaya makes this plea. From the Rig Veda, it calls on an auspicious deity of destruction to bring us longevity and freedom from mortality. The mantra asks, "Oh three-eyed one, who is fragrant and nourishing, like a cucumber is picked from the vine, may I be freed from death, but not from immortality."

[33] Long may we last.

given us profound support. We're all walking on paths toward the same destination.

When I remember that our paths will converge, my inclination to live this life beautifully strengthens. This existence is a finite affair. While we have it, shall we love it dearly? The gift does not last long.

The persistence of death is present in every moment. As the breath comes, we live. As the breath goes, the moment passes.

May I let it go with grace.

This is preparing for death.

We share a 100-percent mortality rate. We are wise to cultivate an appreciation of this reality.

I'm grateful to my teachers and all those brave enough to stand for the premise that death is a highly misunderstood friend. Death is our final provocateur. It may come without warning, harvesting us regardless of our readiness. We can practice becoming ready.

Even when we come to understand the limitations of our likes and dislikes, the absurdity of the roles we play, and the sweetness of our true nature, we still have to contend with our moment of passing. While a fortunate few may have insight into the process, most of us will move toward death without a clear itinerary for the journey.

For this reason, preparing for death offers a lovely opportunity to surmount the obstacles this agent scatters along our path. Maybe we become aware of our nightly sleep as a comparable passage to unknowing. Maybe we allow ourselves deep rest after exercise or meditation. Maybe we become grateful for the persistence of change, recognizing a birth and death in every moment that comes and goes. Or perhaps we begin to inquire into nature itself, to see how it constantly renews itself and us, by growing and dying and returning again—daily, monthly, seasonally, or even along timelines incomprehensible to our perception.

May we ripen into perfect sweetness on the vine before we are picked, and may we be prepared to let go peacefully.

Yoga with Shadows

Like all of the practices described in this book, the following is appropriate for consistent use.

Perhaps more than any other practices included, this one may feel confrontational, emotional, or fraught. This practice guides you to look at the shadows on your path.

If you find yourself challenged by shadows, please consider using this practice in the company of a trusted friend, therapist, or guide. This practice is highly benefited by journaling at the end. Please jot down what you learned to acknowledge and accept the wisdom you acquired.

Your wisdom is the light that illuminates the path.

There are three important factors to remember as you undertake this work.

First, we all have shadows. Every person has history and is a product of it.

Second, a shadow is usually larger than the object casting it. This means that our perception of the source of shadow is often exaggerated by the way we see the shadow looming. What is behind us is in the past.

We've already survived it. The shadow is simply our reminder that we're meant to learn from what we've moved through.

Finally, your chaos agents are a part of your shadow creation. Let yourself know them.

Please seat yourself comfortably, or you may choose to lie down.

Take a few moments to settle in, and let your body feel the support of whatever holds you. Begin to notice your breath. As you breathe in, see what it's like to think the word *grateful*. As you breathe out, see how it feels to think the word *peaceful*. Become aware of how you are grateful for every inhale. Also notice that every exhale leaves you a bit more peaceful.

Now let yourself contemplate the existence of shadows in your life.

You may see them quite clearly, or you may be uncertain. You may prefer, like my friend, to blame the sun.

If you aren't sure, you can let yourself consider what type of behavior holds you back. This isn't someone else's behavior; this is yours.

You may see there is frequently a feeling of injury or insult that keeps you from moving forward.

You may see there's been impatience in you, causing you to make haste and fail to appreciate progress.

You may see patterns of laziness, unworthiness, fear, or regret.

Let yourself notice the shadows that have colored your path up until now.

Take a moment, please, to choose just one. For now, one.

Ask yourself this question: *What is the source of this shadow?*

Now let yourself watch for a moment. At first you may not know what you're watching for. That's not a problem unless you make it a problem.

Be patient. Then notice. You'll start seeing earlier moments in your life when you learned how to behave under the influence of this shadow. Take a look at these moments.

Can you see the behavior served a purpose at the moment the shadow was being created?

We befriend our challenges by marveling in the shadows. We see how they served us in the past. We heal our past from the present.

As you discover how you learned this behavior, can you take a moment to say thank you for what it allowed you to accomplish in the past? Sometimes our impatience stems from a demand to quickly accomplish tasks when we were children. Sometimes the source of our feeling of unworthiness can be spotted at the dinner table, as we listened to our parents remind us never to think we're special. They meant well, but the lesson cast a shadow.

Now see if that thank you can also become a welcome.

What would it be like for you to welcome the event, the people, the lesson into your life completely? What would it be like to gratefully accept the shadow, its source, and all you've learned to arrive at in this moment?

As you complete this process, take time to feel your body again. Return to feeling your breath—thanking every inhale, relaxing with every exhale. If it feels appropriate for you, consider offering your thanks to other circumstances in your life that support you to feel peaceful.

Write about your experiences so you can deepen your relationship with the source of your shadows.

Doubt

A final point on those things that get in the way: it is common as we confront our shadows that we may feel our light fade. We can become overwhelmed by how long we've lived in the shade. We can feel that we'll never understand the sources of our limiting behaviors. Please don't fret. This is just the arising of doubt. It is one more shadow that many of us face on our path.

Doubt is a stealth tool of those provocateurs and will arise for each of us. Doubt shares the strategy of a carpet bomb. It can sever our connections to ideas, communities, teachers, and even sensations that have served to fortify our practice. Our progress can be quickly waylaid by the appearance of doubt.

The remedy for doubt is faith. We strengthen our faith by building on what we've learned.

When it arises, as it will, steady yourself by noting how far you've come. Realize how you've always been a source of light and how you've refined various ways to steady its glow.

The soul is a lamp whose light is steady, for it burns in a shelter where no

winds come.

—Bhagavad Gita

You may like to return to those sources of wisdom that have been meaningful to you. Open a book, talk to a mentor, share your concerns. The very act of revealing your doubt and seeking consolation or guidance will steady your faith. It will create the space in your heart to progress.

Like every other shadow we face, doubt—when welcomed and invited in—deepens our inquiries and, consequently, our ongoing discovery of who we really are.

Wisdom to Bring Home...

- We all experience certain obstacles as we wander our paths. We stumble on occasion. With every fall, we gain more wisdom about the best way to proceed. We acknowledge that our obstacles are of our own creation and that they cast shadows on our path that can be as treacherous as the obstacles themselves.
- Looking at our obstacles as provocateurs or shadow casters can be helpful. We become aware of the particular ways we interact with them and how they may cause further trouble.
- In the wisdom traditions of the East, these provocateurs are listed as ignorance of who we are, believing ourselves to be otherwise, maintaining preferences to solidify this belief, and fearing the certainty of death.

- As we turn our awareness toward these provocateurs, their shadows diminish. We see them more clearly and realize how we can move along our path with more grace.
- Doubt occasionally visits. When it does, consider how a provocateur may be at work, diverting you toward a route you're now ready to navigate.

To continue contemplating identity and spirit, please see the study guide at the end. The practices presented in this chapter reappear for your contemplation. Sit with them. Be you with them.

9. What Comes and Goes?

Ah, world, what lessons you prepare for us,

even in the leafless winter,

even in the ashy city.

I am thinking now

of grief, and of getting past it;

I feel my boots

trying to leave the ground,

I feel my heart

pumping hard. I want

to think again of dangerous and noble things.

I want to be light and frolicsome.

I want to be improbable beautiful and afraid of nothing,

as though I had wings.

—Mary Oliver

So, hug someone. Let your heart find comfort with another heart. We're all in the process of losing everything.

It All Comes and Goes

Take a look around.

No matter where you are, in the next fraction of a second, something will change.

Close your eyes and open them. What did you notice?

Close your eyes again and open them. What changed?

We forget this confounding aspect of reality—that every moment is a passing of the last. We resist this. Have you ever found yourself clinging to an ounce of pleasure, feeling it fade and then trying to replicate the experience? Have you ever justified your behavior by saying, "I can't help it; it's just the way I am."

Have you ever wanted this moment to last forever?

Maybe even said, "Nothing good ever stays with me." I'm sorry if you've felt this way.

Hopefully this will help. Life is constantly changing for all of us. Not one moment will repeat.

Even that thought comes and goes. The feeling it provokes as well; here it comes, and there it goes.

How quickly all things disappear, in the universe the bodies themselves,

but in time the remembrance of them.

—Marcus Aurelius

This is the nature of our world. It changes, and we change.

Our mission is to learn to watch with love and appreciation.

Every moment arrives and departs. It's how time passes, creatures grow, learning deepens. In the process of coming and going, life happens. Life could simply be called shift. In the shift, depending on our attitude toward life's every addition and subtraction, we suffer or celebrate. We may celebrate first and suffer later, or vice versa.

Our relationship to change is shaped by the work of those provocateurs we met in the last chapter. They have the potential to plunge us into deep despair if we don't remember how they behave.

For example, we may resist change because it threatens to alter the person we think we are. You can see how an identity founded on a professional role might be reluctant to appreciate layoff or retirement. Likewise, attempting to hold on to youth restricts us from appreciating the benefits of age. We may love the idea of finding a new home, a new partner, a new experience but suffer as soon as the home, partner, and experience become familiar. At the same time, we may fear one or all of them being taken from us as keenly as we fear death.

Regardless of every posture we take toward change, however, it will still come. And go.

Our efforts to curtail the dramas of nature are futile. We might better direct these energies to finding the ways we will love and appreciate every change. We suffer the drama of change when we resist it. We may even enhance its volatility with our reaction.

What if we learned to rest with, dance in, wander through, and say thank you to the persistence of change?

What if we cultivated a peaceful presence even as the persistent shift enveloped us? What if we developed a comfortable position from which we might appreciate the change?

A beautiful woman I'll call Fatima maintained a relationship with a man for years. From the beginning, he promised her that he would never marry. She believed she could convince him otherwise. She waited for him. Over a few years, their relationship strengthened. Her lover's disinterest in marriage did as well. Fatima couldn't celebrate their happiness.

On the contrary, she suffered. Fatima wanted to be with her lover, and she wanted to be a wife. She found herself unable to find comfort with him. She was disappointed by her lover's strong will and her own inability to accept his position. She was unable to move beyond it and unwilling to forgive herself. She left the relationship.

By this point she was exhausted by the pendulous nature of her emotions. Fatima's despair weakened her. I asked her what she would suggest to me if I stood at the center of the same circumstances. Suddenly she saw it clearly. She said, "I'd say you're a control freak. Your relationship is better without your demands. I'd say, 'If you love him, that's enough.'"

At that moment her healing began. She spent a year learning about the shadows on her path and how she'd long allowed them to shroud her. As she looked toward their source, she saw her desire to control someone, her need to create a personality that didn't honor her spirit, and her fear of being someone alone.

Fatima learned to forgive herself for every effort she exerted to assert her will over the way things simply were. What's done was done. She'd done the best she could. She learned that taking control was the way her provocateurs conspired to fight change.

As she forgave herself, she backed off her pattern of control. As she did, she also saw that accepting her lover and his choices became easier. She saw that he too was doing the best he could. And he had had his own fear of change that prompted his different forms of resistance. In other words, Fatima became compassionate. She practiced loving herself and every roadblock she'd ever encountered. This made it easier for her to accept and love everyone else in her life more deeply.

In the process she discovered peace. All the volatility she'd suffered had arisen because she had refused to be content with the way things simply were. When she believed all stayed the same, she didn't like it. When she noticed change, she didn't like it. When she accepted how things were, she no longer had to spend the energy grieving what she'd wanted. When she stopped regretting what she'd lost or never gained, she found herself steady at the center.

In the midst of change, she could stand still and love herself: her body, her mind, her every experience. She became deeply grateful that life and all its change would never require her force, her control, or even her desire.

Change happens with or without us.

As my lovely friend witnessed, relationships come and go. Despite our promises to one another, change happens. Sometimes, in response, we part ways; sometimes we stay together. The way we respond to change is less important than the quality of our response to change. If we part ways peacefully, we'll be peaceful with the change. If we stay together in conflict, our relationship will remain conflicted.

Because change has been a constant since our first moment in life, this wisdom is familiar to all of us.

We were small, and now we're not. We were dependent on our parents, and now we provide for others. Almost every cell in our body has died, and another has been regenerated to take its place in the shape of us. You speak differently than you did when you were an adolescent. You likely hold new opinions, have scars in place of injuries, learned lessons from difficulty. Whether we're in a relationship with a person, an environment, a job, a nation, ourselves, what is guaranteed within and between us is change.

How shall we engage with it? In peace or in turmoil?

Our thoughts come and go. Our moods come and go. Our friends, lovers, money, jobs, homes, cars, pets, opinions, and beliefs all come and go.

Our breath comes and goes.

We come and go.

We are constantly in the process of growing and breaking apart, growing and breaking apart again. Eventually the life we know will end. Even this is simply another breaking apart. Growth begins anew.

We prefer to pretend otherwise. The pretense isn't wrong, exactly.

It's a sweet suspicion: something lasts.

Be still to see change.

If we sit still, we become the observer. Observing is familiar. We notice a sensation of being established, of finding a comfortable position, and from there, of being aware, of being the one watching. We witness, and we remember something.

We don't understand clearly what we're remembering.

It is absolutely true that an aspect of us is eternal and infinite and constant. Please take a moment and feel the impact of this truth. It's a truth that asks for your discovery. The proof is for you to find.

Until you do, perhaps you allow for the possibility?

Contrary to what is commonly desired, what is eternal, infinite, and constant isn't wealth, status, or partnership. Sometimes those things last throughout our lives, but more commonly they don't. Whether they do or not, we don't carry them along when we pass along. At the moment of our death, we lose our claim to the material treasures we accumulated.

Also, the material debts.

We go.

Of course, there's a mystery implicit in this transaction.

Every wisdom tradition cautions us to be mindful of our actions because something tags along as we move on. Consider these our intangible treasures and debts. They are the cause and effect—the resources that flow from the past to influence the quality of our future. These resources impact the manner of everything that comes and goes as we shift. In other words, our intangible treasures travel with us.

In one word, *karma*.

As we pay attention to our actions, we can have a sense of how they may affect us, wherever we go. We have only to look at the contagion of anger to see how this works. If I experience anger, and I act in anger, it's likely that someone near me is going to feel the anger and spread it. The anger may return to me, and it may carry beyond us. The spread will continue until someone chooses not to react in kind. In the meantime I can be assured that I'll see an angry world simply because what I'm giving is anger. I'm likely to feel some anger returning to me with every moment coming and going.

Now expand this moment. What if I'm consistently operating in anger? What if I'm spreading anger frequently? What resources are these actions accruing for me? And what debts?

My consistent experience of anger will likely provoke me to strengthen skills of offensive, defensive, and protective maneuvers. I'll learn what I can to protect myself from anger for as long as it takes me to realize that the anger is actually mine. It's sourced in me.

When I realize the source in me, I begin to develop new resources. I may learn how to accept what I cannot control, how to remember peace in difficult situations, how to arrest the spread of anger with kindness.

These are the resources that will now travel with me.

If you want to know about your past life, look at your present condition.
If you want to know about your future life, look at your present actions.
—Padmasambhava

With every coming is a going. At every arrival, a departure. With every birth, a death. How will you respond to these changes to lighten your load? Will you realize a treasure to share or incur a debt that will demand payment?

Notice how this has played out in your own life. You leave town and become resident elsewhere. You have a child, and your activities transform. You lose a parent and learn how to parent yourself. You lose a partner and discover new friends.

As soon as we leave, we start again. How have you responded?

This is the way of our world. Things come and go. Ideally we learn to be in the constant motion without getting too ruffled by loss and gain.

For most of us, our education is deficient.

We may learn a bit of economics and a little psychology, but when possessions and people leave our lives, we don't always take it well. Even the threat of their departure worries us. We spend an abundance of energy spinning through possibilities of losing what we have or failing to get what we want. In the leisure hours, we find ourselves regretting what's gone or never arrived. We don't really get it.

And yet a look around is all it takes to remember that every little thing is in process. Our ability to observe depends on the quality of our perception and our willingness to see beyond our personal time frames. To refine these qualities, we have to sit still for a moment.

Find that comfortable resting position. From there ask: "Am I willing to watch? Am I willing to watch carefully? Can I see beyond my limited frame of reference?"

Ten thousand flowers in spring, the moon in autumn,

a cool breeze in summer, snow in winter.

If your mind isn't clouded by unnecessary things,

this is the best season of your life.

— Wu-men

Waves crash and depart. That we can see. Trees bud; leaves shed. Puppies become dogs. Babies turn into adults. Mountains become sand. And what about that rock? Have you considered the changes it's experienced? Can you see its future in the dirt? Look up at the stars. Whatever you see is long gone. Whatever you see has been transformed into what you are.

Whatever is to come is unfathomable.

Even your schedule is a lesson in transience. You arrive for an appointment. You depart for another. What you did is gone. It won't return. What comes next? From moment to moment, we move through life, and all of it is changing. We spend most of our time in the past or the future, and we pretend like our current situation will last forever.

To See Change Is to See Life

The daily coming and going is life itself. We think of ourselves as constant, our lives as constant, our situations as constant. We think of ourselves as stable. Our only stability is recognizing our fluctuations.

Please name the opposite of life.

Odds are pretty good you'll say *death.*

Are you right?

Like wildflowers bloom, grow, and perish, we are born to life and moving toward death. Our birth brought our bodies into this world. As soon as we arrived, death—along with a winding journey toward it— became our destiny.

At a certain point, our wonderful minds offered us the ability to recognize it. Maybe we've done our best to ignore the fact of death, but

255

we know. Maybe our intellect has us convinced that we might be different than every other living being. Maybe some of us believe death won't come. Maybe we even think that death is meant for everyone else. Just not us.

Forgive me for being a persistent messenger.

Death will come.

It will.

And death will return the body to dust. Or, if you like, molecules.

The nitrogen in our DNA, the calcium in our teeth, the iron in our blood, the carbon in our apple pies were made in the interior of collapsing stars.

We are made of starstuff.

—Carl Sagan

The events of our birth and our death are inherent to the cycle of life as much as a wave rising and crashing on the shore is part of the tide. We can't come in without going out.

Which means that death isn't the opposite of life. Death is just a part. It's the same door as birth, viewed from the other side. If there's an opposite to death, it's birth. And if there's an opposite to life...well...

Remember how the tide always returns to the sea. The ocean is at once the wave, the tide, and the quiet depths. We pay attention to it. We become conscious of it all. We watch.

I leave it to you to consider. It's deep. Deeper than the ocean's depths. And it asks you to contemplate what you know of the qualities of life. There is an impulse toward its source. It fuels us and doesn't mind how long we take to return.

The Tao is like a well: used but never used up.
It is like the eternal void: filled with infinite possibilities.
It is hidden but always present.

I don't know who gave birth to it.
It is older than God.
—Lao Tzu

What are we if we will eventually lose our bodies to the stars? What are we if we share our source with infinite galaxies? Perhaps, in that connection, we might find that we are consciousness playing in both.

Our privilege in these precious lives is to become aware of the universe within us and to know it as ourselves. Consciousness is our soul's medium. It's through consciousness that our soul travels.

What is Life?

This life is a gift that offers itself anew every morning when we awaken. With every breath, it establishes itself. With the arrival of every moment, it calls to us.

What are we doing to move toward this life? To honor it? To say yes to its invitation? To smile toward it, listen to it, dance with it, and appreciate its every manifestation?

When we turn down the gift of life, we miss the chance to center ourselves in its opposite. When we sit and watch life, we can free ourselves of the identities we form—from our demands that life must sustain these faulty identities, from disappointment that life is going to take all we have. We see the wonder of the source and have no need to alter it. We are its abundance, and it provides for us perfectly, eternally. It is sacred, and so are we.

For me, discovering grace in, with, and through change was the unearthing of treasure I'd walked over daily. It means cherishing every moment I have throughout a life that is unlikely, fleeting, and fragile. It means paying careful attention to each moment to feel the nourishment of the same holy abundance that creates galaxies.

More practically it may also mean we care for our body at least as well as we care for our car. We recognize that it will not last, but we certainly don't want to rush its demise. We have an opportunity to learn about our minds and how to tend to them. We can meet and befriend the many players enacting our identity. And at the center of it all, we can daily move toward the heart and choose to dismantle whatever obstructs that journey toward home.

We have this beautiful opportunity to acknowledge, in one form, the constant change that is life itself. And in this form, to realize the witness is the constant.

Establishing a relationship with change allows us to understand the way we resist it.

We might like to force change. We might like to escape it.

Have you ever set a New Year's resolution? Any motivation to lose weight, quit cigarettes, find a partner, start yoga, whatever...it's all very laudable. Often when we set these goals, we imagine we're the ones who decide the perfect moment for some new thing to happen. Our work is to become ready and to confront the shadows that obscure our path. When we force change upon a shadowed path, we are likely to experience an equally strong reaction against it.

Our readiness to interact with change means that we create the conditions to accept and welcome the comings and goings, whatever they may bring. This beautiful Rumi poem, often cited as a salve for heartache, offers kind instruction for proper hospitality toward life—all of it.

This being human is a guesthouse.

Every morning a new arrival.

A joy, a depression, a meanness,

some momentary awareness comes

as an unexpected visitor.

Welcome and entertain them all!

Even if they're a crowd of sorrows,

who violently sweep your house

empty of its furniture,

still, treat each guest honorably.

He may be clearing you out

for some new delight.

The dark thought, the shame, the malice,

meet them at the door laughing,

and invite them in.

Be grateful for whoever comes,

because each has been sent

as a guide from beyond.

It may be that the heart occasionally aches, but an elated heart is also a passing state. Our emotional, physical, and intellectual states are guests who come for a visit. When we push sadness out or try to hold opinions hostage, we can't call ourselves good hosts. These visitors are meant to come and go. The more comfortable we become with the flow of our experience, the more deeply we can engage with the experience as it is. We aren't trying to make it into something it isn't. We aren't trying to shut out what's already in, nor are we trying to keep what is on its way out.

We open our doors and stand aside, watching the arrivals and departures. We see that every coming and going bears gifts meant for us and for distribution. May we welcome every moment along with the lessons it has for us. May we give every breath our gratitude and love to carry as it departs. May we know that we are always part of the process of life moving everywhere and this is how we progress.

We don't obstruct the passage of anything, in or out. Instead, we create the conditions in which we can learn and share in every experience, and we watch ourselves shift. What once frightened us will become welcome. What worried us is welcome. So too is every bit of wonder.

Like a spring leaf buds, unfurls, waves, and fades, so every experience moves through its process in us. Do we have to interfere, or can we simply watch the process?

Do you have a sense that you can simply watch?

This is a great challenge for most of us.

We're taught to aspire and achieve. We're taught to hold on to what we have and to fight when someone tries to take it. We believe we are the measure of our possessions, our wealth, an identity we've chosen and developed into a status others will recognize with respect.

If any of these things are threatened, we suffer. We also suffer if we don't realize these aspirations. We suffer failures of respect. We suffer desire, loss, and a persistent fear that our deficiencies are keeping us from a fulfilled life. Have you heard this one: "I'll be great when…"? Or how about this: "As soon as I get the job, wife, car, guitar, fill in the blank, I'll be happy."

A friend likes to say this: "If I can just get through this week, I'll be okay." She's said that every Sunday for fifteen years. I have another friend who says, "When I make a million dollars, I'll have arrived." I ask, "Where you headed?" He says, "I don't know. But I'll be satisfied when I'm there." Yeah, right.

Just like the end of this week will deliver heaven.

Just like the new car will satisfy your every desire.

Just like you'll call it a day at a million.

Laugh with me. We all do this.

Now and every moment that comes is our chance to observe more carefully. In this moment and every moment lives peace, fulfillment, abundance. In this moment is heaven. We become quiet and pay attention to who we are in the midst of every change.

Be still and know that I am God.

—Psalm 46:10

This is the true complement (and compliment) to life.

We are a constant.

As we learn to pay attention, we discover that our consciousness—our seat of attention—is always ready.

At any moment, it returns us directly to spirit.

Who Doesn't Die?

I know a woman who believes she'll subvert her body's aging process if she takes certain medications for the rest of her life. She wants to keep her body alive forever, so she doesn't have to die. Yet she doesn't want to get old.

I asked for her opinion on accidents, heart disease, and cancer. She said, "Why would those horrible things happen to me?"

Well, I don't know the answer to that, nor can I speak to their horror. But they're very common ways that human lives come to a close, and this is a natural process we each have the honor of learning.

I asked this woman if she knew anyone who'd never known death.

She said, "I can be the first."

I asked if she'd never lost a person, pet, plant she loved.

She said, "That was their death. I'm different."

I asked, "Have you never changed due to loss?"

She said, "That's different."

I stopped asking questions. Maybe she is different.

Maybe she's also lonely, missing the wonderful company we all keep with each other with our every loss and bereavement.

Whether we enjoy it or not, there is profound comfort in our shared fleetingness. Look around you. Everyone you see will pass. Before they do, they will lose someone important to them. Just like you.

Their hearts will hurt. They'll grieve.

And so will yours.

It's enough to make you want to hug someone.

So hug someone. Let your heart find comfort with another heart. Let yourself grow stronger in the connection.[34] We're all in the process of losing everything.

Here's a sweet story from the Buddhist tradition. A woman mourning her son asked the Buddha to revive her little boy. Buddha acquiesced with one condition. He said, "Bring me a mustard seed from a house that hasn't known death." The woman set off. Every home she visited offered her compassion for her loss and a seed. No one, however, could assure her that death had not been around. The woman

---

[34] Ayurveda teaches that hugging improves immunity. One more reason to bring our hearts together.

understood the lesson and returned to the Buddha with thanks. She wasn't alone. The whole world was with her.

We too shall pass. Before we do, many of those things we love shall pass. After they do, many things we could never anticipate will arise. If we stand in the way, we will never experience the wonder of these natural processes. If we hold ourselves out as all powerful, we'll never experience the true power of life.

What is it that compels us to intervene?

Recall, we have these personalities in the driver's seat, following routine pathways that seem safe or at least convenient. We don't really know where we're going, but we're told it should be some destination worth a salt. We aren't certain whether the destination we've aimed toward is worth salt or anything else, but we still drive, with some reluctance, toward it. Because we aren't particularly jazzed about our destination, we look for things, people, anything to make us feel purposeful and motivated. We consume everything we see, but we rarely pay attention.

Along the way, we outsource our happiness by purchasing, impressing, or forcing some kind of sensation into our experience. And because we had to work so hard to get that sensation, we fear its departure. Even though we have no idea why we're here or where we're going, we even fear our own departure. Out of fear, we prioritize our desires. Out of fear, we try very hard to stop things we like from leaving us. Out of fear, we try to stop things we don't like from coming.

They lose the day in expectation of the night, and the night in fear of the

dawn.

—Seneca

Out of fear, we suffer.

We follow our well-worn routes, and we do our very best to ignore the obstacles and the long shadows cast from them. In our neglect we remain in the trenches.

You Can Know Yourself

We want so badly not to suffer, but we have no idea how to set about relieving ourselves of pain, sorrow, worry, despair, anger, laziness, injury, illness, discontentment. So we simply outsource again, calling upon anyone and anything to fix us. We never expect that we may not need a fix at all but simply a shift in perspective.

Sadly, many of our trusted helpers want so badly to feel useful that they don't suggest a perspective shift. Instead they offer help that doesn't do much to change anything for the better. They try to solve our problems. They never suggest that we're the ones with the solutions.

You are the solution.

This may be a familiar story to you. I have a friend with severe anxiety. He can be called Anthony. Since childhood, whenever Anthony's stress increased, he cycled through phases of worry about his health. Although he recognizes himself as a healthy man, he fears any unfamiliar pain or bodily function as the disease that will take him. For a time Anthony's doctors were unaware of his feelings and made various suggestions for labs and tests and scans. He was even placed on pain medication for a time because his experience of pain—despite having no injury or abnormality apparent in imaging results—was severe enough to prompt the doctor to suggest epidural shots and daily opioids.

Instead of relief, my friend simply found new reasons to be concerned for his health. He worried over addiction, stigma, and liver damage. Additionally he recognized that whatever the source of his pain might be, it wasn't being treated. He was simply being numbed.

Anthony then started experiencing discomfort related to his digestion. Quietly he was convinced that he might have cancer. Doctors told him otherwise, but he was unpersuaded.

It took another few months, but Anthony finally managed to admit to his doctors that he couldn't accept the possibility that there was no diagnosis. At that point his doctors suggested he take medication to stop worrying. Not once did a doctor suggest that he talk to a counselor. Not once did they mention that his fear could be addressed without medical intervention.

Anthony was exhausted by his worry.

He made the decision to attend to his condition and committed to being its project manager.[35]

He sought assistance through yoga and meditation to strengthen his body and calm his mind. He asked for his doctor's support to wean himself off the pain medication and shots. With the assistance of a therapist and spiritual guidance, he allowed himself to observe the shadowy spaces along his journey. In these places he suspected he might

[35] His words. He applied one of his useful skills to his troubling issue and discovered it worked well.

266

come to understand the origin of his anxiety and its relation to illness. In these shadows he encountered childhood trauma, abuse, anger, and misery. He also saw that these experiences were awaiting his acknowledgment and acceptance.

He appreciated each one he found because he knew his awareness indicated progress in his project. He worked with them. He asked for help at every turn, but he was the one who took every step through and beyond his darkness. He was the one who learned how to cast his light.

Ultimately he discovered that every step forward benefited from quiet introspection. He realized and shared, "I have to pay attention." He said, "My whole life, I tried to ignore everything life gave me. I thought it was all suspect because I'd been hurt so many times. What I had to do to live well is to appreciate everything life gave me. I had to develop the ability to do exactly the opposite of what I'd learned as a kid."

He noticed his journey would stall when he forgot to give himself space to contemplate the shadows on his path. And he became a very good afficionado of his life.

Of course, had someone suggested that he simply sit still and watch for a moment, Anthony may not have been ready. He may not have been able to hear the simple perfection of the advice. Then again, maybe someone did. And the seeds eventually bloomed for him at just the right time.

So.

Sit still and watch for a moment.

Sit still and watch the moment.

Sit and appreciate everything in the moment.

Sit, be in the moment, and pay attention.

Please.

Like seeds, helpful words bear fruit when the conditions are right. Attend to the soil. See where you can reclaim your personal wisdom and fortify your courage to serve yourself. See where you can solicit the guidance of others rather than relying on others to simply serve you. See where you can find space to be quiet, spacious, welcoming of every moment, shadows included.

Discover how you can appreciate your life and all it gives you.

Do You Know Yourself?

You'll recall, at the root of fear is a deep dependence on that tenured provocateur: our entrenched ignorance. We've forgotten who we are. With all our wandering, we've forgotten the way home.

How do we remember?

We're told we should carve our niche, assert our position, and stand our ground. But the raw material for the niche, the location of our position, and the ground beneath our feet had nothing to do with us. We didn't make these things.

We work with the raw material, but the raw material is not of our creation. If you're a jeweler, you may set beautiful stones, but you did not make them. A goldsmith works with gold, but she doesn't make gold. Likewise, we have the means to become masterful artists of our existence, but we have to appreciate and respect the materials of our craft.

We don't create the source of life, but it moves in each of us. How do we become skillful with it?

First, we realize the changing nature of our bodies, minds, and intellects, as well as everything around us. Then we learn to work with these changes skillfully.

Even the most rambunctious of us are habit-driven; the ways we behave are plain and simple patterns that make it easier on us to move through life. If I don't have to think about where I'm going or why I'm going there, I don't have to spend any energy wondering how or why I'm actually doing it.

Consider the many simple chores you do throughout the day. Isn't it a wonder that neither of us have to learn to brush our teeth every day? The practice is a habit, and the method we use likely works pretty well.

Until an arm doesn't work like it's supposed to.

When I broke my arm, my well-tested method fell apart, and I had to develop a new technique. The whole endeavor challenged me for a few days until a new pattern formed. In that process, I discovered all sorts of new toothbrushing techniques. I also realized how mindless the practice had been for me up until that point. What had been a series of steps that flowed in perfect sequence became as clumsy as a beginner ballroom dancer.

That was when I started brushing my teeth while standing on one foot, switching hands, noting the sensations in my mouth, and savoring the taste of the toothpaste. The process of toothbrushing became a method to hone my focus and concentration.[36]

---

[36] Of course, my partner finds the whole process entertaining. He calls them "bathroom shenanigans." He has no idea what I really get up to in there.

By breaking the old routine, I learned to incorporate more attention into my new one. The new one, of course, will have to be relinquished as well—eventually.

Recognizing our habits makes them easier to source. Better yet, we see them with grateful eyes. After all, they served us in some important way through a certain duration of our lives.

If we see them as a little vein of gold, we can mine it to the motherlode. Deep at the core of us, we share a yearning. We want joy, love, and the bliss of peace.

That's the raw material of our lives. When we recognize a habit and trace it back to the raw materials, we discover how we mined these materials in our unique, wonderful ways. As we travel within, we can imagine passing those provocateurs heaving their picks in the wrong direction, not quite sure where to access joy, love, and peace. We can move right on past and look toward the ways our patterns first served, in whatever small way, our access to joy, love, and the bliss of peace.

Let's not blame the habits so much. We may think they cause the trouble, but they were originally formed to serve us. What causes trouble is our unwillingness to pay attention to our patterns to see what they have to teach us.

Like this.

At a certain point in my adulthood, I realized how much I craved validation. I wanted people to like me.

I don't think I'm special in this craving.

Where I got lucky was that it was making me unstable. I felt unhinged. Whenever I succeeded, I wanted more. My success felt empty if no one approved of it.

The instability saved me.

I looked at the pattern and traced it back. I saw how much I wanted to please my family. I was loved, and I was awkward, and I was different. I wore mismatched socks, wrote sonnets, and wandered everywhere by public bus with three or four books in my bag.

My family wanted to guide me to be comfortable. I wanted them to guide me to be free. I kept myself free and tried to impress them with my achievements. I kept reading on the bus, but I also won swimming championships and debate competitions. My family still saw my socks.

I was looking for love in their approval. But love was always right there for me.

It took a while for me to figure it out, but eventually I understood. The only validation I required was mine. I could know that I was okay. I could be free. And I could accept that anyone's ideas of how I should be were really not my business. What was my business was accepting their love in whatever manner it was offered.

So I learned that love is delivered in various packages. I learned to appreciate all the packages, and I no longer needed someone else to love me in just the right way.

It's a gift to be loved. Watching all living beings come and go from our lives strengthens our appreciation for this gift. Indeed, it's the greatest treasure of life. How others choose to share the treasure with you is up to them. How you choose to accept and use the treasure is up to you.

You can treat it like a pitfall or a means to paradise.

Up to you.

While the world changes around you, what remains the same is your ability to choose how you experience it—love and opinions alike.

Yoga with Change

Here's a way to quietly contemplate change.

Sit in a quiet place while straightening your nice, long spine. Sit with respect for your journey. Ideally, you'll sit on a surface that allows you to keep your spine tall without too much difficulty. A chair is a great tool for sitting! If sitting is too difficult, lie down on your back with your legs supported by a pillow.

Close your eyes, and take deep, nourishing breaths. Begin to deepen your inhale and lengthen your exhale.

Discover the moment in the coming of your breath. Discover the moment going with the departure of your breath. In the pause following each, wait in one moment for the arising of another.

As you observe the moments passing, notice qualities of your inhale and exhale. Describe these qualities to yourself. How does your inhale feel? How does your exhale feel? Discover in your breath's constancy its persistent change. Every intake of air is eventually exchanged for a release. Every inhale brings the world to you. On every exhale you offer yourself to the world. Eventually release control of the breath, and let your body breathe for you.

As you deepen your inhale, open your eyes. As you lengthen your exhale, close your eyes.

Say to yourself as you inhale, *Breathing in, I observe the world.*

Say to yourself as you exhale, *Breathing out, I observe the world.*

You may not think anything is changing at first. Please continue to pay attention as you breathe, opening and closing your eyes.

Become aware of the small changes in your perception. Watch for a few minutes. At a certain point, release your breath and contemplate what you observed.

Notice the things that have gone in the last hour, the last day, the last week, month, and year.

Then, call to mind the things that have come along in the last hour, the last day, the last week, month, and year.

See the connection between the passing and arising, the going and coming.

Finally, close your eyes and become aware of what did not change in the process.

Ask yourself this question: *What's come, and what's gone?* No need to provide answers. Simply sit quietly and watch the answers appear in your consciousness. Notice how what has come and what has gone are always intertwined. There is not one without the other. Just as we inhale to exhale, we must also let go to find space. We must find space to let go. When change stops, we are no longer alive.

Notice the constancy of your consciousness and your gratitude for what has come and gone.

Now notice what has remained the same throughout every coming and going you've experienced.

This is who you truly are.

This is the process of quietly contemplating change.

Wisdom to Bring Home...

- Every aspect of life requires constant change. Life itself is change. We are part of that change, and we are the change.
- The way we accept and move with change is the way we accept and move with life. When we observe the ways of change, we see ourselves more clearly as beneficiaries of this change. We learn how to be in awe of our fortune in the midst of change.
- Sitting still in the moment offers the best view of change.
- Welcoming every change that moves us from moment to moment will free you from the anxiety of what's to come and of the despair at what's gone.

To continue contemplating identity and spirit, please see the study guide at the end. The practices presented in this chapter reappear for your consideration. Sit with them. Be you with them.

10. What Remains?

The sensible man doesn't pay attention

to what increases or decreases,

since both pass like a quickly moving stream.

Whether the water of life runs clear

or is tumultuous as a flood,

don't bother speaking of it—

it doesn't endure more than a moment.

—Rumi

You're the most interesting person you'll ever know.

You Remain

This will feel a bit fantastic, maybe, but your perception of yourself as a being subject to time and its effects is a choice you make. Truly, it's all you know.

You've got a calendar; you plan ahead; you run late and hurry along. You forget to appreciate the miracle of this current moment. In this moment is everything you'll ever know.

The truth is, in this moment you are.

Whatever you've been or will be informs the quality of the moment, but what lasts is an understanding that you are. In this moment alone, you are. And you always are. Everything around you will die.

You Will Die One Day

You've been born into a belief system that welcomed you at birth with a coo and a promise. The promise included all the benefits of life—all the comings and goings. The promise, however, did not include your attention to these comings and goings. You are given the tools for this but their way you use them is for your discovery.

What a game. Life gives us change. We learn how to adapt. Eventually, maybe, hopefully, we learn how to apply this adaptation to the ultimate change we all face: physical death.

We've discussed this great and shared inevitability. We've explored our great and shared aversion to this inevitability. It unites us all. Indeed, we're all collaborating toward this inevitability.

If we were rational in our projections, we might endure this unity a bit more peacefully. We might commit to living long and well, so we might learn what we must. We might commit to serving each other along the way.

Here's an idea: we might honor the inevitable and all those sharing our journey.

Instead, we mostly loathe the power of it. We mostly commit to a belief that our journey is somehow separate.

We prefer to insist on a concept of free will with its pretense of control. Death reminds us that we have no control. It also asks us to think a bit more deeply about our continuity, which concerns our sense of identity.

We see the moon cycle around us. We see the rain arrive, pass, and appear again in the green grass. We trust the sun to return. Yet we position ourselves as different, separate, unique from nature. If we might have been someone else before we arrived as who we are now, how are we to reconcile two selves?

I'm not afraid of death because I don't believe in it. It's just getting out of

one car and into another.

—John Lennon

Instead of bothering with that thought experiment, we maintain an uncomfortable relationship with death. We fear it, we resist it, and deep down we resent we can't escape it.

Which is true. And false.

Your body will go but you are free to realize continuity. The mind will go as well, but you are free to realize continuity.

When she first died, do you think I didn't grieve like anyone else? But I
looked back to her beginning and the time before she was born. Not only
the time before she was born, but the time before she had a body. Not
only the time before she had a body, but the time before she had a spirit.
In the midst of the jumble of wonder and mystery a change took place
and she had a spirit. Another change and she had a body. Another

change and she was born. Now there's been another change and she's

dead. It's just like the progression of the four seasons, spring, summer,

fall, winter.

—Zhuangzi

The realization of your continuity asks that you surrender your grasp on what you perceive as you. Can you discover the deepest experience of you? Can you accept what the experience offers?

Who Is This You?

Not the you of body or mind.

And not the you of intellect.

As we've seen, these dimensions of you are subject to constant change. These dimensions of you are inherently changeable. It's the very nature of these aspects of you to undergo persistent change as you experience the world. They adapt to the conditions you create or those created for you.

If you're paying attention, you've discovered that your very mutability is your greatest teacher. Seeing the ways you change or don't, the ways you resist it or rush, the ways you thank or resent it...these are all the best lessons you have to guide you back home. The fact of change is a simple truth that helps us to become conscious and aware that every step is not guaranteed and every step matters.

The whole future lies in uncertainty: live immediately.

—*Seneca*

In other words, what if you consider your life's journey as your immediate and ongoing means of learning to navigate through and beyond the shadows?

If you're willing to watch yourself carefully, you'll discover the ways you've plotted your course with respect to every shadow. Maybe you'll find that you managed to learn a thing or two about seeking help, finding alternatives, overcoming, or giving in.

Every moment going forward becomes your path to wisdom. Allowing a moment to reflect on the ways your wisdom has developed builds a certain faith. We can see that every decision offers a lesson on the journey. Your past illuminates your path if you choose to see the light shining in every experience. If you choose instead to see only the dark, your future navigation continues in the shadows.

How do you discover light?

The light is gratitude.

This is frequently the point when people protest: "You don't know what I've been through."

I know life is hard. And I'm sorry you've felt it so keenly.

All is perfect. This is perfect. When something perfect is taken from what

is perfect,

only perfection remains. Peace and peace and peace.

—*Isha Upanishad*

You Don't Know You

This, of course, is true. I don't. It may be the case that neither do you.

You don't really know what you've been through. Until you do. Which means knowing your past in its fullness, with great curiosity and a certain objectivity. No need for any prefatory remarks about its horror.

Just for a minute, consider how everything that ever happened got you here.

You made it to this moment.

That's an important acknowledgment. You know many, very likely, who did not. You made it to now because of all the events that came and went. You have no idea where or how you would be if you'd done a single thing differently. Any fantasies about changing the past are simply games of regret. You can play those games, certainly, but the instructions and conclusion are one in the same: regret. You regret the past, so you pretend like you can change it and find a different moment. Looking for a different moment is another form of regret. Really, what's wrong with this one?

We should make all spiritual talk

Simple today.

God is trying to sell you something,

But you don't want to buy.

That is what your suffering is:

Your fantastic haggling,

Your manic screaming over the price!

—Hafez

Everything you are exists in this moment. Everything you can feel is present in this moment. You will never be in the past again. It's gone, available to memory, fantasy, and dream but only in the moment that hosts the memory, the fantasy, and the dream. And the future: it will never arrive. The very definition of the future requires that it remain out of our reach. When the future comes, we will be in this moment.

So feel this moment. And ask, do you really want to regret anything?

Unfortunately too many of us review the past and express our regret. We say, "It was awful…" or "I was so hurt…" or "It was bad…"

Regret is another pattern. You can trace it back to the motherlode if you like. Can you find the way your expression of regret has afforded you an occasional moment of joy or love or peace? Look for a moment.

You'll see. And you'll also see what the past was teaching you.

The path into the light seems dark,

The path forward seems to go back,

The direct path seems long...

—*Lao Tzu*

We love to pretend like we're the only ones who have suffered. As if suffering weren't a part of everyone's existence.

And these sufferings are usually things we refuse to see again. As if suffering didn't eventually show us a new way forward.

It's time we learn otherwise.

When it comes to those difficulties we've faced, we've got to go easy on ourselves. Let's be kind first.

We didn't want to experience it the first time, and our defense mechanism in response is often to shut off the memory in various ways so we don't have to relive it. Those who suffer trauma will be familiar with the uncomfortable arising of the replay. It returns without invitation or warning. Still it returns.

One of the most unfortunate realities of our current condition is we make all kinds of effort to stop its return.

Our aversion is an attachment. Remember how this trips us up? We wanted life to flow differently for us, but it didn't. We regret that we still can't control the way things went, even as a memory. Even though they went the way they did. Even though the past is gone.

This doesn't mean we have to thrill to the experience; we simply start by acknowledging that it happened. The fact of its occurrence means it was necessary for us in one way or another. Will we understand the necessity?

We might ask ourselves, "What are we resisting? Why?"

We try so hard to ignore what we resist. It pushes back with equal effort. Whatever we resist will constantly seek our attention. It's a tagalong.[37] It goes where you go, trying to befriend you but feeling like a drag. It appears everywhere. You didn't invite it along. You find it annoying. You think it's aggressive. It just wants your attention. Then it gets pushy. It calls at all hours, knocks on the door, comes with you to work. You want it to leave you alone, and it sticks to you tighter.

The stronger our resistance, the stronger it becomes.

Some of us try to ignore it by dulling our awareness of its presence. Maybe we medicate with alcohol, marijuana, food, distraction. Maybe we seek medication from a doctor. We do whatever we can to keep it outside our awareness.

We don't ask, "Why do you keep returning?"

We don't even think of the possibility of friendship. We never consider that it may have something to offer us.

When will we learn?

---

[37] Some might say *creep*, but here's a kinder perspective. I was the youngest in the family by a longshot. My brother and sister had to take me with them everywhere. I was the tagalong; I wasn't a creep. I know they didn't always want me around. Still, there I was! I wanted to love them and be their friend; they wanted to leave me outside sometimes, I'm sure. In the end they both raised wonderful children, and I like to think that my constant presence was their early training!

Here's where we put our lessons into play. As we've journeyed together, we've discovered the wonder of our bodies, the rhythms of our energy, and the ways of our minds. We've acknowledged the facets of our personality. We've also learned that obstacles may trouble us from time to time but we can surmount them by practicing with kindness, honesty, generosity, moderation, and gratitude.

With this practice, we discover what is always waiting for us: joy, peace, and enduring love.

When we observe the presence of a tagalong, what if we choose to respond from the wholeness of our being? What if we observe the tagalong as a guide directing us toward the dimensions of ourselves that require attention? What if we choose to be kind, honest, and thankful for whatever our tagalong wants to teach us?

When we realize we've got a tagalong, a generous move is to turn and welcome it in. Throw open the doors, hold out our hands, and make friends. Receiving the memory, the pain, the concerns, the fears that the tagalong carries doesn't mean they're moving in forever. Paradoxically, with our welcome, the tagalong will be less inclined to stay. If we'll listen, it will deliver its story. It will become one of our many guides to a life of joy and peace and love.

It will stop hanging around so stubbornly. It may return, but we'll be ready and grateful to learn when we encounter it again.

Blessed is the man who has suffered and found life.

— *The Gospel of Thomas*

Zen master Thich Nhat Hanh tells the sweet story of Buddha's lifelong reception of the powerful demon of temptation Mara. Before becoming the Buddha, Siddhartha was a wandering yogi. Before that he'd been a prince. He left his family because he couldn't bear the suffering of the world. He wanted to find a solution. In his wanderings he tried all sorts of austerities. He'd grown exhausted by disciplines that only hurt his body and mind. On the eve of his enlightenment, he decided that he would simply sit still under a tree until he had a solution to suffering.

That night Mara appeared in Siddhartha's meditation and tried to persuade him to cease his pursuits in favor of power, women, and wealth. Siddhartha politely declined and became the Buddha.

Throughout the long remainder of his enlightened life, he received visits from Mara. Upon his arrival Thich Nhat Hanh said, "The Buddha did hugging meditation with Mara."

He welcomed him with open arms.

To the dismay of his disciples, the Buddha would invite Mara in for tea, offering him the best seat and listening to him like a friend. If we could watch the two talking, says Thich Nhat Hahn, we "would have had the feeling that Buddha and Mara were a couple of friends who need each other—like day and night, like flowers and garbage."

Flowers and garbage. Each one exists with the other and becomes the other.

There is the mud, and there is the lotus that grows out of the mud. We need the mud in order to make the lotus.

— Thich Nhat Hanh

So many sage ones want us to hear the truth. Listen to them. Rumi asks us to become a guesthouse even for a crowd of sorrows, shame, and malice. Khalil Gibran reminds us that the strongest souls emerge out of suffering, "seared with scars." Walt Whitman simply recognizes the experience we all share as we review our trials and fathom our reality as humans: "I am the man, I suffered, I was there."

Although the world is full of suffering, it is also full of the overcoming of it.
—Helen Keller

What we've suffered will be surmounted. What we've suffered will guide us toward greater joy, love, and the beautiful experience of peace.

From that enduring place of joy, love, and peace, is there any better response to suffering than thank you? When we arrive home, are we not relieved—grateful for the journey that brought us there?

When we open ourselves to every experience with a kind heart, an honest mind, a generous personality, and a grateful heart, all that may come and all that's gone is a perfect gift.

Please Meet You

Certainly, this deeper experience of ourselves wouldn't keep pushing in if it didn't have something to offer. If it didn't, why would the mind return to it? You're the one in this experience.

You're the one who stars in all the stories you've lived through.

It's a beautiful paradox. We seek so much attention of others, offer so much attention to others, and refuse to attend to ourselves.

Imagine watching a movie and deciding to ignore the protagonist for the two-hour duration.

This is what we mostly do. We act as if life happens around us and to us.

There is no authority who knows you better than you know yourself. You're in there with you. No one else occupies your space like you. We may be moving through a time in which we've surrendered our minds to the vagaries of studies, but we are truly sovereign in our lives. This means we rule our domain. Our reign comes with great responsibility. We cannot be mindless. We cannot cede our authority. We must understand our condition.

No one is better placed to do so.

Assuming the throne challenges each of us in our particular ways. Please accept this wonderful privilege.

Some of us who have been trained only in the way life hits us will recognize how we constantly hit back. We contribute to every failure and trial in our domain. Some of us who like to play strong will have to acknowledge that our domain has its vulnerabilities. Some of us who blame others will realize that every sovereign is in a relationship with every person who has ever entered the kingdom.

It isn't easy to lord over ourselves. And yet we cannot lord over anyone else and expect to experience the contentment and love that we find in ourselves.

We find this contentment and love at home.

It is our birthright.

We only have to decide to exercise our sovereignty.

We review our ways to begin to understand what has been constant in us. What is constant grants us the keys to our kingdom.

When we don't like the way the narrative went down, do we pretend like it didn't happen? Do we imagine we've been irreparably damaged by it? Or both?

We exist in the dissonance of our intellect's disinterest in facing facts. But what happened, happened. What is happening, is happening. Our negative feeling toward the events and circumstances around us doesn't change a thing. They simply arrest our ability to contend with the lesson at our feet. Will you accept what you're experiencing with gratitude for its provocative education in survival, evolution, wisdom, and compassion?

To do otherwise simply prolongs the battle between you and the world. Your perspective keeps the game going.

What is your perspective?

Let's say you've had your colorful life. You had sticky fingers as a teenager and later become a police officer. You busted teenagers who did what you did and worse. Now you've retired as a gardener. You want to make the neighborhood lovely, but you don't want anyone to walk on your lawn or pick your flowers.

Every one of these experiences is important, but none of them defines the constant in you.

They will be helpful, however, as you discover the manner of your sovereignty. Consider for a moment how you rule your kingdom. Take the time to realize who guides you through your many disparate roles in life.

Who is it, actually, aware of all of your shenanigans? Not acting them out, but aware of them. Are you the teenager, the cop, or the gardener? Or something much, much more?

You're the one who's endured through all the roles. You're the one who continues.

You're the spirit in there, guiding your way.

Even if it feels like an intrusion, a forced entry, an unwelcome guest who wants to trash your house, every encounter is a guide to remind us of exactly who we are. Every encounter is us—spirit returning us to spirit.

Your role is to coordinate every dimension of your existence to clear the path to spirit. Work with your body, settle your mind, and shepherd your personality to remove every obstacle that blocks the light from shining in and out of you.

This is the superhero's journey and the only journey worthy of you. You prepare your kingdom for spirit.

So, what if, as the poet Rumi advises, and as we do with our tagalongs from the past, we invite everyone in—knowing, always, that this is spirit seeking spirit? Invite everything in and listen carefully. Remember, and notice that whatever is happening is for your illumination. Everything is pointing you toward the light, if you choose to see it.

Your Purpose Is Greater than You Suspect

What may be the greatest fugazi of our time is the shared suspicion that our lives have no purpose.

Your purpose is inherent and intact. You are important and meaningful.

If this feels foreign to you, the discovery awaits. Please become aware that your present inability to experience your purpose doesn't preclude its existence. Chances are pretty good that you've never personally discovered an atom, the mechanics behind flight, or the roundness of the world. And yet you accept (and likely appreciate) the reality of each.

The greatest gift we offer life and those who support us as we move in and through it is to affirm our certainty that we are meant to be here. We are part of the play. We are essential and connected. We are as imperative as every virus, lion, and star.

To believe otherwise is to discount every smile and kind word you've offered a friend. To believe otherwise is to dismiss every shared laugh, tragedy, and wonder.

You may not know the impact you've made, but you are necessary.

Otherwise you would never have come into being.

Please jog your memory for a moment.

Take a look at the connections you've made with people and places. Realize the enormity of the net you've created around you. Even if these connections have weakened or expired, you can still see the continuation of the knots you've created. You found others; they found you. There is a coherence to your existence that will become clear and supportive as you look at the ways you've met and interacted with others in your life.

Consider this. Your presence is imperative.

"To what?" you ask.

To everything.

The very fact of your existence is highly unlikely. You've read about this in chapter two.

What becomes fascinating as we think about our purpose is that we often think of ourselves in isolation. We forget that we aren't operating separately from anything. We may think of ourselves as a man, a woman, nonbinary, queer, gay, straight, asexual. As sons or daughters. Of a certain race, status, community.

We forget that we are also beings on a planet constantly spinning through its own existence, just as we spin through ours. Our existence touches others in the same way that the earth's spin touches ours. We may not know our impact at every moment of the spin. Regardless, we're part of an intricately connected web of interbeing that requires our existence for as long as we last.

If it didn't, we would no longer be here.

The whole idea of compassion is based on a keen awareness of the interdependence of all these living beings, which are all part of one another, and all involved in one another.
— Thomas Merton

Our ideas of isolation veil our appreciation of the whole. When we marvel at the whole, we become more curious about our participation in it. We become aware of how we might relate to and impact the world around us.

If you're willing, you can start this discovery now. You can investigate how you relate to and impact your world and begin to understand how your manner of relation and impact is quite unique.

You have your ways.

You have your purpose.

And the world is evolving with you, just as you evolve with it.

There are lines that run through our lives, serving to connect us to others. These lines indicate the directions we take in order to connect. These lines help us identify our path.

Once again, we may regret that we don't come with an instruction manual that prescribes the mission of our lives. We've all been exposed to expectations and social duties, but these may not entirely correlate with our true purpose. To figure it out, we have to pay careful attention to who we are. We look at how we use our bodies and minds. We consider how we share our energy and apply our vast and wonderful personalities.

Take a look at the ways you've tailored your life. Maybe you got married early or ran away to join a cult. You may have money or not. Maybe you've been a lawyer. Or a combat soldier. Maybe you've maintained a family, an art gallery, a food delivery service. Do you collect things or lose them? Are you organized and ready? Do you heal? Are you an innovator? Are you a builder? A listener? A musician? A runner? A dancer? A player? A friend?

For clues to your purpose, look at the ways you've chosen what may be appropriate for you. It isn't actually about what you do but how you do it. Look at the ways you conduct your business. Let's say you love food. You became a chef. Your mission may be nourish the world or it may be to figure out how to accept nourishment in your own life. Whatever role your personality plays, your mission is to be aware of the ways it plays.

No need to judge and no need to want otherwise.

People who do not feel the music of the world do not want to dance. That's fine. Not everyone will develop and manufacture the next big tech gadget. That's fine too.

My favorite story of mission discovery comes from my mom. After six decades as a nurse and nutritionist, she retired. Over coffee on one of her new free mornings, she said to me, "I'm very good at helping others to heal. What I've only just realized is that I never learned to properly heal myself." At the culmination of her career, she understood how her mission was developing and, better still, chose to persevere. She committed to listening as carefully to herself as she did to her patients and to provide all due care.

Each of us contributes in our sweet and powerful ways. These are the ways we participate in the dynamic of life. Whether you believe it or not, you are the only one who can do what you do. Your tasks may be menial, but the way you do them is yours.

And it's important.

An individual has not started living until he can rise above the narrow confines of his individual concerns to the broader concerns of all humanity.

—*Martin Luther King, Jr.*

Creation would not have you doing it any other way. You may be forcing yourself to do things that don't work. Eventually you feel this and understand. You realize it doesn't work for you and see the reasons why you attempted to do something contrary to your nature.

Creation wants you in integrity. Without this integrity, we lose sight of our connection to the whole. We lose sight of how we must contribute. When we lose sight, we lose sight of everyone who shares this wonderful world with us. We lose our compassion and the peace, joy, and love it delivers.

Ask yourself: *What do I do in my natural state? How do I share this with others?*

Review the things you've done to get a glimpse of your purpose. Allow yourself to acknowledge the ways you've followed particular directions in your life. Notice how you've failed and reorganized yourself. Notice how you've increased your skills and reach. Finally, consider how you might further refine these directions to eliminate any of the complications that you may have added for the wrong reasons.

As part of this unified world, how would you offer your gift to creation? In what manner would you like to fold yourself into existence? Because you are here for a reason, and you have a choice in the way that you share yourself. Your contribution is fundamental to this existence.

Your participation helps all of us to learn and evolve. We all belong, and we are meant to share our purpose. When we share our purpose in integrity, we feel content.

We feel love. These are the constants of our eternal state. These are the comforts of being home.

You're the Most Interesting Person You'll Ever Know

I say this with an abundance of love and compassion. You've suffered, and I'm sorry. Whatever you've been through, please allow me to thank you for making it to this point. You're strong and you're resilient.

I have little doubt that you've experienced overwhelming pain and occasionally gut-wrenching sadness. I have no doubt you've felt cruelties inflicted on you and witnessed the same. Most likely, you have also been cruel. You have probably yelled and possibly hit. You have probably said words intended to hurt someone. You have probably said words to yourself that are even worse.

But here's the truth of it all: you're alive.

You exist in an expansive community of humans who have also suffered pain, outbursts, despondency, and despair. We're at our best when we're willing to be honest in our self-assessments and be compassionate toward what we discover. Not a single human exists who hasn't suffered. Being alive is our opportunity to learn how we'll greet our suffering, accept its lesson, and experience the profound peace of gratitude for every moment we find.

Everything we have within us is ours to discover. Look around and see how richly detailed this world is.

See the colors, notice the smells, and feel the texture of your clothes and the air on your skin.[38] Now become aware that a more abundant treasure resides within you. The element of you that is eternal and constant is your ability to look within—with curiosity, compassion, honesty.[39]

This eternal element of you will become increasingly alive as you deepen your appreciation for every experience you've ever had. Each experience gives you the foundation to live in your purpose.

For instance, I used to practice law as a social-justice attorney. I struggled with my mission because I focused so much on the conflict I saw around me. Everything was a mess. I wanted to help. I was compelled to serve. But daily I felt anger. I carried rage for the hardships my clients faced. I boiled with hatred for the many obstacles that held them back. Certainly, the anger and hatred fueled me. It also burned in me. Clients lost their homes, lost their incomes, lost their families and resources. I fought daily to find support for them. Finally, the anger was my hurt. I shared misery and anxiety with friends and family. I felt injured, and I injured others with my sadness.

Without fully comprehending what was happening, I was engaged with my mission. I cared for everyone, but I didn't care for those who interfered with their well-being. I was applying my mission with too many conditions. I didn't understand that I needed to burn first.

---

[38] You may enjoy a practice of saying thank you to each sensation you find.
[39] You may enjoy a practice of thanking your curiosity, your compassion, and your honesty for what they've taught you.

I burned and burned until the anger burned out. I burned until I saw that whatever transpired for my clients was part of what they had to burn. I realized in the stark numbness that followed that we all have our missions. I have mine. My clients had theirs. I was part of the interference I'd loathed. Every fight I won or lost was to teach me about my mission, not interfere with theirs.

That was when I knew I had to learn to care without conditions. For everyone. Always.

As I evolved, I found the means to love without the fight. This doesn't mean I like every action of mine or of anyone else. It means I know how to look for the ways it contributes to the fulfillment of my mission.

It was a few years before I realized I had to deal with my suffering. I trembled through panic attacks until I finally decided to sit quietly through one of them. I chose to be grateful for whatever it might bring...even death, which felt entirely possible.

Instead of reacting, I watched. It came and went. I saw the holes in myself, like broken windows and failing doors. I saw how my best intentions kept escaping me through these hatred and anger-worn holes.

I had to become whole.

That was a holy realization. It was truth. I knew it immediately. It woke me up to every blessing I had. The sensation of it was vital, magnetic, and as serene as moonlight on water.

That was my first conscious choice to come home. I couldn't attend to others with any integrity or endurance until I could get home and heal what was broken or failing.

I chose to walk a peaceful path.

Eventually I would learn how to share it. Eventually I learned we can all love everything.

On that path I had to dismantle the anger and hatred. Like oil in the earth, they were a resource created by a once vital habitat. Like oil used too abundantly, they became toxic. I could be thankful for the ways they allowed me to develop and grow, but I no longer needed to abuse them. On my peaceful path, I sought kinder resources to fuel me.

> *If the red slayer think he slays,*
> *Or if the slain think he is slain,*
> *They know not well the subtle ways*
> *I keep, and pass, and turn again.*
> —*Ralph Waldo Emerson*

When you wake up to a trial and recognize its value, you're on your way. When you welcome it as a messenger with a highly personalized lesson, well, then you're on a well-lit path toward home. When you connect to what is eternal in you, then you're ready to know you.

Be patient with yourself. The journey takes a lifetime.

Yoga with the Eternal

Here's how you might sense the eternal.

Make yourself comfortable and take five nice deep breaths. Sometimes this practice can feel good to do as you walk. Other times you'll feel more supported in a chair or even lying down.

As you breathe, become aware of the condition of your body in the moment. Notice also the condition of your breath. Make a commitment to yourself: *I am attentive and curious; I'm coming home to myself.*

Now please call to mind a person, a place, or an idea that brings you joy. See this clearly in your mind. If you can't visualize easily, then simply allow yourself to remember the person, place, or idea. Now feel the effects of finding your friendly thought. Feel this inspiration deeply as you breathe. Allow your whole body to feel it. Notice how the feeling expands as you offer greater concentration to your joy-filled inspiration.

Be with this feeling for a while. Notice this sensation is yours. It is generated within at your impulse. You are the catalyst to bring it to being. And you are the one who sustains it. Feel this.

From this place, sensing joy, become aware of the persistent change around you. Listen in to sounds or notice the air moving. Notice the changes within you as well. You make certain shifts in your body. Tension arises and eases. The breath constantly moves you. Remain centered in your sensation of joy as you experience the constant change.

And now choose one changing factor in your life that often causes you to suffer. It may be that you've fought with a loved one. Maybe you've lost a job or are becoming aware of the effects of your age. Maybe you've lost someone. We all experience various difficult emotions as a result of persistent change. Choose one now.

As you inhale, allow yourself to experience the challenging emotion. Breathe it in.

As you exhale, recall the sensation of joy you experience when you call to mind your inspiration.

As you continue this process, realize the changes in your body as the emotion you've chosen begins to shift with every exhale. Be with this process for five, ten, or fifteen minutes. There is no limit to the time, and sometimes, depending on the emotion you choose, you may discover that the process can be quite quick or quite slow.

Without interrupting your focus, simply become aware of the changes you perceive as you continue.

Notice that it's you, a creature of joy, working with this emotion. This is the eternal. It is you, in that space of joy, love, and peace. Notice what you feel as you experience what is ever-present. Realize this eternal is always available to you.

You may like to offer this experience of joy through a prayer for those you love, for those in your community, or for all living creatures— that they too will find their way to realize their ever-present peace.

With a deep breath, offer thanks to your attention and will. Become aware of the sensation of your breath coming and going. Become aware of the position of your body and the space around you.

You may like to write about this experience. Or simply sit for a moment to rest.

Wisdom to Bring Home...

- You are more than you know. Look beyond the uncertainties to see what is eternal and stable in you.
- You are the sovereign of your domain in this life. You choose the manner of leadership you exercise over the many dimensions of you whom you've come to befriend. The more competent you become in befriending yourself, the more competent you will feel as you befriend others.
- As we become grateful for every moment and every experience, we no longer need to learn how to forgive.
- As we awaken to the truth of change and to an abiding presence that permeates it, we learn to cast the light of our awareness toward behaviors and relationships that honor this truth. We learn how to love without condition. This is who we are.
- We practice loving—joyfully and peacefully—in every moment.

To continue contemplating identity and spirit, please see the study guide at the end. The practices presented in this chapter reappear for your consideration. Sit with them. Be you with them.

11. You

What lies behind us and what lies before us are tiny matters compared to

what lies within us.

—*Emerson*

Our heart guides us home.

Remember You

Please say these words: I am.

Say them again.

I am.

I am.

I am.

Feel what it is to simply be. We are not a label, description, role, concept, or idea. We simply are. What does it feel like to be the host of everything? Coming home is a process of remembering this.

What we remember is the sublime importance of realizing who we are. The way we remember is by deciding we're ready. We choose to ask ourselves questions. We listen to our responses. We begin the beautiful process of getting to know ourselves. We open our eyes to ourselves. We see the world as our mirror. Every friend, partner, challenge, bird, tree, flower comes alive again, and so do we.

We say the words, *I am*.

In this discovery, we become aware we are constantly realizing ourselves. We've always been right there; we just didn't remember where or how to look.

When we remember the way to come home, we perceive ourselves, and it feels paradoxically new and completely familiar. The paradox exists because we're experiencing a new frame of reference. It's no longer based on what we've been told but on what we perceive, from moment to moment, in the abundance that life offers. This familiarity simply reminds us that the abundance is our birthright. The whole world lives in us.

The real voyage of discovery consists not in seeking new landscapes but in

having new eyes.

—Marcel Proust

We shift our gaze. We see again. Welcome home.

The process is much like confronting a beautiful poem for the first time. Although the manner of expression may overwhelm us at the start, what is expressed conveys the clarity of a truth we've always known. Coming home is realizing we are the poem and our poetry speaks the divine language of truth. There is no other poem like the one that speaks of you. And the way you interpret your lines and turns of phrases are for your investigation. Learning your poem is learning your life.

By now we can acknowledge that the poem of this life will end. The epic, however, continues. Homecoming awaits.

We're all going to die eventually. Long may we last. In the interim, all of life is waiting for each of us to come home. It's a simple idea that asks for commitment, patience, and faith. All of these will strengthen as we proceed.

The ancient wisdom advises that it's possible for some—a very few—to simply make the decision to return to their true nature. To simply say, "I'm home" and to see that there is only eternity in every moment, that there is no good or bad, that there is only connection in an illusion that persuades us of our idiosyncratic separateness. From these very few, who are also us, we might learn that the moment of their decision is the same as the moment of ours. We all make it again and again. Until we eventually acknowledge the truth: "I'm home." The complexity of the journey, for most of us, isn't in the steps we take but in the quality of our commitment. We don't even need to move an inch to remember our true nature. There is no requisite retreat to the high mountain caves of the Himalayas or ashrams serving gassy vegetarian meals.[40] Indeed, the journey asks for much less doing than we realize. No running around or puzzles or prayers or gurus or games required.[41]

Without opening your door, you can open your heart to the world.

Without looking out your window, you can see the essence of the Tao.

—Lao Tzu

---

[40] Please note, the discomfort of both journeys could be exactly what will help you shift your patterns of expectation and complaint. And vegetables do help lighten every step we take.

[41] Please note, the puzzles and prayers and gurus and games may all help you shift your patterns so you can see more clearly. All may be helpful; none are demanded.

We have a choice to remember, again and again, that we are always at home and the universe is at home with us. It may be easier to choose alternatively. It is certainly more common.

If we make the choice, however, we will be one person closer to making it common. Even better, we'll become more adept in the many skills that enable us to continue making it. Skills like empathy, gratitude, kindness, and equanimity strengthen us. The choice becomes our path.

Our best efforts can be directed toward observing ourselves honestly and shifting our weight away from the collective sham that we are these things we pretend to be.

It's a process of noticing and dismantling. It's a process of acknowledging and allowing. It's a process of deconditioning and release.

What's left when we let go of everything?

You.

Everything.

And us.

Luminous and clear and completely intertwined.

And this is so unfamiliar and occasionally uncomfortable. We recall we are uncomfortable in the shadows, uncomfortable under the control of those chaos agents. While we may be uncomfortable in the process of undoing, undressing, and shedding—that is, letting go—we will be our own agents. And we will begin to cherish the discomfort for what it teaches us. We'll discover a much greater ease.

So let us be grateful for teachers and everything we don't know, simultaneously. In both we find support as we confront our discomfort.

Guidance is precious, and puzzles, sometimes, are a relief. In a puzzle, at least, we settle into the awareness that we aren't meant to understand until we do. We go beyond our common sense to the humble place where we ask questions and await solutions. Often a teacher enters.[42]

While the finger pointing to the moon isn't the moon, it is certainly a kind gesture if we hadn't been looking up. And the mystery of the moon's mesmerizing size when it hangs low at the horizon is a wonder that generates great awe. We are humbled once again. We come back to the wonder of our existence.

The plain fact for many is that it's easier not to bother. It may be that we have customs that have us sitting around, grumbling, and complaining—moving without attention through each unique moment of life. We don't see a thing.

If the path before you is clear, you're probably on someone else's.

—*Joseph Campbell*

With all that distraction, how could we? Most of us keep one anxious eye on the future and one sad, slightly disappointed eye on the past. When we don't see, it's easier to stay put. And it's easier, for sure, not to see.

Have you noticed, however, that ignorance is only blissful until it's not?

---

[42] It is said that a teacher appears when we're ready. I like to remember that everyone is a teacher, and this keeps me in constant readiness.

You wouldn't be reading this if you'd found contentment in ignorance.[43] Your heart has guided you to this moment—to a recognition that home is awaiting you.

Once we have a sense that our ignorance isn't serving us, going back is untenable. You've awakened; if you try to return to sleep, your heart will call you in your dreams. Even if you squeeze your eyes shut, your path is ongoing. You'll trip more in your refusal to see. At some point your eyes will pop open again.

> *However long the night, the dawn will break.*
> *—African proverb*

Still, if you feel compelled to stay in the dark, please try. Report back and let me know how it works.

From what I've experienced, it feels as awkward as it is cynical: forced smiles, tense bodies, a lot of pretending, and anger that creeps up like a thief. We know we've delayed our journey toward home.

We know this is a detour.

Maybe it feels easier than committing to ourselves. But it begins to hurt. The pain—physical and emotional—increases as we become frustrated by a repetitive cycle.

---

[43] And pharmaceutical companies wouldn't be making huge profits on pills that aim to diminish despair. And our energy of consumption wouldn't flow toward purchases of more things we don't need. And we'd remember to say thank you before we complain about any of the conditions of our life.

Regardless of the terrain, the path continues. Even stuck on a roundabout, the path is ongoing. We have to choose, again and again, to listen to our heart's call. We continue our journey home. And we have the privilege of choosing, if we remember, the quality of our adventure. Doing this requires the deep strength to surrender to every moment. The heart grows more robust in its guidance.

What is this heart?

Take this moment and feel the space of your physical heart. Notice its bump bump bump. Just to the center of this space, you can feel into another heart—a quieter one, the place of an unstruck sound in us. Feel this heart space for a moment and notice the sensations you find. In the Yoga Sutra, we're taught that thorough meditation on this heart space brings us an understanding of our pure minds.[44]

Another way of putting this: When we honor our hearts, we learn to become aware of everything life has to offer.

We learn that everything is offered for the benefit of our awareness. This is what the heart shares.

Will you direct energy toward engaging thankfully with every moment?

Every bird song and every car horn, every happy dog and every dog barking all night, every complaint and every criticism: these are all packages wrapped up especially for you. How will you appreciate them? Will you try to return them all, or do you have the means to appreciate the gift and find a lovely way to integrate it?

---

[44] Find this verse at Chapter 3, Verse 34 of the Yoga Sutra of Patanjali.

Practice Being

I have a dear friend who wants to claim happiness. He really, really, really wants it. He reads about it and thinks about it. On his days off, he tells his friends about it. And then every weekday morning, he gets up and decides anew: happiness is mine.

This friend can be called Joshua.

What a lovely mission Joshua has. This happiness is his heart calling. It's asking for his attention.

Throughout the day, however, Joshua's hunt for happiness falters as he starts to perceive life stalking him. He feels like the target of misery. He receives calls from his colleagues and family and hears their pain. He stands at his job and sees his dissatisfaction reflected in his customers' faces.

By the end of the day, he wonders if he deserves to find happiness. When he comes home late, tired, he feels like a failure because another day passed without the appearance of happiness. He has a glass of wine. Then another. He tunes out, and soon he's asleep. He says he always wakes up on the couch just before midnight, with a realization that he did the same damn thing again.

This is how his obstacles and all the shadows they cast overwhelm the sweet song in his heart. His mission is overwhelmed by the patterns of his personality.

The next morning he renews his quest for happiness.

And promptly gets lost again in the search.

His morning commitment was simple and sweet. Joshua just didn't have a good set of directions to take it into the world. He knew his destination but wasn't clear on how to get there.

This is where the simplicity of choice demands the beautiful complexity of commitment.

Please rest assured that the only complexity will always be of your construction. Still it's worthwhile to see how you engineer your own obstacles, so you can understand how you're the one with the power to dismantle them.

For Joshua, to take his quest beyond his front door meant consenting to allow the world into his adventure.

Happiness isn't a quality that stands idly on a street corner waiting to be recognized. Happiness is a quality to be discovered within and poured onto every surface of life.

Joshua's decision to become happy was simply the first choice in a series of choices to be made. He saw that happiness was available to him. His next action was to experience it within himself.

To find it, he started a stillness practice. In the quiet clarity of his mornings, when his commitment renewed with the new day, he started to spend a few moments quietly contemplating the moments of happiness he'd already found in life. In these quiet moments, he felt the physical sensations that arose with his recollection of happiness. He felt them again.

He also noted the thoughts that would come up to dismiss these feelings. He could see that these thoughts would move in quickly but didn't have to distract him. It was always his call.

With this practice, he realized he was the agent of happiness. He could call on it when he wanted. It wasn't waiting for him in the world out there. It was alive in him at every moment that he chose to feel it.

This became his epiphany: the portability of happiness. What he discovered in these quiet morning moments was completely contained within him, thus convenient to carry and access throughout the day. His heart brought him home. His home is within.

He simply had to choose to return.

Complexity arises once again.

As is the experience of so many of us, Joshua's mood would often sink when he was exposed to the sinking moods of others. Again, as in the case of so many, this whirlpool effect made him think he would have to isolate himself from the world in order to keep from drowning in the despair of his friends, family, and others.

The opposite is true.

While it may be the case that isolation is serene, most of us don't live like hermits. Nor do we have the means to do so.

Our world is full of people and activity. We share the world with these fellow earthlings doing their earthly chores.

Periods of retreat are beautiful antidotes to the racing pulse of society, but they aren't feasible for most of us over the long term. If they are, and you choose this, enjoy and be well. For the rest of us, a life of total renunciation is less appropriate. Where would our children, lovers, and pets wait for us?[45] Our task, therefore, is to learn how to engage with the race without being run over.

Can you engage with each moment as it comes and accept all of its possibilities?

We're the only ones who live this life. The journey we make through it is the mission of our heart. Our heart is guiding us home.

It may seem as though every moment of our lives is dictated by activities beyond our control. We may insist that our life has delivered more challenge to us than anyone should suffer. We may protest that we have nothing to do with any of it. Folks like to say, "What did I do to deserve this?" I say, "You received the precious gift of life."

Before Joshua discovered he was the vessel of his happiness he used to complain that I didn't get it. He would say, "I didn't choose any of this."

I would ask, "Would you prefer the alternative?"

He would say, "I work to make money, and I have this family who complains all the time. It's not like I can ditch it all."

I would ask, "So why not accept it all on the friendliest terms?" We're the ones who can become the friend.

We're the ones who can be happy.

We're the ones who can carry happiness within us.

We're the ones who can freely consent to this life and all it offers.

---

[45] A Catholic nun once shared with me that her choice to renounce the family life made her spiritual work much easier. She enjoyed ample silence uninterrupted by partners or children. She wondered whether she might be required in another life to become a mother of many children to test the strength of her faith.

The other option is a fight, and we won't win. It's a rejection of the forces that created us.

We're the ones living this life. Will you consent to live it?

You're the one living your life.

This world may present every horror to your doorstep; you have a choice. Will you embrace every aspect of this world or choose to reject it and stumble over every bit of reality you don't like?

Your way is the way. The wisdom of the prudent is to discern his way.

—Proverbs 14:8

We may not be able to pave our path, but we certainly choose how to travel on it.

In every decision we make, a potential arises that may send us toward a gentle winding walkway through a meadow or up a barely discernible pass on the face of a sheer cliff.

What are you ready for? Choose wisely. That's the simplicity available to us.

Complexity arises because we lag in our commitment to embrace simplicity.

Many of us who've been congratulated for working hard come to believe that our worth is dependent on the way we push our agendas. We become forceful instead of graceful. We spend our energy aiming to conquer instead of dismantling whatever is preventing us from letting the energy flow with the world around us.

Often the easiest possibility is the one we don't perceive as accessible.

We've all had the experience of watching a friend, or maybe ourselves, work through a problem in the most ridiculously clumsy way. If we're lucky, when we arrive at the solution, we see how we might have saved ourselves a bit of burden. Sometimes, we even see the problem wasn't a problem. It was a solution awaiting discovery.

There's a story a friend told me a long time ago. She said, "When we're walking our path up the mountain, we think there's only one way to go. And we worry about getting lost. We choose a hard route and fall. We choose another route and find ourselves circling the same tree for a while. At a certain point, we summit. When we look down, we see so many paths we didn't take. We realize they all lead to the same place."[46] Which brings us back to our paths.

How does it feel to discover we're on it? Feel the path beneath your feet and choose how you'd like to navigate. Will you quiet yourself enough to hear your heart's guidance? Whatever we find along the journey is part of our heart's mission. We may not understand it as we choose, but whatever choice we make is meant for us to understand.

The level of responsibility can be daunting. Every step asks for a consideration. Then again, every step offers a reply. Our path is our personal feedback loop.

When we start to pay attention, we notice guideposts are everywhere. We might discount them as funny coincidences for a while. Eventually, we realize that coincidences are wonderfully meaningful

---

[46] She added, "Remember, from the summit we always see clearly another mountain to climb." So be it. Thank you to every teacher who reminds us to persevere.

points of validation. One incident occurs at the same time as another, and we're in the right space and time to perceive it...what an absolute boon.

We've discussed how fortunate we are to even be alive. We are so unlikely, and yet we are. How can we possibly dismiss the power of any event when we acknowledge the odds against every occurrence?

We have the freedom to shift our route at every moment.

Sometimes we cower at freedom because it's so uncertain.

It ensures possibility and requires our ability to respond. It can mean loneliness in our courage. It can provoke suspicion or derision among friends who don't trust our faith.

In freedom we must always remember that our business is ourselves. What others think about us is their concern and their weight to carry.

We may not know what our path will bring, but in our freedom to pursue it, we trust that every experience will be the lesson we require. We step forward with trust in ourselves to remember that every opportunity is a gift. Our lives unfold as we become willing to experience the sun and all the shadows falling away from the obstacles on our path.

We realize that life is living through us.

So look around. Walk a good course with an open heart. Consider your physical, emotional, and energetic well-being. Engage with the obstacles and learn about the shadows they cast. Listen to careful and experienced guides. Share your experiences, so we all learn from each other.

Rest assured, even with our best intentions and our best efforts, we'll continue to encounter obstacles on our path. We'll stumble again and again. Sometimes we'll fall down. Consider every fall a blessing. Each time we find ourselves sprawled out on the floor, we can acknowledge how we continue to overcome our beliefs. That it's safer to build walls than to open our hearts to the world, that we must first judgment instead of compassion, that we sometimes point a finger when the responsibility is ours. We can even say thank you to this training. It was important and helped us at a time when our resources were scarce. It helped us arrive in this moment.

Little by little,

You will turn into stars.

Even then, my dear,

You will only be

A crawling infant,

Still skinning your knees on God.

—Hafez

In this moment we can savor the hum of life in everything. We feel it—as distinct within us as it is around us.

We commit to this moment again.

We've seen how navigating the way back requires a patient practice. The practice happens every moment we respect our bodies, use our minds, tame our opinions, and expand our hearts. Each of these tasks is a practice. The practice is our effort to make.

We must make the effort and let go of any expectation of results. We make the effort not because we expect anything. We make the effort because we're the only ones responsible for ourselves.

We can't hire an attorney or a doctor or a housecleaner to fix the world, rid us of woes, or clean up our act. Or we can. But we'll be disappointed when we continue to find ourselves feeling the persistent nag of our heart. It will tell us again and again that we aren't comfortable. We'll fire the help and still find ourselves homesick. We haven't remembered how to get home.

We make the effort ourselves. We make the effort *for* ourselves.

We pursue the personal practices that help us realize our connection with all of existence. We learn to release whatever prevents us from offering kindness to everything and everyone. We discover that lovers and far-flung strangers are not just a part of us; they *are* us.

We commit to ourselves, and we do it because this commitment to ourselves, in all our dimensions, is the first step in serving others.

When we remember ourselves, we also remember that everything and everyone we've ever encountered is also us. As we become comfortable exploring what is within, we discover our greater comfort in the world beyond. As we befriend ourselves, we discover our competence as friends. We understand we share with others an inclination to love.

We understand the within is also above and beyond us.

Within you and around you are the spaces hosting all that has always been sacred to you. This spaciousness supports your every move. Within you and around you, filling this space, is your connection to grace.

Pause for a moment and consider your response to that.

Not merely to the concept of what is sacred. Consider your response to the word itself. Also to grace.

Are these words you frequently use?

As removed as the words may be from our regular conversation, the concepts are ingrained in us. We're the ones limiting ourselves from gaining the elevation to include them in our dialogue. And yet we feel these words. Truly, we feel them.

We have an easier time feeling these words than we do trying to feel an electron or proton. And yet electrons and protons have our easy, intellectual confidence. We can't understand the formulas that surmise their presence. We can't see them. Still we are certain of them.

That's called faith.

So what's in the way of accepting grace?

Grace we actually feel.

Consider times you've experienced the humbling realization that you're exactly where you're meant to be. Consider the playful connection in a baby's gaze. The kind eyes of a stranger holding the door for you.

The sacred...we feel that.

Consider the sunrise, a storm on approach, a grandmother's hug.

Like love. Feel that. The absolute support of it.

We rejoice in the presence of these holy events.

Let's rejoice together in them.

They are eminently familiar to us and available in our surrendered thought. The issue is we prefer to think and think and think under some pretense that we might know.

We won't.

It may be that the best function of our thoughts is to lead us to the realization that thinking doesn't get us home.

The best we can do is be good people, offer kindness all around, and embark on a process of self-evaluation using whatever techniques will serve us until we realize that grace is what transforms us. Our transformation is another holy event. Our role is simply stripping ourselves of everything that keeps us from feeling whole and holy.

At that point we'll realize that it isn't what we do, but how we created space for grace.

I'll say it again: *It isn't what you do; it's what you allow.*

Finding your way to grace is finding your way home. Whatever practice you pursue, whatever discipline you maintain, does it make room for grace or create additional barriers to its entry?

May the consequences of your every effort open you to grace.

Maybe you let go of pride and ask for help. Maybe you release guilt and take action to make peace. Maybe you free yourself of fear. You choose.

Decide to practice and make space.

Don't worry about the results. Just keep walking in a homeward direction. That is, go within. Or go outside to head inside. Light a candle to head inside. Find a beautiful prayer, and head inside. Seek assistance as you head inside. Notice the others walking near you. Know that we return home and find them with us. We don't follow them. Our shared journey is the holy event.

Remember You and Your Connections

As we proceed, cultivate deep thankfulness for your connections. These are our true foundations. We may create them with people or animals or trees or bugs. Or all of the above. We may have a fervent and abiding correspondence with the stars. Or maybe we feel the wind in our bones and the sun in our blood.

However we connect with the world is up to us and our attention. The fact of our connection with the world is the source of our very vitality. It is the warp and woof of love we've offered and received.

We are the tapestry.

We are the net. We support each other. We catch each other. We embrace each other.

We are the entire world, and our purpose is nothing more than to discover and share it with every experience and creature that weaves itself into life.

We may be discouraged by a habitual respect for authority. The authority is also you. We are of the divine and inspired by every divine creation. We are energy formed as matter. We are a composite of the entire cosmos, and the cosmos is also us.

We are already one. But we imagine that we are not. And what we have to recover is our original unity. What we have to be is what we are.

— Thomas Merton

We're connected. We're perfect in this moment.

Will you accept life as a gift and write an openhearted thank-you note? Will you honor the source of love by becoming one? Will you share what you've learned so love's volume will increase?

This is our power. We don't cause the sun to rise, but we can welcome the light. We don't choose the end of day, but we can respect the darkness. We have a purpose, and the purpose is life itself. To learn it and share it. To love it well.

When we realize, we no longer need to suffer. We have a choice. We find ourselves at home with the whole universe.

Come home.

Yoga to Come Home

Sit comfortably and feel your breath. Say thank you to your body for allowing you a vessel from which you can appreciate the coming and going of every breath.

Say thank you to your inhale for the vitality it brings you.

Say thank you to your exhale for all it removes.

Say thank you to your mind for finding the breath and knowing how it serves you in this vast, infinite world.

Say thank you to your wonderful patterns of behavior, emotion, and thought with this vast, infinite world that weave together to support your ability to arrive home.

Say thank you to your home, for always waiting for you. Listen to how it thanks you for returning.

Say thank you to your mother and father for creating this unique existence of you. And to their mothers and fathers for finding each other, so you could find home.

Say thank you to your teachers, for guiding you, disciplining you, challenging you, loving you, so you found the strength and resilience to come home.

Say thank you to your friends for laughing and crying with you as you wandered toward, around, beyond, and, finally, near home.

Say thank you to every other creature who, like you, is moving homeward.

Thank you is always the prayer.

We are all one. And we're all heading home.

You are sacred. Grace is everywhere. We are the holy event. Thank you for being you.

Wisdom to Bring Home...

- Coming home is a process and a practice. Listen to your heart and the guidance it provides. Choose to come home day by day, moment by moment. Enjoy the journey through every moment.
- We all have access to our own wisdom, our own gratitude, our own love. Each of us—no matter who we are, where we live, how we worship—carries the memories of our journey home.
- Pay attention to the ways you serve yourself. This will show you how you serve others.
- You are sacred. You are holy. When you remember this state by feeling it, you will share the feeling freely.
- We are all at home together. We are all collaborators, companions, friends, family.

To continue contemplating identity and spirit, please see the study guide at the end. The practices presented in this chapter reappear for your consideration. Sit with them. Be you with them.

Epilogue

You are the poem.

I love you.

May you become aware and grateful for every wonderful high and low you've known.

May you cast your light on every support that carries you through life—your body, your mind, your personality, your spirit and the spirit of every living creature. May you say thank you.

May you learn to dissolve every barrier you've erected and feel your eternal connection with everything. May you appreciate every knot in the tapestry of your life.

May you appreciate every movement, every breath, every discovery you make as you realize the wonder of your home. May you realize how precious they are.

May you realize you are the poem.

May you always say thank you as you awaken.

May you love all.

When I walk outside

all I want

is to be with everything.

Don't you?

To be is fine.

To be with

is heaven.

No need to choose.

Only, open the doors.

A bee, humming in pleasant busyness,

over an elated cosmos.

A pinkening life, with all her sisters and brothers and cousins,

celebrating the good fortune of togetherness.

A dragonfly eager to guide me though the narrows.

A puddle awaiting its return to the sea.

Let's say the queenly moon even, beautiful in every aspect.

And when I sit inside,

all I want

is everything

being me.

The hum.

My limbs loose in the breeze.

My memories rising and catching currents to be crunched under someone

else's foot.

So when I breathe,

the air coming in is everything.

We mingle.

So when I breathe,

the air going out is everything.

We go home.

And I don't mind anymore

that everything comes and goes.

I mind only that I remember,

eternally,

to let it.

—Megan Doyle

Practices to Explore

Do your practice and all is coming.

—Sri K. Pattabhi Jois

Each of these practices is intended to take you toward self-awareness. If we don't venture honestly through our ways, emotions, thoughts, and patterns, we'll never know what is standing in our way and what is moving us along our path.

You're welcome to read through them again and again to familiarize yourself with the process, but that can be a challenge. To make it a little easier, you can also visit them as recordings at: **knowthyselfyoga.com/homepractices.**

Please be patient and muster whatever compassion you can; please be a friend to yourself.

In the process of befriending ourselves, we come face to face with our mistakes, our challenges, our weaknesses, and our bad behaviors. We may not see ourselves in a very friendly way. Rest assured, we've all made mistakes, faced challenges, and behaved poorly. The more we acknowledge and accept these facts, the more competent we become as friends…to ourselves and others. We see how much we all struggle and overcome. We see how much we all want to turn away from pain. We learn to be friendly toward all experiences, whether they bring the giggles or the pain.

You are wonderful and perfect. You will marvel at yourself as you learn to become an honest and loyal friend.

One: Yoga with Presence

You exist.

Here's your first practice. Please follow along.

Take a deep breath. Realize the fact of your existence.

You are, right now, a human being. You exist.

You dwell within a composite of some tens of trillions of cells that create the form of you over and over again. Smile at the wonder of this form.

You are breathing. You expand and contract with every breath. Notice this. Smile at your breath, coming and going.

Your attention is noticing. Notice this as well. You may have a dull awareness or a sharp recognition of the fact that you're watching you. That's you too.

You may like it or not. Also you.

And you may, possibly, experience a comfort in the exercise. A sweet gratitude to see and be seen. You.

You are someone who has loved, been loved and loving, regardless of reciprocity or propriety. You.

Notice you, among everything in your surroundings right now. And notice how you are, remarkably, connected with all of it. As soon as you put your attention on every form and face around you, you establish a relationship in this very moment. It may be as fleeting as the moment itself, but still. You.

Please smile at the presence of you.

That's it. The most basic exercises are not the easiest. But they are worthwhile.

Will you commit to practicing every morning for a week? A good time is when you first wake up. You can make note of the practice and keep it next to your bed. You might choose the following shorthand message to yourself: *Remember all of you.*

When you wake up, read the words and remember: you.

This is you deciding to connect.

Two: Yoga with Breath

Every breath brings you home.

Let's do a small practice together.

Please become aware of your breath.

As you feel the breath moving into your body, silently say, "My body receives this breath."

When it feels right, please exhale. As you feel the breath moving out of your body, silently say, "My body releases this breath."

Do this about five more times. Feel both sides of your breath in your body.

Where do you feel your body receiving and releasing the breath?

As you inhale again, please thank your body for breathing.

"Thank you, body, for breathing in."

Feel your thanks expand as you acknowledge how precious, fulfilling, and lifesaving every breath actually is.

As you exhale again, please thank your body for breathing.

"Thank you, body, for breathing out."

Feel your thanks expand as you realize how much relief every exhale offers.

Please do this about five more times.

Every breath—your inhale and your exhale—gives you access to your most essential nutrient in this life. We can live without food for a while, without water for a shorter time. Without breath, we don't last long at all.

"Thank you, body, for letting every breath arrive and go. I'm grateful you breathe."

Three: Yoga with the Body

Your beautiful body is instrumental to your journey home.

Let's practice yoga with the body.

In a comfortable position, either on your back or in a chair, please consider these questions, one at a time, for a few moments before you continue with the sequence of simple movements below.

- What is this form you inhabit? What is your body made of?
- Can you feel its weight, any areas of tension or ease?
- Can you sense its layers, the movement of your breath through it, and the subtle vibration of energy in it?
- How do you treat this body? What do you commonly say to it? What don't you say?

- How does it feel to say thank you to this body? Let "Thank you, my good friend" be your mantra as you continue to the exercise below.

Now try these simple movements.

<u>Position One</u>

Rest on your back, with your legs gently straight on the ground or with knees supported by a pillow.

Find your breath. Recognize your inhale and exhale. You'll move with the breath.

On an inhale, please bring your arms up and over your head toward the floor behind you. As you exhale, please bring your arms back to your sides. Do this about eight times, moving carefully with your breath.

<u>Position Two</u>

Stay on your back, but bend your knees, so your feet are flat on the ground and about hip-width apart.

Find your breath again. You'll continue to move with the breath.

On an inhale, gently lift the bum up by pressing the feet into the ground, strengthening your legs and lengthening the spine. On an exhale slowly lower the bum back to the ground.

Do this about eight times, moving carefully with the breath.

<u>Position Three</u>

Still on your back, bring your knees toward your chest. Place your hands on your knees.

You'll continue to move with the breath.

On an inhale, feel the expansion of your ribcage. Let the knees move gently away from your chest, just to the point where your fingers can still rest on your kneecaps. On an exhale, let the knees move gently toward the chest, keeping the knees hip-width and the feet relaxed. Once again, do this eight times, moving attentively with the breath.

Now feel the sensations in your body after these small simple movements. It doesn't take much to enliven our bodies. Please say thank you to your bodies, and then take some time to rest for a bit.

Four: Yoga with Words

Focus on the sound and meaning of what you say to yourself.

Let's be in the moment together.

Read the following words aloud: *I am.*

Read these words aloud again: *I am.*

Feel who, what, and how you are. Watch how quickly you want to identify yourself based on notions of the past or present. Instead allow yourself to notice what you are now.

Your body is probably sitting or reclining. Your breath is coming or going. You are engaged in the act of being you.

Read these words: *This is.*

Look around and see what is. Not how you'd like it or how it was. Just everything around you perfectly as it is. Notice how it cannot be any other way than it is right now. It will change and is in the process of doing so, but right now it is.

Read these words aloud: *I love this moment.*

Feel that. Notice what comes up from the past and future to persuade you otherwise. Or, if nothing arises, simply love this moment.

Five: Yoga with the Mind

Pay attention to your habits of mind.

Let's consider reactions and responses.

Someone steps in front of you in line at the store. You feel anger arising.

You feel the injustice of losing your hard-earned position. This minor injustice morphs into a generalized anxiety that you are not doing enough, and now you're worried that you don't have enough money to pay for groceries that someone wants to sell at such a high price.

Now your heart is racing; you're mean to the cashier, who makes less money than you do and only wanted to know if you needed a bag. Suddenly you're disappointed in this grocery adventure, and you anticipate the traffic in the parking lot. (You'll probably scratch your car door when you get to the parking lot.)

I'm sorry, my friend. That was a reaction gone awry.

Your uncontrolled mind did that.

Here's another option.

This morning you decide, "I'm good for whatever this day delivers." You head to the store. The girl cuts in line, and you start to feel the injustice but remember your promise. "I'm good."

You smile at her instead. You ask about her day. The girl apologizes and says she's spaced out because she had an odd experience at work and her boss is mad. You say nice things because you've been there.

Now the cashier loves you, and you get a free bag and smiles all around. The girl invites you to a party over the weekend that her boss is giving. He's actually a prince, and it's in his castle. She says, "Don't worry about what to wear. Just wear jeans." Now you're awesome, and you're heading to a prince's party.

New pattern developing! That's a mind you're guiding.

Six: Yoga with a Friendly Mind

Here's a practice to move toward greater cooperation with the mind. It's so simple and can serve us a lifetime. At its heart it's a concentration exercise. But it will also help you refine your sensory awareness and your powers of acceptance.

Sit quietly and comfortably. As you breathe, become aware of the condition of your body in the moment. Notice also the condition of your breath. Make a nice commitment to yourself: *I am attentive and curious; I do this practice to come home to myself.*

Become aware that you live in your body. Be aware that you reside in a physical existence and from this place you watch your interactions with the world around you. Sense the ground beneath you. Sense the moisture in your body. Sense the heat in you. Sense the feeling of air on your skin. Sense the space around you and within you.

Notice the breath.

Now become aware that the mind is offering an abundance of thoughts in relation to these experiences.

Watch them arise, grow, move, fade. Remain passive, neutral, equanimous. If you find yourself judging the thoughts, observe this with a simple statement: *I am judging this thought instead of observing it.* If you find yourself following a thought, simply come back to your point of observation and forgive the mind for wandering.

I like to say this: *Oh dear mind, I've let you run off again. Please return, so I can watch what comes and goes.*

And then I watch. Without judgment. With pure love.

As you watch, begin to notice a space developing between every thought.

And say thank you. To the abundant capacity of the mind to experience this world. To the world for offering you an experience. To the way you're remembering how to see beyond the mind.

Seven: Yoga with the Moment

Every moment offers a map that will guide you home.

Here's a practice to become connected to the moment.

Sit comfortably, or even lie down if you're sure you won't fall asleep.

Now tune your senses in, one by one, to everything around you. Awaken to your surroundings.

First, notice the ground beneath you. Feel its stability and support. Now turn your attention toward the scents that the earth provides. No need to try to find smells. Just notice what smells are available to you.

Feel into the qualities of water within you. You may notice the moisture in your eyes, nose, mouth. Become aware of taste simply by checking in with your tongue.

Now find light by opening your eyes as you gently inhale and closing them as you gently exhale. No need to control or strain your breathing. Simply notice the light beyond you and within you.

Become aware of the feeling of air on your skin. Notice that the surface of your skin is as much a bridge as a barrier to the space that surrounds you.

Finally, become aware of the sense of spaciousness surrounding you. Hear any sounds, and do so without classification or identification. Simply listen.

Spend a few moments now experiencing the moment as a whole, a compilation created by your sense of smell, taste, sight, touch, and hearing. See if you can allow your senses to share information with your mind without any interference. If a loud noise or offensive smell arises, allow it without judgment. If you feel uncomfortable, allow it, and move if you must. Welcome all sensation if you can. I like to say these words, *Oh, hi, you're here too. Thank you for being here.* Choose your own words to allow all sensation to simply be with you.

Spend about five minutes a day with this exercise and notice how your perception of activity begins to shift.

Eight: Yoga with Energy

Life moves through you, around you, and within you.

Let's take a moment to consider our relationship with energy.

The elegant and ancient system of Ayurveda, a sister science of yoga, offers a useful framework for our self-analysis. By asking us to consider our preferences and traits, it helps us to identify the way energy moves in us.

Please answer for yourself the following questions.

10. Are you…
    A. a bit slow to start but sure to finish
    B. actively ready for whatever project comes your way
    C. curious about everything but committed to very little
11. Do you like to…
    A. sit around
    B. keep intellectually busy
    C. stay in constant motion
12. Do you prefer…
    A. lots of friends
    B. only the right friends
    C. friends who come and go
13. Would you choose…
    A. to admire and collect art
    B. to critique art
    C. to make art
14. Are you…
    A. slow to learn and slow to forget
    B. curious and ready to learn more
    C. quick to learn and quick to forget
15. Do you eat…
    A. too much and when you don't feel hungry
    B. so you don't get angry
    C. occasionally, when you remember
16. Do you…
    A. comfort others
    B. intimidate others
    C. play with others

17.   Would you rather…
   A.   ignore conflict
   B.   win arguments
   C.   let things pass
18.   If someone hurts you, do you…
   A.   hold a grudge
   B.   maintain a justified resentment
   C.   forget there was ever an issue

Now consider your answers. Tally up your As, Bs, and Cs. It is absolutely normal to have a predominance of one or two. Some folks will have an even distribution.

Part two of this practice is to think a bit imaginatively. Ayurveda suggests that energy moves through you as it does in nature. You are a creature of nature.

In Ayurveda every person is said to be a composite of the five elements of nature: space, air, fire, water, and earth. The elements are evolutes or manifestations of essential life conditions: activity, stability, and consciousness. Think of it like this: life vibrates. Slow down a vibration, and you find the rise, the fall, and the space between them. Like breath itself. We inhale and expand, exhale and contract, and there's a space between each expansion and contraction in which we simply are.

All of life is created by the interweaving of these life conditions, and every experience is born of the shifting dominance of one or more of them. For example, if you feel weighted down by a challenging conversation, you are sensing an overwhelming feeling of stability. If you feel enraged by a bad act or distracted by pain, you're encountering a surge of the active force. Maybe you can think of the harmony and calm you feel while listening to a beautiful piece of music. This would be the clarity of the conscious force.

Every form in the universe is said to be made of all three, vibrating at various frequencies. As a creature of nature, you are a realization of these frequencies. You're a unique vibration of energy. You're a tapestry that takes its shape through the elements born of the three primary forces. You're energy manifested through a beautiful composition of earth, water, fire, air, and space.

Returning to the results of our quiz...

Lots of As suggest an earthy, watery person. This person may be a bit heavier in the body, with energy that moves somewhat slowly. Stagnation can happen; laziness can happen; depression can happen. These are the folks who give great hugs and know how to comfort others, often with food.

Lots of Bs suggest a watery, fiery person. This person may be a strong leader, prone to anger, and quick-witted. Because of that wit and that heat, these folks know exactly how to hurt someone. They may intimidate others, but they get their work done.

Lots of Cs suggest an airy, spacy person. This person is usually thin, highly creative, very good at brainstorming, and not always certain to execute the plan. While these folks may not prove the most reliable, they always know how to set things in motion. This is an innovator but not someone to hold to a schedule.

Nine: Yoga with Kindness

Your kindness is the first step toward home.

Please take a moment to review the kindness you've extended over the last twenty-four hours.

Please be kind to yourself as you make note. Include even the simplest act. A door held open. A small smile toward a stranger. A pause to allow someone to pass.

Now notice the spaces that could have used your kindness. It's okay if you didn't give it. Just notice. Maybe you see a scowl on a cashier's face. Maybe you saw a mother struggling with her kids. Maybe it was you, feeling low.

Even if you missed the opportunity earlier, you have the opportunity now. While we can never go back in time, we always heal through the present moment.

Take a moment to choose a few responses you could have offered in the spaces that wanted kindness.

Watch yourself offering your kindness.

Share your kindness and watch how it spreads beyond you.

Feel your kindness growing through the ripples you created.

Ten: Yoga with Obstacles

Sometimes we get in our own way.

A useful practice is to make a commitment every morning to love everything. Although this may seem like a practice in loving, the challenge is actually to strengthen our discernment.[47] To love everything, we need to know how to choose wisely.

---

[47] Truly, we don't require practice in loving. It's who we are. We may be sheltered by so many obstacles that we've forgotten but under all the rubble, there's the love.

Take a moment to see how an obstacle has appeared on your path lately. Consider what has kept you from deeply loving every moment you've experienced in the last day. As you do this, remember you're not alone with your obstacles. We all have them, and we all have the responsibility of learning how to dissolve them.

Maybe you judge everyone you meet. Judging others is a surefire technique to ensure our own suspicion that everyone is judging you. We find ourselves vulnerable to embarrassment, guilt, shame, fear that someone is going to realize our weaknesses.

Maybe you keep telling lies. Our dishonesty often leaves us with a sense of instability and shame. Our hearts know the world is all right the way it is, but our lies insist on making it otherwise. We've all done it. We tell a lie and gently excuse ourselves with an insistence to our conscience that it was really nothing. But we still feel the sting.

Maybe you feel insecure in your job or relationship. This insecurity can bleed into other experiences and lead to an overall sense of distrust in the way things are. You may even find camaraderie with others when you complain about your work or partner, but it doesn't really feel like fulfilling friendship.

Maybe you're going so hard in your activities that you can't remember how to have fun. Alternatively, maybe you're feeling dull. You can't even remember what fun feels like. Sometimes we compensate for these imbalances by settling more deeply into them. When we go hard, we feel like the way out has to be just as hard. Likewise, if we're dull, we may just give into the couch. We make patterned choices that deepen the pattern itself. And we wonder why we keep feeling pain and discomfort.

Maybe you're just feeling like you can't win. Your progress is slipping, and you feel like quitting. Sometimes we feel disappointed when we start to compare ourselves with others. We start thinking we aren't succeeding if we don't measure up to the standards of others. We forget to see how much we've learned, how well we've recovered from challenges, and how *our* standards have improved because of *our* hard work.

As you look toward your day, you may discover that every single obstacle is an opportunity to make a difficult choice. We can choose to feel limited by our behaviors and feel the challenge of them, or we can choose to change our behaviors and feel the challenge of the work. We have the privilege of getting to choose wisely.

Based on your observations, choose one of the following mantras, or shape one to suit you. Invite the mantra to become your guide to sharing love.

Today, I am kind. Today, kindness guides me.

Today, I am honest. Today, honesty guides me.

Today, I am generous. Today, generosity guides me.

Today, I am balanced. Today, balance guides me.

Today, I am grateful. Today, gratitude guides me.

Now take a seat and examine your breath. Feel the movement of your inhale and your exhale in the body. Expand your awareness beyond your breath to the guidance you've chosen.

As you inhale, silently say the first part of the mantra to yourself.

As you exhale, silently say the second part of the mantra to yourself.

See how it feels to make this commitment. At the end of the day, notice how your responses to the day improved due to your commitment. Notice when you failed to follow the guidance you chose. Become aware of the thoughts, emotions, or judgments that steered you away from your commitment.

Affirm to yourself: *I have a choice at every moment. I will choose wisely.*

Eleven: Yoga with Our Players

We forget that we're performing.

Please take a moment to respond to the following thoughts.

Describe the qualities of your ego.

Describe the qualities of your intellect.

Describe the qualities of your identity.

Now contemplate these ideas of yourself and notice how they're different players in the same story. We can think of them as actors in the story of you.

Also notice how your resistance to the word *ego* is probably slightly greater than it is toward the words *intellect* and *identity*. Maybe you were a little more reluctant to consider your ego's contributions. We tend to have a certain notion about the ego being a bit of a stage hog. Our concern with the ego often allows it to grandstand.

Let's watch your identity for a moment. Here's the player who defines your walk, your glide, your stomp, and stumble? Here's the player who is most easily recognized by others as you.

Now let your intellect play a role. Here's the player who helps us see the opinions and judgments driving our story. The intellect is the player who motivates us to laugh and cry, to understand our motivations and to question if they're right.

Now cast the ego in a role. Watch the ego mediate between the world around it and the world within. The ego creates our story's conflict by drawing lines of ownership. The lines are often drawn a bit tightly to make our story distinct and unique. Ego creates our drama. We may think the ego only wants a blockbuster story that everyone loves but it really just wants to keep us safe and steady. Ego may do this by broadcasting our story to billions or keeping it in the shadows.

When ego is taught that steadiness and safety are assured, it will become an important player in nurturing our connections.

All three words—*intellect, identity, ego*—come together to tell our stories to others.

But who wants to put on a show?

Fortunately, these players also give us access to deeper connection and union with the world around us. First, we have to acknowledge the show. Then we can direct them otherwise.

This is our responsibility.

Twelve: Yoga with the Will

We return home under the power of our free will.

Let's explore our will. Are you willing to be aware of the ways you cultivate joy?

As you breathe, become aware of the condition of your body in the moment. Notice also the condition of your breath. Become aware of the activity in the mind. Are your thoughts erratic or focused? Are you consumed with one or two ideas, worries, thoughts, or is the mind bouncing from subject to subject?

Now make a commitment to yourself: *I am attentive and curious; I do this practice to come home to myself.*

Consider the events of your day.

Ask yourself: *Did I remain joyful and peaceful throughout the day?* If you did not, ask yourself why you chose to let go of joy or peace.

You may hear yourself responding: "It wasn't *my* fault." Acknowledge the message and notice that a decision to surrender joy and peace is a choice you don't have to make. You have other choices.

To maintain your peace, you must have the will to choose for yourself.

Even if someone else does something you don't like, what can you do in response that you do? What will cultivate and sustain joy and peace in a moment that challenges joy and peace? What can you do to choose your joy and peace in the moment of provocation?

How can you create that pattern?

Thirteen: Yoga with Space

When we clear ourselves of ourselves, we make room to become full.

Imagine yourself standing on the sidewalk. A car goes by, and someone yells.

Be honest: What's your reaction? Do you yell back? Do you think they're yelling at you? Do you believe they should behave better? Do you laugh at their good time? Do you simply stand?

How we react to these unintentional provocations tells us a lot about our patterns. When we're stimulated by a sudden event, we can choose to make space before we offer our response. In that space we often realize no response is necessary.

Our patterns thrive when we forget to make space for another option.

So, we breathe and remember to find space in this moment. This is how we come to be. We remember that the likelihood of our existence is so minimal. We see that those around us are just as fortunate to exist. This is enough to make us precious and worthwhile. There is nothing we need to accumulate or deliver to prove our worth. Nor is there anything that anyone else needs to do to justify their purpose.

Being is enough. Be fully as you are. And remember that you are a precious life in a wondrous world. This is enough and will fulfill you for your entire life if you allow it.

Now how do you respond to the yelling and screaming?

Everyone, including you, is truly doing the best they can.

Everyone will experience a life that, occasionally, delivers horror and awe. Will you guide yourself to make space for the error and the wonder? For the shits and the giggles? For all of it?

Fourteen: Yoga with Personality

Home is behind all the masks we wear.

Let's play with our masks.

Please get comfortable. Be with your breath for a moment and notice how it moves through you.

With each inhale, feel these words: *I am spirit.*

With each exhale, feel these words: *I play a role.*

Be with these ideas for about ten to twelve breaths.

Now notice that there's a voice in your head.

Notice that it's incessant and always has something to say about you, your actions, your decisions, your future, your past. It may also have a lot to say about everyone and everything around you. Notice that it won't always be kind.

You may hear thoughts like "Ugh, he always does that" or "Will she ever learn?" or "That's not my problem" or "Gosh, this is a terrible neighborhood."

That's the voice of your identity, judging, defending, separating.

It rambles, oblivious to any of the quiet magical moments of things like hummingbirds and baby smiles. It goes on and on. It tells you what you like and dislike, how you are, how you aren't, how bad things are, how great things are, how much you have to do. Seriously, it's exhausting.

Now I'd like you to notice what this voice says about you.

It's decent odds this voice of yours has worse things to say than anything anyone else could muster. After all, you know yourself better than they do.

These things you hear essentially are a ceaseless monologue of thoughts you've gathered. These thoughts are a great defense against the judgment you anticipate from others.

You stand in the throes of critical self-judgment while being afraid and imprisoned by a perception of judgment from others. And the truth is: you're perfect.

All this judgment distracts from your true mission of learning to love to yourself, without condition.

So, listen to the monologue of thoughts again and interrupt it. Just for a moment: *I hear you, and we're okay right now. Let's know this moment.*

Watch what happens.

If it argues with you or offers resistance, repeat the line.

I hear you, and we're okay right now. Let's know this moment.

When you get to the space where your body takes a deep breath, you've made a little progress. At that point offer your personality an intention to establish a new pattern.

From here on out, you might suggest, *what other people think of us is none of our business.*

Watch the patterns arise to tell you why this might be wrong and apply the original sentence again: *I hear you, and we're okay right now.*

As your new pattern establishes itself, set about watching the personality quiet down. It has a new agenda.

In the stillness notice how you occasionally hear the quiet breath of guidance from some place deeper. Notice how this sound guidance is always there for you. Notice how this guidance supports your kind reminders to remain present to the moment. Enjoy spirit.

You may also become aware of other players appearing. Perhaps a teenager dismissing this exercise. Perhaps a supervisor who wants to shut it down as a waste of time. Welcome these players. They are aspects of your personality coming forward to indicate places ready for healing.

As you welcome them home, the voice of spirit will enliven. Your sacred space at home will be infused with your spirit's wisdom.

When you become comfortable hosting a bit of silence, you'll start to cherish its wisdom. You'll also start to tune into the wisdom of everything around you.

All of life is awaiting your decision to connect.

Fifteen: Yoga with Shadows

When we see our shadows, we know there's light.

Like all of the practices described in this book, the following is appropriate for consistent use.

Perhaps more than any other practices included, this one may feel confrontational, emotional, or fraught. This practice guides you to look at the shadows on your path.

If you find yourself challenged by shadows, please consider using this practice in the company of a trusted friend, therapist, or guide. This practice is highly benefited by journaling at the end. Please jot down what you learned to acknowledge and accept the wisdom you acquired.

Your wisdom is the light that illuminates the path.

There are three important factors to remember as you undertake this work.

First, we all have shadows. Every person has history and is a product of it.

Second, a shadow is usually larger than the object casting it. This means that our perception of the source of shadow is often exaggerated by the way we see the shadow looming. What is behind us is in the past. We've already survived it. The shadow is simply our reminder that we're meant to learn from what we've moved through.

Finally, your chaos agents are a part of your shadow creation. Let yourself know them.

Please seat yourself comfortably, or you may choose to lie down.

Take a few moments to settle in, and let your body feel the support of whatever holds you. Begin to notice your breath. As you breathe in, see what it's like to think the word *grateful*. As you breathe out, see how it feels to think the word *peaceful*. Become aware of how you are grateful for every inhale. Also notice that every exhale leaves you a bit more peaceful.

Now let yourself contemplate the existence of shadows in your life.

You may see them quite clearly, or you may be uncertain. You may prefer, like my friend, to blame the sun.

If you aren't sure, you can let yourself consider what type of behavior holds you back. This isn't someone else's behavior; this is yours.

You may see there is frequently a feeling of injury or insult that keeps you from moving forward.

You may see there's been impatience in you, causing you to make haste and fail to appreciate progress.

You may see patterns of laziness, unworthiness, fear, or regret.

Let yourself notice the shadows that have colored your path up until now.

Take a moment, please, to choose just one. For now, one.

Ask yourself this question: *What is the source of this shadow?*

Now let yourself watch for a moment. At first you may not know what you're watching for. That's not a problem unless you make it a problem.

Be patient. Then notice. You'll start seeing earlier moments in your life when you learned how to behave under the influence of this shadow. Take a look at these moments.

Can you see the behavior served a purpose at the moment the shadow was being created?

We befriend our challenges by marveling in the shadows. We see how they served us in the past. We heal our past from the present.

As you discover how you learned this behavior, can you take a moment to say thank you for what it allowed you to accomplish in the past? Sometimes our impatience stems from a demand to quickly accomplish tasks when we were children. Sometimes the source of our feeling of unworthiness can be spotted at the dinner table as we listened to our parents remind us never to think we're special. They meant well, but the lesson cast a shadow.

Now see if that thank you can also become a welcome.

What would it be like for you to welcome the event, the people, the lesson into your life completely? What would it be like to gratefully accept the shadow, its source, and all you've learned to arrive at in this moment?

As you complete this process, take time to feel your body again. Return to feeling your breath—thanking every inhale, relaxing with every exhale. If it feels appropriate for you, consider offering your thanks to other circumstances in your life that support you to feel peaceful. Write about your experiences so you can deepen your relationship with the source of your shadows.

Sixteen: Yoga with Change

Be still and watch how everything comes and goes.

Here's a way to quietly contemplate change.

Sit in a quiet place while straightening your nice, long spine. Sit with respect for your journey. Ideally you'll sit on a surface that allows you to keep your spine tall without too much difficulty. A chair is a great tool for sitting! If sitting is too difficult, lie down on your back with your legs supported by a pillow.

Close your eyes, and take deep, nourishing breaths. Begin to deepen your inhale and lengthen your exhale.

Discover the moment in the coming of your breath. Discover the moment going with the departure of your breath. In the pause following each, wait in one moment for the arising of another.

As you observe the moments passing, notice qualities of your inhale and exhale. Describe these qualities to yourself. How does your inhale feel? How does your exhale feel? Discover in your breath's constancy its persistent change. Every intake of air is eventually exchanged for a release. Every inhale brings the world to you. On every exhale you offer yourself to the world. Eventually release control of the breath, and let your body breathe for you.

As you deepen your inhale, open your eyes. As you lengthen your exhale, close your eyes.

Say to yourself as you inhale, *Breathing in, I observe the world.*

Say to yourself as you exhale, *Breathing out, I observe the world.*

You may not think anything is changing at first. Please continue to pay attention as you breathe, opening and closing your eyes.

Become aware of the small changes in your perception. Watch for a few minutes. At a certain point, release your breath, and contemplate what you observed.

Notice the things that have gone in the last hour, the last day, the last week, month, and year.

Then call to mind the things that have come along in the last hour, the last day, the last week, month, and year.

See the connection between the passing and arising, the going and coming.

Finally, close your eyes and become aware of what did not change in the process.

Ask yourself this question: *What's come, and what's gone?* No need to provide answers. Simply sit quietly and watch the answers appear in your consciousness. Notice how what has come and what has gone are always intertwined. There is not one without the other. Just as we inhale to exhale, we must also let go to find space. We must find space to let go. When change stops, we are no longer alive.

Notice the constancy of your consciousness and your gratitude for what has come and gone.

Now notice what has remained the same throughout every coming and going you've experienced.

This is who you truly are.

This is the process of quietly contemplating change.

Seventeen: Yoga with the Eternal

Be still, and know you are eternal.

Here's how you might sense the eternal.

Make yourself comfortable and take five nice deep breaths. Sometimes this practice can feel good to do as you walk. Other times you'll feel more supported in a chair or even lying down.

As you breathe, become aware of the condition of your body in the moment. Notice also the condition of your breath. Make a commitment to yourself: *I am attentive and curious; I'm coming home to myself.*

Now please call to mind a person, a place, or an idea that brings you joy. See this clearly in your mind. If you can't visualize easily, then simply allow yourself to remember the person, place, or idea. Now feel the effects of finding your friendly thought. Feel this inspiration deeply as you breathe. Allow your whole body to feel it. Notice how the feeling expands as you offer greater concentration to your joy-filled inspiration.

Be with this feeling for a while. Notice this sensation is yours. It is generated within at your impulse. You are the catalyst to bring it to being. And you are the one who sustains it. Feel this.

From this place, sensing joy, become aware of the persistent change around you. Listen in to sounds or notice the air moving. Notice the changes within you as well. You make certain shifts in your body. Tension arises and eases. The breath constantly moves you. Remain centered in your sensation of joy as you experience the constant change.

And now choose one changing factor in your life that often causes you to suffer. It may be that you've fought with a loved one. Maybe you've lost a job or are becoming aware of the effects of your age. Maybe you've lost someone. We all experience various difficult emotions as a result of persistent change. Choose one now.

As you inhale, allow yourself to experience the challenging emotion. Breathe it in.

As you exhale, recall the sensation of joy you experience when you call to mind your inspiration.

As you continue this process, realize the changes in your body as the emotion you've chosen begins to shift with every exhale. Be with this process for five, ten, or fifteen minutes. There is no limit to the time, and sometimes, depending on the emotion you choose, you may discover that the process can be quite quick or quite slow.

Without interrupting your focus, simply become aware of the changes you perceive as you continue.

Notice that it's you, a creature of joy, working with this emotion. This is the eternal. It is you, in that space of joy, love, and peace. Notice what you feel as you experience what is ever-present. Realize this eternal is always available to you.

You may like to offer this experience of joy through a prayer for those you love, for those in your community, or for all living creatures—that they too will find their way to realize their ever-present peace.

With a deep breath, offer thanks to your attention and will. Become aware of the sensation of your breath coming and going. Become aware of the position of your body and the space around you.

You may like to write about this experience. Or simply sit for a moment to rest.

Eighteen: Yoga to Come Home

Sit comfortably and feel your breath. Say thank you to your body for allowing you a vessel from which you can appreciate the coming and going of every breath.

Say thank you to your inhale for the vitality it brings you.

Say thank you to your exhale for all it removes.

Say thank you to your mind for finding the breath and knowing how it serves you in this vast, infinite world.

Say thank you to your wonderful patterns of behavior, emotion, and thought with this vast, infinite world that weave together to support your ability to arrive home.

Say thank you to your home, for always waiting for you. Listen to how it thanks you for returning.

Say thank you to your mother and father for creating this unique existence of you. And to their mothers and fathers for finding each other, so you could find home.

Say thank you to your teachers, for guiding you, disciplining you, challenging you, loving you, so you found the strength and resilience to come home.

Say thank you to your friends for laughing and crying with you as you wandered toward, around, beyond, and, finally, near home.

Say thank you to every other creature who, like you, is moving homeward.

Thank you is always the prayer.

We are all one. And we're all heading home.

You are sacred. Grace is everywhere. We are the holy event.

Thank you.

Notes

In a random, slightly historical order, here are reading materials by special people who have found home and chosen to leave breadcrumbs to guide you. You may love the taste of some crumbs and not others. You decide. And then consider what kind of trail you'll leave for those who follow you.

The Tao Te Ching by Lao Tzu

Zhuangzi

The Yoga Sutras of Patanjali

The Upanishads

The Bhagavad Gita

Ashtavakra Gita

Dhammapada

Meditations by Marcus Aurelius

On the Shortness of Life by Lucius Annaeus Seneca

The Gospel of Thomas

The Cloud of Unknowing by Anonymous

Rumi's Little Book of Life by Rumi

"Walking" by Henry David Thoreau

"Song of Myself" by Walt Whitman

As a Man Thinketh by James Allen

How to Win Friends and Influence People by Dale Carnegie

Autobiography of a Yogi by Paramahansa Yogananda

Thoughts in Solitude by Thomas Merton

The Book of Secrets by Osho

Living in the Material World by George Harrison

'Watching the Wheels' by John Lennon

'The Highwayman' by The Highwaymen

Loving What Is by Byron Katie

The Seat of the Soul by Gary Zukav

A Course in Miracles

Be Here Now by Ram Dass

The Heart of Yoga by TKV Desikachar

A Return to Love by Marianne Williamson

Living Buddha, Living Christ by Thich Nhat Hanh

The Power of Now by Ekhart Tolle

Inner Engineering by Sadhguru

You may also seek a teacher. Seek out Gary Kraftsow or Juris Zinbergs. Seek out Shawn Roop. Seek out Sally Kempton or Shari Friedrichsen. Maybe you'd like a shaman. Look up Julie Kramer or Sandra Ingerman.

Or maybe you'd like a friend on the path. Start talking with your neighbors, your sisters and brothers, mothers and fathers, aunts, uncles, and cousins. Discover how much you learn in every loving conversation.

You can find me too. I'm always around.

cf4e760d-8985-46c2-8078-8e567a1761eaR01